2301·91
AD.

TECHNOLOGIES OF POWER: INFORMATION MACHINES AND DEMOCRATIC PROSPECTS

COMMUNICATION AND INFORMATION SCIENCE

Edited by
BRENDA DERVIN
The Ohio State University

Recent Titles

Laurien Alexandre • The Voice of America: From Detente to the Reagan Doctrine
Bruce Austin • Current Research in Film Volume 4
Barbara Bate & Anita Taylor • Women Communicating: Studies of Women's Talk
Donal Carbaugh • Talking American: Cultural Discourses on Donahue
Kathryn Carter and Carole Spitzack • Doing Research on Women's Communica-
tion: Perspectives on Theory and Method
Benjamin M. Compaine • Issues in New Information Technology
Gladys Ganley & Oswald Ganley • Global Political Fallout: The VCRs First
Decade 1976-1985
Gladys Ganley & Oswald Ganley • To Inform or to Control Revised Edition
Gerald Goldhaber & George Barnett • The Handbook of Organizational Com-
munication
Enrique Gonzalez-Manet • The Hidden War of Information
Gary Gumpert & Sandra Fish • Talking to Strangers: Mediated Therapeutic
Communication
Cees Hamelink • The Technology Gamble: Informatics and Public Policy–A
Study of Technological Change
Carrie Heeter & Bradley S. Greenberg • Cableviewing
Robert Jacobson • An "Open" Approach to Information Policymaking
Meheroo Jussawalla, Donald L. Lamberton & Neil D. Karunaratne • The Cost of
Thinking: Information Economies of Ten Pacific Countries
Manfred Kochen • The Small World
John Lawrence and Bernard Timberg • Fair Use and Free Inquiry Second Edition
Robert Picard et al. • Press Concentration and Monopoly
Carl Erik Rosengren & Sven Windahl • Media Matter: TV Use in Childhood and
Adolescence
Michael Rogers Rubin • Private Rights, Public Wrongs: The Computer and Per-
sonal Privacy
Ramona R. Rush & Donna Allen • Communications at the Crossroads: The
Gender Gap Connection
Jorge Reina Schement & Leah Lievrouw • Competing Visions, Social Realities:
Social Aspects of the Information Society
Jennifer Daryl Slack & Fred Fejes • The Ideology of the Information Age
Charles H. Tardy • A Handbook for the Study of Human Communication
Majid Tehranian • Technologies of Power: Information Machines and Democrat-
ic Processes
Sari Thomas • Studies in Mass Media and Technology, Volumes 1–4
Carol Weinhaus & Anthony G. Oettinger • Behind the Telephone Debates

TECHNOLOGIES OF POWER: INFORMATION MACHINES AND DEMOCRATIC PROSPECTS

Majid Tehranian

Department of Communication & The Institute for Peace
University of Hawaii at Manoa

Foreword by Johan Galtung

Ablex Publishing Company
Norwood, NJ 07648

Printed in the United States of America.

Library of Congress Cataloging-in-Publication Data

Tehranian, Majid.
   Technologies of power : information machines and democratic prospects / by Majid Tehranian.
      p.   cm. — (Communication and information science)
   Includes bibliographical references.
   ISBN 0-89391-634-X
   1. Information technology—Political aspects.   2. Information technology—Social aspects.   3. Democracy.   I. Title.   II. Series.
   303.48′34—dc20   89-18080
                                                                      CIP

Ablex Publishing Corporation
355 Chestnut Street
Norwood, New Jersey 07648

For my favorite communitarian tribe,
Katharine, John, Maryam, Terrence, and Yalda,

Table of Contents

Foreword

This book is a portrait of its author who, in turn, has lived the book. The book is located in the interface between democracy theory, development theory, and communication theory. And the author is located in the interface not only of the theories but also of the practice of the three. An Iranian with experience from his work in Iranian television, he certainly got exposed to all three through their negation. There was no scarcity of rhetoric of democracy and development, only so little practice. As a matter of fact, those who are furthest removed from either often use the adjective "true." What to others might look like arbitrary authoritarianism often operates under the cover of *true democracy*, probably because it is guided by the strong. And what to others might look like a system taking 15–20% of the population for a ride into consumerism, buoyed by an ideology of materialist individualism (or individualist materialism; it amounts to the same) is touted as *true development*, probably because it rewards the strong. The net result is status quo, frustration, and aggression. And down the road—a revolt, which may be a very costly way of bringing about change.

Electronic communication was, of course, mainly by and for those with power and privilege. An ad for credit cards on the Shah's television pointing out how practical those cards are when you order your theater tickets for your next trip to London, is as good an example as any of blatant noncommunication with people. But Iran also offered interesting counterexamples. The cassette recordings of Khomeini's voice over direct-dialing telephone—Paris-Tehran; the burning of pictures of the Shah in front of TV surveillance cameras in public places gives some insight in the dialectic of communication. One is the flip side of the other.

Majid's academically, politically, and personally rich life trajectory also passed through UNESCO where he was an international civil servant; through England and France and several parts of the U.S., both as a student and a professor; and then landed him in Hawaii, recently as chair of the Department of Communication at the University of Hawaii, Manoa. A true cosmopolitan, a global person at home anywhere, he is also holistic in his approach, meaning that he is a modern social scientist, adequate for and to a shrinking world where issues and problems, not to mention their solution or resolution (or dissolution), tend to not respect disciplinary borderlines drawn by science and university administrators. This also applies to his epistemology in trying to come to grips with the intricacies of that interface. For any of the usual dichotomies under which so many are slaving (such as, materialist/idealist) Tehranian has a truly buddhist approach: neither one, nor the other, nor both-and, nor neither-nor—possibly all of the above, depending on the concreteness of the situation. His many concrete examples bear ample testimony to his ability to practice the rules he lays down.

But his heart is with the communitarian approach, not for that reason is he rejecting the big media. The small media are clearly what he sees as the technologies of empowerment for democracy and development. Small groups tied by affinity, not necessarily by vicinity, should possess the media enabling them to do three rather important things:

1. *Enrich their own life,* among themselves—doing across space and time what conversation can do, the palaver, the Spanish *tertulia* of people simply sitting outside chatting when the cool evening air makes outdoor life possible in a Spanish village at summer time;
2. *Enrich society at large,* by getting their message out, as unmediated as possible, as they want the message to be heard or seen;
3. *Participate, struggle if necessary,* for their own rights and for the rights of others, for the human betterment as they see it.

According to Majid, human and social needs should direct the technology, not vice versa. But the communication technology has been developed for the big media, for the corporate and bureaucratic needs of modern society. Paradigmatic is the political propaganda in pre-glasnost Soviet Union and the commercial propaganda in the U.S.: the highly mediated message, hitting hard on ears and yes, filtering through to brain and soul in spite of our defenses. And it is, and of course, unopposed. No dialogue. No communication. Except in that terrible sense made popular and even accepted in an unreflected manner through a frequent expression in the U.S.—*mass communication. Mass Communication Does Not Exist* is the title of a book by Danilo Dolci, the Italian social critic and practitioner, a Gandhi after Gandhi and a Freire before Freire. Communication means having things in common; it means reciprocity. Above all it means dialogue, as a minimum.

An aside from the author of this preface: What kind of totalitarianism makes us accept this horrendous idea that commercial propaganda, ads, are not to be discussed? Of course, those who produce goods and services have not only the right but even a social duty to communicate their existence. But, equally obvious: We, the receivers of these messages, have not only the duty but also the right to challenge, to dispute, to doubt, to ask. For each commercial, a debate! Bring noncorrupt consumers' associations and just plain, ordinary consumers who can tell about their experiences with this and that product into the picture! Use commercials as an invitation to democracy not, as now, as an invitation to authoritarianism, to training in blind/deaf acceptance. A product is no more holy than my views are right here, on this page; all there to be challenged, not only by buying or not buying. If democracy is so important in capitalist societies, why not practice it? When is glasnost coming to this very important sector of capitalism?

To Tehranian, then, *interactive communication* becomes absolutely crucial. The call-in radio or TV show are examples and not among the worst. However, Tehranian demands more. He wants *community ownership and management;* according to the "he who pays the piper calls the tune" rule—a rather good piece of social science. He wants *deprofessionalization* of programming and production so that anybody can run it like a conversation, a debate. Think of all the money put into technical perfection at the expense of alienating most! Which is a good example of how little participation counts for those in charge of technological decisions.

On top of this, Tehranian wants *empowerment of audiences,* even to the point where he challenges the very concept of an audience as a manipulative concept, as the opposite of communicative citizenship. He wants *decentralization* into small and presumably beautiful communicative circles. And he wants all of this to serve, respect, indeed to foster, cultural and structural pluralism. Only that way will it be possible, according to him, to realize the twin ideal embedded in the slogan "think globally, act locally."

Obviously, cable television did not make this kind of dream come true. I am not so sure that the many electronic networks via telephone lines and computers meet the bill either; maybe too cold, too technical. But somewhere there is a technology waiting to be born, one that would meet these demands. In doing so I think there is little doubt that Tehranian's basic contention would come true: New life blown into both democracy and development not only because more can participate, but mainly because they can participate the way they want, in a more organic manner. Such as, affinity cycles, as mentioned, in addition to the vicinity cycles among neighbors that may be in for a revival.

Of course, the position is not unproblematic, as Tehranian himself points out in his discussion of two of his favorite examples: the Greens in Germany and the Sarvodaya in Sri Lanka. I am a consultant to the former and a board member of the latter and love them both. But the Greens, so far at their best in local politics, are of course victims of Big society as when some of them become parliamentarians and their base feels left behind, even to the point of communicating through ads in the newspapers (whether this was necessary or not). And the same may apply to sarvodaya: anybody trying to keep equal contact with base and top, participating both in the big and the small media, maybe having to stretch to the point of breaking.

However, this big dialectic is precisely what this important book explores so well. The theme has met its author. It has been thought and written by the right man who took up the challenge. The challenge to us is to help his dream come true.

Johan Galtung
Honolulu, June 1988

Preface

The project for this book has been in the making for the past few years. Its gestation has coincided with a veritable technological revolution in communication, a crisis of confidence in democracy in the advanced industrial societies, and a decline of optimism regarding the democratic prospects in the less developed world.

The book that has emerged deals with all three of these immensely difficult themes—information technologies, democracy, and development—within a comparative, theoretical, and global perspective. It deals with the hopes as well as the fears for democracy and development that have emerged out of the current technological revolution in information and communication. In the process of addressing that problem, however, the book's focus has had to be broadened to include some perennial questions of far-reaching theoretical import: What is democracy? How do we define development? How do information technologies enhance or constrain democratic development? What are the historical conditions peculiar to capitalist, communist, or mixed economies at the centers and peripheries of world power?

PERSPECTIVES

The writing of this book started as a daring enterprise but has ended as a humbling experience. Perhaps the book's successive working titles would best reveal the education of its author. The manuscript began somewhat optimistically with the title of "Electronic Democracy." But in the process of rethinking the problem, it became apparent that the promise of *direct democracy* held by the new interactive communication technologies has to be weighed against their much more immediate and real threats of electronic surveillance and its creeping ultimate form—an Orwellian nightmare.

A second working title, *Communitarian Democracy*, was meant to argue for a new form of democracy in order to promote grass-roots, direct, community participation through mediated and unmediated communication. This title imparted three sets of unabashed biases. First, it suggests a new and emerging form of democracy—as yet unborn—that might in some respects complement the strengths and correct the weaknesses of the present democratic systems. It implies that democracy should be viewed as a continuing historical process rather than as a finished historical achievement. To the dismay of some readers, therefore, the book speaks of capitalist as well as communist democracies as the two contemporary expressions of the same unfinished and continuing process of democratic fulfillment.

Second, it puts community rather than technology at the center of democratic development, while arguing that the new interactive technologies may indeed serve as new channels for the revitalization of global communities of affinity as well as for the traditional communities of vicinity.

Third, in so far as community and communication share common linguistic roots and epistemic connotations, that title also implies that *information* technologies have to become *communication* technologies before "information society" can become a communication or communitarian society. If we have indeed embarked upon a post-industrial, information society in the advanced industrial countries, and if this is the prospect for the rest of the world, we must go beyond this stage to achieve a truly interactive communication system before we can claim to have achieved higher levels of democratic development.

As a final title, with which I am prepared to live, *Technologies of Power* suggests that information technologies, like all other technologies, extend and augment our powers—for good and evil, for better or worse, for democracy or tyranny. But such theoretical neutrality, fair and scientific as it may seem, does not get us very far. Communication, democracy, and development are fundamentally normative concepts. Attempts at theoretical neutrality are doomed to failure from the start. It is intellectually more honest to state our normative preferences, argue our case as best as we can, and let our readers guard against the biases we might impart. Caveat lector!

My biases for a reform of the present democratic systems and for a transformation of the predemocratic societies are still alive and kicking in the following pages. They are, in turn, informed by a central argument which, at the risk of oversimplification, may be summarized as follows: Communitarian democracy is a concept and an ideal embedded in the French revolutionary slogans of liberty, equality and fraternity (or, in a less sexist language, community). Whereas capitalist democratic systems have historically emphasized liberty (including a domination of private property), communist democratic societies have stressed equality (including a domination of state bureaucracy). As the single most important, decentralized, and irreducible unit of human organization, small communities have been often trampled upon by both the capitalist and communist democracies. Robert Michels' "Iron Law of Oligarchy" has worked through the rise of centralized technocracies in both industrial systems to achieve Big Business, Big Government, Big Labor, or Big

Party machineries that do not represent their respective constituencies—that is, the stockholders, the electorate, the working class, or the rank-and-file membership. The most persistent resistance to the domination of the industrial system has thus come from the repressed and peripherized communities, that is, from the oppressed ethnic, racial, and national communities that do not share the values, norms, and interests of those anonymous, abstract, and self-perpetuating technocracies of power.

Information technologies have historically played a dual and paradoxical role in this process. On the one hand, they have provided the indispensable tools and channels for a centralization of authority, control, and communication typical of the modern industrial state. But on the other hand, they have also supplied the alternative channels of cultural resistance and ideological mobilization for the oppositionist forces. Generally speaking, the major media (the national press, broadcasting, and mainframe computers) have served the centralizing forces, while the small media (the alternative press, the small scale audio-video production/transmission, and—increasingly—the personal computer networking) have provided the channels for community resistance and mobilization.

The current technological revolution in information processing presents yet another round in the dual impact of the communication media—this time under the rubric of what might be called "Information" and "Communication or Communitarian" societies. The book thus rejects both the technophilic (e.g., Naisbitt, 1982) and technophobic (e.g., Ellul, 1983), views of the information technologies and presents a structuralist and contextualist perspective. It argues that the new information technologies, like the old, should be viewed neither as technologies of freedom nor of tyranny but primarily as technologies of power that lock into existing or emerging technostructures of power. They may serve to enhance democracy only to the extent that democratic social forces employ them to achieve greater access, participation, community, and democratic will formation.

Recent studies of information technologies and social change have often presented sustained intellectual arguments for or against their democratizing effects. Ithiel de Sola Pool's (1983) *Technologies of Freedom* is, for example, a case for the democratizing impact of information technologies *provided* government regulation is kept at bay. Vincent Mosco's (1982) *Pushbutton Fantasies* presents, by contrast, a warning against their negative impact on equality of access *unless* public control over their ownership and management is insured. This book begins not with the technologies but with their social context. It problematizes not the effects of information technologies but the social purposes which they serve. It is argued here that technologies, from the moment of their inception in scientific laboratories to their time of entry into the consumer markets, are inextricably tied to the social structures of domination and dependency. Technologies are thus viewed as neither good, nor bad, nor neutral! To understand their role in society, we need to contextualize their uses and abuses. For this reason, the book presents a mix of theoretical explorations and historical case studies—none of them conclusive on the questions of final effects which are viewed in the light of a dual-effects hypothesis, leading to democratic as well as counter-democratic effects. This approach presents perhaps a less tantalizing conclusion, but it calls for a more critical understanding of the contexts of technologies and their linkages with social structures.

A footnote on "technology" is called for here. In common usage, the term suggests gadget and gadgetry. In scholarly usage, however, the term has achieved a broader category of meaning, including the "software" that goes with the "hardware," the "know-how" that must accompany the machine. An even broader usage of the term appears in the works of Jacques Ellul (1983) and Michel Foucault (1979)—the two leading French critics of technology. Technology is assumed to represent an overwhelming and generalized system of ideas and techniques. As Mark Poster (1984, pp. 52–54) has pointed out, in the work of Foucault particularly, "technologies of power" is a key concept for the understanding of systems of domination in history.

Foucault's view postulates an intermediary position between idealism and materialism; it proposes the logic of discourse/practice for unraveling the modes of domination in history. It holds that systems of ideas and discourses, such as those of "sexuality" or "punishment" or "democracy," are deeply tied to a grid of technologies of power that act upon the social field to ensure compliance and domination. In contrast to traditional idealism or materialism that tend to be universally reductionist, this view sees technologies as locked into specific systems of discourse/practice. This approach attempts to avoid the Aristotelian logic of postulating discrete causes and effects; it proposes a matrix of understanding in which every cause can be an effect and every effect can become a cause in complex "webs of significance" (Geertz, 1973). The burden of such an analysis clearly falls, therefore, on contextual studies of historically-specific situations.

While I believe that the poststructuralist tendency towards idealism and political passivity should be critically viewed, there is much in the perspective of discourse theory that recommends itself to any serious analysis of technologies. But to provide for human agency and a democratic outcome, it has to be supplemented with a more positive vision of a hypothesized community such as that of Jurgen Habermas's (1979) "ideal speech community." The book thus presents its normative biases without pretending that they are *either* the only possible, ethical position to take *or* arguing that they present in any sense an inevitable *telos* of history. In the perspective of this book, information technologies consist of *messages, media,* and *modes* (i.e., social networks and structures of communication). Their impact should be therefore analyzed in the context of historically- and culturally-specific situations, the spaces they occupy, the social linkages they establish, and the powers they enhance or limit. No universal effects theory is thus possible. That is why this book constantly alternates between theoretical discussions and empirical case studies. The text may occasionally lapse into the older Aristotelian/Cartesian logic of postulating causes and effects, or to the Hegelian/Marxian dialectics of postulating inevitable synthesis and progress, but the author is highly skeptical of both of these approaches. A more holistic approach to the problem of understanding comparative social and communication systems would have to go deeply into the material as well as into the symbolic universes of discourse, into the socioeconomic as well as the cosmological contexts.

Orthodox liberal and Marxist theories have paid particular attention to the former while largely neglecting the latter. Evolutionary progress and economic determinism have often served as the twin theoretical premises of both schools. Some liberal theorists have of late argued that a postindustrial information society has already overtaken the industrial system. This book takes issue with that proposition. As Stephen Cohen and John Zyzsman (1987) have persuasively argued, the statistical facts of a transition from manufacturing to service and information industries in the United States (from about 50 percent of total employment in 1967 to about 70 percent in 1987) do not necessarily mean evolutionary progress. As the current mammoth deficits in the U. S. trade and balance-of-payments demonstrate, the United States has lost much of its international competitiveness to Japan, West Germany, and the newly industrializing countries. In the meantime, the myth of a militarized, high-tech "information economy" has captured the public fancy because it does resonate to some elements of our experience while mystifying larger realities. Similarly, the book takes issue with the Marxist propositions regarding the inevitability of the demise of capitalism and the rise of people's democracies. The path to democracy is perceived here to be fraught with many totalitarian temptations and pitfalls. There are no historical guarantees. The price of freedom, equality, and community is constant vigilance. Free flow of information, dialogical communication, and democratic will formation play a central part in that process. One of the simplest and most eloquent statements on these principles I have run across comes from the Melanesian Council of Churches. It provides a universal manifesto for democratic communication[1]:

---

[1]I am grateful to Suzanna Layton for bringing this statement to my attention.

A DEMOCRATIC MANIFESTO ON INFORMATION
AND COMMUNICATION

We believe that communication is a gift from God and therefore inalienable. Being a gift from God, it becomes a right, on a par with other human rights. We believe that for human beings to unfold their personalities and attain their highest potential, they need to communicate. They have a right to communicate, a right to inform, and a right to be informed. They have the right to free expression subject to the rights of all individuals. Because communication is so fundamental to human existence, we also hold that it should be free from domination, either by foreign or local interests, or by the State. We believe that people should have access to a plurality of communication opportunities and should not be limited by monopoly.

We also, believe that communication should always be wedded to the truth and be sensitive to the culture and values of the people. It must be free from ethnocentric prejudices and respect the interests of women, children and all minorities.

These values, we may add, are also the values clearly articulated by all the member nations of UNESCO, including PNG, at its Special Assembly held in Belgrade in October 1980, when the world's nations called unanimously for a New World Information and Communication Order.

The Melanesian Council of Churches,
Papua New Ginea,
January 1988

PROSPECTUS

Enough caveats! The organization of the volume is simpler and more straightforward. Chapter 1 states the problem and provides a global perspective on what is perceived to be the main trends in technological and social developments. It argues that the impact of information technologies has led to four concurrent and contradictory global trends, including the transnationalization of economies, indigenization of politics, democratization of cultures, and totalitarianization of power. Chapter 2 provides a theoretical framework on "contextualism" and a more focused argument on the concentrating and dispersing effects of information technologies. The dual-effects hypothesis sets the stage for Chapter 3 to provide a historical perspective on the impact of the new information technologies and on the emergence of two competing social formations, technocratic vs. communitarian. Chapter 4 looks at the national contexts of communication and democratization, focusing on the capitalist democratic, communist democratic, communitarian democratic, and totalitarian models. By presenting a series of case studies, Chapters 5 and 6 concentrate on the promises of direct democracy and the perils of an Orwellian nightmare. Chapters 7 and 8 analyze the new technological possibilities in the historical contexts of centers and peripheries of world power: Chapter 7 argues that the new information technologies have prompted three significant trends in North America, Japan and Western Europe—from scarcity to abundance of channels, from regulation to reregulation (as an outcome of deregulation!), and from public to private spheres; Chapter 8 focuses on the peripheries and semiperipheries while arguing that the mass media and the new information networks have led to the increasing incorporation of peripheries into centers as well and have mounted mobilization and resistance. It also provides a ninefold typology of development strategies, focusing on high accumulation, high mobilization, and high integration policies that have combined with dissociation, assimilation, and selective participation strategies vis-a-vis the world system. In conclusion, Chapter 9 examines the prospects for a communitarian democratic vision of society in which economic and political democracy are combined with cultural and communication democracy. To provide an insight into the promises and difficulties of this vision, the chapter also provides case studies of two contemporary communitarian movements—the Green Party of West Germany and the Sarvodaya Shramadana Movement in Sri Lanka.

ACKNOWLEDGEMENTS

The intellectual and material debts accumulated in a project as long and tortuous as this one are too many to be capable of full acknowledgement. Nevertheless, it is a pleasure to thank, however, inadequately, those institutions and individuals who helped the most.

I am grateful to UNESCO, whose pioneering studies in community media originally inspired, initiated, and partially funded this study. Alan Hancock and Maxine Shatton of UNESCO were particularly helpful in their watchful encouragement. At the University of Hawaii, I am particularly grateful to those colleagues who gave me the benefits of their wisdom on the successive drafts of the manuscript. These include Andrew Arno, Ted Becker, Jim Dator, Johan Galtung, L. S. Harms, Vincent Lowe, Peter Manicas, Deane Neubauer, Richard Vincent, and Dan Wedemeyer. Thanks are also due to Don Topping, director of the Social Science Research Institute at the University of Hawaii, for his support of my research by providing release time from teaching. Many of the ideas in this volume were tested out first in the University of Hawaii classrooms where my students shared in their critique and refinement; I am grateful to all of them for their sympathy and support in its pangs of birth. To the anonymous reviewers of the manuscript during its submission to several publishers, I am most grateful for their frank and honest critiques—some laudatory and some critical! I have tried to respond positively to the helpful criticisms by revisions wherever possible.

Thanks are also due to Jay Blumler, Anne Branscomb, Wimal Dissanayake, Herbert Dordick, Youichi Ito, Edward Ploman, Jan Servaes, Robert White, and Frederick Williams for their thoughtful comments and critiques. Ablex's editor, Brenda Dervin, deserves a special word of thanks for her big heart, critical mind, and constant encouragement. Sarah Bott, Teresa Takaki, and Anthony Pennings helped me immeasurably as research assistants; Sarah, by extensive editorial suggestions; Teresa, by preparing the references; and Anthony, by his patient indexing. Susan Shinogi and June Tanabe protected me from the intrusions of the office of a department chair when the going was rough.

Whatever merit there is in this volume belongs to my visible and invisible collaborators. My wife, Katharine, has been my closest collaborator and severest critic. Many of this book's central ideas belong to both of us, but I am sure she will develop them with greater sophistication in her own right. John and Maryam, who were patient with my undemocratic demands on their leisure and playtime, wanted the book out sooner than I could dare or produce.

I have to take full responsibility, alas, for whatever errors of fact or interpretation that remain!

Majid Tehranian
Honolulu, Hawaii
May 1988

I

Theoretical and Historical Contexts

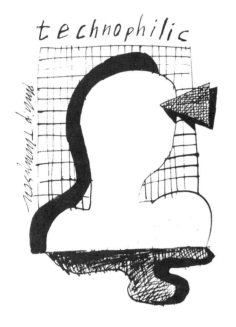

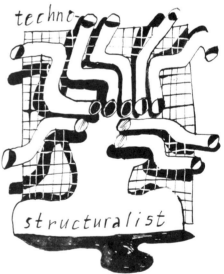

Source: From "Information Technologies and World Development," by M. Tehranian, May 1988, *Intermedia*, *16*(3), pp. 30–31.

1

A Global Perspective*

As for the future, your task is not to foresee but to enable.

(Antoine de Saint-Exupery)

If Karl Marx were alive today, he would have probably written his *magnum opus* on *Die Information* and not *Das Kapital* (Ploman, 1983). While the first industrial revolution was driven by accumulation of capital, the second industrial revolution seems to be propelled by the exponential growth of "information" in the forms of science, technology, and organization. The current technological revolution in information storage, processing, and retrieval is clearly affecting all aspects of our economic, political, and cultural life. The first industrial revolution was fueled by the mounting power of the new electromechanical technologies; the second revolution has been driven by the accelerating speed and efficiency of the new electronic technologies in information processing. Both revolutions, however, have vitally depended on accumulations of capital *and* information.

But that is where the historical parallels must pause. The first revolution involved structural changes in economy, society, and polity. It led to the major social revolutions of modern history, defining the systemic features of the modern world. What does the second revolution portend? The world economy is currently driven by the massive application of new information technologies to the old problems of design, manufacturing, and marketing of products and services. Our political institutions everywhere are undergoing transformations which may be, in part, attributed to the impact of the new information technologies. And finally, our cultural life has not been left immune from the impact of telephones, radios, televisions, computers, VCRs, compact discs, and their increasing convergence into a huge, worldwide information and communication network. In what ways, if any, can the new technological revolution contribute to the processes of development and democratization that were assisted by the invention of the print technology?

*Originally delivered as keynote address to The Fourth World Communication Forum, The Japan Society for Communication and Information Research, November 25–26, 1987; published in *Intermedia*, 16, 3, May 1988.

To provide a global perspective on these questions, this chapter will look at the promises, perils, and prospects of the impact of information technologies on world development and the processes of democratization. By information technologies, I mean the whole range of technologies from print to fifth-generation computers—all of which fail to become communication technologies until we use them in interactive modes. By world development, I mean not only quantitative advances in economic growth (as measured by such conventional indices as Gross National Product) but also equitable income distribution (as measured by such indices as the Gini co-efficient). By democratization, I mean a process of increasing political participation that allows for considerable autonomy, diversity, and freedom while providing a supportive environment for critical public discourse, consensus building, and democratic will formation.

FOUR CONTENDING PERSPECTIVES

The impact of information technologies on the world economy, politics, and culture has been profound and lasting, yet controversial. With some poetic license, at least four perspectives on the problem can be identified: the technophilic, technophobic, technoneutralist, and technostructuralist. These four positions may be viewed in terms of a matrix derived from responses to the following two propositions as shown in Table 1.1.

The technophiles tend to be the optimists who believe that the present technological revolution in information storage, processing, and retrieval has already inaugurated a "post-industrial, information society" with higher productivity and plenty at the world centers that will eventually trickle down to the peripheries. In the United States, the concept has been developed by such scholars as Bell (1973), Machlup (1962, 1980–84), and Porat (1977). It has been also popularized by such best-selling authors as Toffler (1970, 1980) and Naisbitt (1982). In Japan, the development of the concept as *Johoka Shakai* coincided with the development of its American versions. Ito (1983) has traced back its origins to January 1963 when Tadao Umesao published his seminal article, en-

Table 1.1. Information Technologies and Democratization:
Four Contending Perspectives

| | | Information Technologies Lead to Concentrations of Power. | |
		Yes	No
Information Technologies Lead to Dispersions of Power.	Yes	Technostructuralism	Technophilia
	No	Technophobia	Technoneutralism

titled "*Joho Sangyo Ron*" (On Information Industries). In that article, Umesao argued for a progressive movement from agricultural to material and spiritual industries in order to fulfill the increasingly more complex, organic needs of human survival, locomotion, and cybernetic control. These ideas have been further developed, in English publications, by Masuda (1981) and Ito (1981) with their own unique Japanese perspectives and contributions.

The technophobes are, by contrast, rather pessimistic about such promises of widespread productivity and plenty. They point to the threats that increasing robotization and computer-assisted design and manufacturing (CAD-CAM) hold for rising structural unemployment and socioeconomic dualism; to the perils that the new databases pose for political surveillance and individual privacy; to the dangers that homogenization of culture by media monopolies present for cultural autonomy and diversity. Such scholars as Schiller (1981), Mosco (1982), Ellul (1983), Hamelink (1983), and Roszak (1986) have provided some of the most devastating critiques of the new technologies and their institutional support systems in the modern technocratic state and corporation.

The technoneutrals typically tend to be the consultants, who have few theoretical pretensions and considerable interest at stake not to alienate their clients. They often assume a neutral position with respect to the question of effects: on the one hand this, but on the other hand that. . . . This literature tends to be dichotomous in analysis without much reference to the social and historical contexts of technological impact. For example, a major National Science Foundation research project on the impact of videotext in the United States offers the following dichotomous scenarios (Tydeman & Zwimpfer, as quoted by Mosco, 1982, pp. 4–5).

> It is possible to develop a number of general societal themes that provide some insight into alternative feasible videotex features:
> 1. Social structure: New rural society or the electronic hermit.
> 2. Societal decision making: Real-time participation or Dr. Strangelove democracy.
> 3. Consumer choice: unlimited choice or electronic Babel.
> 4. Equity and access: informational equalizer or the poor get poorer.
> 5. Socioeconomic organization: Mass produced individuality in the competitive market or RAMJAC [America Inc.].
> 6. Financial structure: Cashless society or Big Brother.

The technostructuralist, including some reluctant optimists and pessimists among the above scholars, argue that technologies are by themselves neither good, nor bad, nor neutral! This is because they developed out of institutional needs (in the case of information technologies, primarily military and business needs) and their impact is always mediated through the institutional arrangements and social forces, of which they are an integral part. To understand the impact of information technologies, therefore, we must turn to an analysis of the social structures through which they produce their employment-generating or -reducing, political centralizing or decentralizing, cultural homogenizing, or pluralizing effects. As Galtung (1979, p. 6) has put it succinctly:

> A naive view of technology sees it merely as a question of tools—hardware—and skills and knowledge—software. These components are certainly important, but they are the surface of technology, like the visible tip of the iceberg. Technology also includes an associated structure, even a deep structure, a mental framework, a social cosmology, serving as the fertile soil in which the seeds of certain type of knowledge may be planted and grow and generate new knowledge. And in order to use the tools, a certain behavioral structure is needed. Tools do not operate in a vacuum; they are man-made and man-used and require certain social arrangements to be operational. Even a fully automated production technology implies a cognitive and behavioral structure, namely one of detachment from the production process.

PROMISES: TECHNOLOGIES OF DEMOCRACY

This book assumes a technostructuralist perspective. However, assuming a neutralist position for the sake of argument, it can be demonstrated that the current technological revolution in informatics promises some democratic outcomes in world development. If we view democracy as a cybernetic social system of networks in which there are many autonomous and decentralized nodes of power and information with their own multiple channels of communication, the new media are increasingly providing the technological conditions for such a system. There are at least six features of the new information technologies that might account for this potential: increasing interactivity, universality, channel capacity, content variety, low noise, and high speed.[1]

Interactivity is being made increasingly possible by a convergence of telecommunication and computer technologies. Videotext provides an example of such a technological marriage. By combining cable television with computers and telephone lines, it provides a fully interactive system for teleshopping, telebanking, and teleconferencing. Audio, video, and computer teleconferencing provide other examples of interactive technologies, each with their own possibilities and limitations. The traditional media such as print and broadcasting have been essentially one-

---

[1]Johan Galtung (1987) has also presented some of the same cybernetic principles as conditions for democratic development.

way and vertical modes of communication. The new interactive technologies could lay the groundwork for more interactive and horizontal modes of communication. But neither the old nor the new media can be justifiably called communication technologies until the media systems that use them work out their corresponding, interactive social systems. Most media systems in the world today use information technologies at their command as one-way, noninteractive channels. There are currently many social experiments with interactive technologies to build what has come to be known as "teledemocracy" (Arterton, 1987; Becker, 1987; Lewis, 1984; Ito, 1984). However, they generally point to the difficulties of overcoming power concentrations and political apathy through technological interventions alone.

Universality has long been recognized as a feature of mass communication systems but, with lowering costs, universal access is becoming a possible dream. While high rates of illiteracy have prevented the print media from becoming universal, radio and—increasingly—television have begun to achieve that status. Thanks to Japan and the newly industrialized countries, cheap transistor radios have already become a ubiquitous medium all over the world. But television has also made its serious entry. Take the two most populous nations of the world. Within the past decade, television penetration in China and India has reached, respectively, 50 and 10 per cent of the population (Rogers, 1987). In some Pacific islands where television is absent, the VCRs have taken their place. In some Middle Eastern countries with petrodollars and state-controlled, sanitized programming, VCR penetration is nearly a 100 percent. In the less-endowed countries, the small media such as audiocassettes, mimeograph machines, and the underground press provide channels of some autonomy and resistance. But universality is still a distant dream. The stark fact on world media distribution is that nearly 10 percent of the world population still own nearly 90 percent of the world's media channels (Pelton, 1981; MacBride et al., 1980). There are more telephones in metropolitan New York than in the whole of black Africa; in India, the waiting list for a telephone is close to 1 million. The developing countries have a much smaller proportion of the world's telephones than they do of its income—which may partially explain why they are poor ("Telecommunication Survey," 1987). Access to information and communication is the beginning of empowerment.

Channel capacity has dramatically increased in recent decades by the introduction of broadband cable (more than 100 channels in some major U.S. cities), satellites, fiber optics, laser technology, and more efficient uses of the electromagnetic spectrum and the geostationary orbit. Personal computers are increasingly putting this augmented channel capacity at the service of individuals and businesses—sometimes in interactive modes. The introduction of optical discs, CD-ROMS and WORMs, will soon increase the storage capacity into gigabytes (one billion characters). Eastman Kodak, for instance, has put 150 optical discs into a jukebox to provide a total storage capacity of more than a terabyte (1,000 gigabytes). The company believes this will allow a 250-bed hospital to store more than 12 years' worth of X-rays, body scans, and untrasound examination on the jukebox and find them again in 12 seconds or less ("Will Optical Fibers," 1987).

Content variety is, however, a promise less fulfilled. The GIGO principle (garbage-in-garbage-out) applies to computers as well as to the mass media. Despite dramatic increases in channel capacity, the media diet of the world still continues to be primarily such popular commercial TV productions as *Days of our Lives*, *Dynasty*, and *Dallas*. What uses and gratifications the audiences gain from such programs is largely unknown, but in the United States (the media capital of the world), they have not led to higher educational and cultural standards. The U.S. "information society" is suffering from an increasing rate of functional illiteracy of some 20 percent. Three current studies in the United States, for example, deal with the alarming cultural and educational problems that have arisen out of the emergence of a two-tiered society (Hirsch, 1987; Bloom, 1987; Bok, 1986).

Low noise, by contrast, is a technological achievement that has been more fully obtained because it depends less on our institutional arrangements. The introduction of Integrated Services Digital Network (ISDN) promises even further international standardization and multiplicity of services in the transmission of voice, data, and image over the same channels. But for a long time, due to high cost and complexity, these services will be available primarily to the privileged. Besides, low noise in democratic terms means acceptance of the rules of democratic discourse. So long as those rules exclude large sectors of the world population from public discourse, the disenfranchised and excommunicated will communicate either by apathy (e.g., the ghetto blacks) or by recourse to violence and terror (e.g., the Palestinians).

High speed is another area of technological achievement where institutional arrangements have less hampering influence. The transition from copper cables to fiber optics is rapidly moving ahead. Each hair-spun fiber usually transmits at the rate of 565m bits a second. Some carriers have already doubled that rate, and the technology exists to do so again at least twice ("Telecommunication Survey," 1987). Once the photonic equivalent of the electronic transistor is invented, computers also will probably come to work on light with the speed of light. "They would be switched on and off from a laser rather than electricity. If such devices can be made as small as transistors are now, millions of them could be packed into a microchip. This would provide a new type of memory device. It would store more than an optical disc and have faster random access than a hard disc. And it would not even have to spin" ("Will Optical Fibers," 1987). Beyond that, computers may be relieved from the tyranny of on-and-off dichotomies into the gradations of light. Such computers will be not only speedier but also more subtle and intelligent. But such high speeds cannot serve the cause of democratic development until we have flexible and responsive democratic institutions cutting short the time lags between public demands and official responses. Otherwise, the law's delays and the insolence of office will become an increasing feature of the aloof and anonymous technocracies that new information technologies are making ever more powerful.

PERILS: TECHNOLOGIES OF DOMINATION

From this cautiously optimistic technological perspective, we now have to glance at the more realistic world of asymmetries of global development. If we view the world as a series of concentric circles, the most technologically and economically advanced countries stand at the core, followed by the newly-industrialized countries at the semiperipheries, and the least developed at the extreme peripheries. In modern history, relations between these countries have been largely governed by domination and dependency. Few countries have succeeded to emulate Japan in breaking away from a periphery status to stand at the core. The overwhelming majority of periphery countries continue to be dependent and resentful. Moreover, the division of the world into centers, semiperipheries, and peripheries is replicated within nations with similar patterns of domination and dependency.[2]

The dynamics of these relationships in world development may be best captured by four global trends that seem to characterize our own epoch: (a) Transnationalization of the world economy at the centers; (b) indigenization of politics at the peripheries; (c) democratization of values at the semiperipheries; and (d) totalitarianization of surveillance throughout the world. Information technologies have played a central part in all these processes.

Transnationalization of the world economy has been perhaps the most apparent of all four trends. The accelerating processes of transnationalization have been engineered in the postwar period primarily by the transnational corporations (TNCs) whose growth and prosperity vitally depend on an expanding world development and trade, an inte-

---

[2]The concepts of center and periphery in world development have been extensively explored by Wallerstein (1974, 1979), Amin (1974), Frank (1969), and Galtung (1971).

grated world market, and rapid and efficient transportation and telecommunication infrastructures (Barnet & Muller, 1974; Wallerstein,
1979; Amin, 1974; Brock, 1981; Schiller, 1981). The processes of transnationalization have already achieved high levels of vertical and horizontal
market integration, reasonably flexible world monetary and fiscal systems for necessary adjustments, and a world technocratic and managerial elite with common ties of interests, education, and values. The role of
telecommunication in the TNCs has evolved from an administrative tool
in international corporations devoted to export/import, to a managerial
tool in the multinational corporations for financial control and, finally, to
a strategic tool for cybernetic control of production and distribution
decisions in the global corporation (Sturm, 1987).

However, the present international political system, organized principally around the sovereignty of the nation-states, presents an obstacle
to the unfettered growth of the transnational enterprises. There is thus
an increasing disjunction between the world economic and political systems. The transnational corporations have operated on the basis of corporate autonomy, stockholder accountability, and tendencies towards
concentration and partial global integration. Nation-states presume national sovereignty, embody the political will of national elites, and are
proliferating into a diversity of political and ideological configurations—
from 51 UN member states in 1945 to 159 in 1987.

Information technologies are thus providing, on the one hand, the
essential information and communication infrastructures for an expanding and more integrated world economy. On the other hand, they are
threatening national and personal sovereignties to an unprecedented
degree (Mowlana, 1986). For example, direct broadcasting satellite
(DBS), transborder data flows, remote sensing, and the global realloca-
tions of the electromagnetic spectrum and geostationary orbit have provided grounds for increasing frictions between the world techno-economic and techno-political systems. These frictions came into the open
most notably in the rounds of North-South negotiations conducted in
the seventies. The Brandt (1980, 1983) and MacBride (1980) reports have
amply demonstrated the seriousness of these problems. Those negotiations have failed to produce significant results, but the problems they
addressed cannot be ignored. They will continue to point to the existing
asymmetries of power and mounting feelings of frustration in correcting
them.

The world thus faces a political and cultural lag in its technoeconomic
development that will intensify in the coming decades. The central focus
of these problems has been the conflicts between the transnational
"rights" of free trade and free flow of information and the sovereign
"rights" of protectionism, cultural autonomy, and balanced *cum*

controlled information flows. In short, the TNCs have led the postwar world towards a dynamic but lopsided pattern of growth that is fast reaching its political and economic limits.

Indigenization of politics at the peripheries, both within and among nations, therefore may be considered as a reaction against the forces of transnationalization. Whereas transnationalization trends represent a top-to-bottom process of accumulation and concentration of wealth, power, and information, a reverse bottom-to-top process of mobilization of the world peripheries against the centers is also undermining the world system created at Bretton Woods[3]. We may label this as a process of "indigenization" in that it represents a reaction against the secular, scientific, and technological culture of transnationalization, while calling for a return to indigenous, smaller, and more cohesive cultures and communities. The slogans of "small is beautiful," "self-reliant development," "appropriate and soft technology," "conscientization," "less is more," and "neither East nor West" reflect these sentiments in a variety of sociohistorical conditions (Schumacher, 1973, 1977; Freire, 1972; Illich, 1971a, 1971b, 1973, 1974; 1978; Galtung, 1979). But the emotional intensity and political power of such sentiments can be best witnessed in several neotraditionalist movements.

The Islamic neotraditionalist movements, the Solidarity movement in Poland backed by the Catholic Church, the Theology of Liberation in Latin America, the Jewish fundamentalist movement in Israel, and the "electronic church" in the United States all spring from a similar sense of alienation and yearning for community caused by the dehumanizing effects of modern technocratic structures. In the softer states, the process of indigenization has also led to tribalization. The civil wars in Pakistan leading to the creation of Bangladesh, in Nigeria between the Biafrans and the rest of the country, in Lebanon between the various communal groups, and in Northern Ireland between the Protestants and Catholics all have cultural roots with political manifestations.[4]

This means that *civic* identities imposed by the nation-states and *status* identities moulded by class or profession, are increasingly rejected in favor of the far more potent communal bonds of *primordial* identities, shaped by common language, ethnicity, or religion (Geertz, 1973). As the repository of cherished historical memories, culture has thus become the last ditch defense of the common people against the stupendous and

---

[3]The United Nations Monetary and Financial Conference was held at Bretton Woods, New Hamphire, July 1–22, 1944. The conference established two permanent institutions for international cooperation: the International Monetary Fund and the World Bank.

[4]For the neotraditional movements in Islam, see Tehranian (1984) and Mortimer (1982); for the fundamentalist electronic church in the United States, see Armstrong (1979); for movements towards small-scale communities, see Ferguson (1981) and Sale (1980).

complex sociotechnical forces reducing them to conditions of abstraction and anonymity. These developments have sometimes led to great social and political upheavals such as those in the Cultural Revolution in China, the Nigerian, Lebanese, and Cambodian civil wars, and the Islamic revolution in Iran. In these instances, the small media (wall posters, audiocassettes, mimeograph, and xerox machines) have combined with traditional, social, and religious networks to produce powerful social movements.

Ironically, the very technocratic achievements of the new transnational political economy have proved to be its Achilles' heel. Complex technologies in transportation, telecommunication, and warfare are vulnerable to the challenge of dedicated mass movements or small group activists. Three recent examples illustrate the point: (a) the defeat of the advanced United States war machinery in Vietnam by an indigenous, revolutionary movement coupled with a domestic American peace movement; (b) the fall of the Shah's massive military and civilian bureaucracies in Iran at the hands of spontaneous civil demonstrations employing telephones, audiocassettes, and xerocracy as their weapons of political struggle; and (c) the relatively slower ouster of Marcos from power in the Philippines by massive religious and popular forces in alliance with factions of the military. Revolutionary struggle, disguised in cultural forms, has thus served as the mode of communication of the world's oppressed and disenfranchised against the state terrorism of a complex, incomprehensible, insensitive but vulnerable technoeconomic world.

Democratization of political norms at the semiperipheries may be thus considered as a third global trend. Thanks to the penetration of a worldwide communication network, the slogans of the French Revolution (liberté, egalité, fraternité) have now become part of a universal political culture. But effective demand for democratic participation has manifested itself primarily in those countries that have created a social base for it. These include such critical factors as accelerating rates of economic growth, literacy, and social mobility—the conditions that characterize such semiperipheries as Iran, Nicaragua, the Philippines, Brazil, South Korea, and Taiwan.

But political democracy takes root wherever we have also social and cultural democracy. No matter how democratic our constitutional arrangements, conditions of economic inequality or cultural domination breed political hegemony. Political democracy, understood as a system of effective participation to guarantee social plurality and national unity, has been institutionalized only in those countries that have narrowed the gaps in wealth and income. For some countries, this achievement has come after long periods of primitive capitalist accumulation; for others, it has resulted from long periods of primitive socialist accumulation. Is it possible to invent a development strategy for the Third World nations that bypasses the economic exploitations of capitalist growth and the political oppressions of the communist path?

The key to the unlocking of this question may lie in understanding the role of information and communication in development. It also calls for an understanding of the vital linkages between political, social, and cultural democracy. Information technologies have historically played a significant role in democratization in all three domains. Democratic movements depend on two kinds of interlocking communication networks, interpersonal and telecommunication. Human association by "affinity" rather than "vicinity" has been made progressively more possible by every successive wave of technological breakthrough in communication. Information technologies have facilitated such networks by the formation of nongovernmental, voluntary associations. The introduction of print, for instance, led to the rise of a new secular priesthood—the intelligentsia—who challenged the traditional authorities of the church and the state. The introduction of electronic media made it possible to reach the illiterate people of the world. Revolutionary newspapers and underground radios have historically played a critical role in the organization of revolutionary movements. Small media and personal computer networking today are providing yet another channel of communication for deviation from the norms of orthodoxies. The combined effects of these networks has been a proliferation of epistemic communities, of many cities of the mind. Programs rather than proximity are the common bonds of these invisible networks.

But telecommunication also abstracts and distantiates. Media realities are by their very nature distorted realities. Telecommunication provides the opportunity for the senders of messages to reconstruct reality to suit their own persuasive purposes. Genuine democracy, however, is fully interactive. It begins at the community level. But decentralized, direct democracy is threatened everywhere by the increasingly centralized bureaucracies—including the mass media bureaucracies. Mass communication is a contradiction in terms. It imposes a cognitive tyranny by the senders of uniform messages to hypothesized, undifferentiated, and inert mass audiences. The ultimate form of this hidden tyranny is an Orwellian nightmare—a totalitarian system of mind control.

Totalitarianization of communication and surveillance is, therefore, a fourth global trend that owes much of its origins to the rise of modern information technologies. Totalitarianism is a uniquely modern political formation that should be distinguished from the traditional, authoritarian forms of government. As Tocqueville (1956), Arendt (1966), and Friedrich et al. (1969) have pointed out, a totalitarian regime claims and exerts a historically unprecedented degree of monopoly over the means of violence, production, and communication. This is made possible primarily by the modern industrial means of warfare, organization, and telecommunication. The most barbarous authoritarian regimes of the past, from Oriental despotisms to European monarchical tyrannies, never had the means for total administrative penetration, military enforcement, and ideological manipulation that modern totalitarian regimes have at their disposal. Totalitarianism should be thus viewed as an inherent potentiality of all modern industrial societies, regardless of the liberal, Marxist, nationalist, or religious ideologies they might espouse.

Totalitarianism is an ideology of crisis resolution that thrives under the conditions of social fragmentation, individual isolation, and national disintegration. It represents a mass, hysterical movement searching to regain a sense of community and solidarity by focusing attention on hypothesized enemies external to itself. It thus operates on scapegoat psychology. It works best under conditions of economic, political, or cultural crisis. Capitalist, communist, as well as populist regimes have all been prone to this ideology.

The monopoly of the means of communication in the hands of modern totalitarian regimes clearly provides the most powerful means for mind control ever known in human history. Whereas traditional authoritarian regimes had to work with much more indirect and less efficient systems of communication, the modern totalitarian regime combines the mundane authority of the state with the mystification of its mission to achieve a higher degree of authority and efficiency. To cite just the best-known examples: the Third Reich aiming at global Aryan supremacy, the Stalinst state constructing a world socialist bastion, McCarthyist America defending the free world by purging internal enemies, and the Khomeinist state attempting to purify the Muslim world.

Modern invisible totalitarianism is, however, far more subtle in its techniques. It operates on the basis of systematic distortions in communication through mediated and falsified constructions of reality. Information technologies play a dual role in this process: surveillance and dissimulation. The surveillance functions of the state have become perfected by such factors as electronic eavesdropping (e.g., Watergate), national identity numbers (e.g., social security numbers), computerized data banks, correlation modeling of the data to identify the deviants, and remote sensing and spying on a global scale.[5] The dissimulation functions have become far more sophisticated through the application of

---

[5]Due to their possession of satellite remote sensing capabilities, for instance, the United States and the Soviet Union were probably better informed than the belligerents about the conditions of the war between Iraq and Iran.

subliminal advertising techniques to political campaigns, including the packaging and programming of candidates to appeal to the audience's greatest anxieties and fears.

PROSPECTS: TECHNOLOGIES OF TRANSFORMATION

Information technologies are thus dramatizing the two stark tendencies in world development. On the one hand, they promise an era of higher productivity, direct democracy, and cultural diversity. But on the other, they threaten massive unemployment, totalitarian surveillance, cultural homogenization, and cognitive tyranny.

The current debate about "information society" represents a recurrent pattern in the history of major technological breakthroughs. The second industrial revolution, as the first, has found its celebrants among those who tend to assume technological determinist views of history. They tend, therefore, to underestimate the institutional fetters in the way of spreading the full social benefits of the new technologies. They are the technological optimists. At the other extreme, however, we have the technological pessimists. The Luddites[6] of the information revolution see in the new technological transformations the sinister designs of a new age of slavery. Both schools of thought tend to overestimate the power of technologies to shape our lives.

Out of these debates, four distinctly different scenarios of the future have emerged, which may be labeled as continuity, reform, collapse, and transformation scenarios. But a caveat on futurology is called for here. We have neither a past nor a future; we have only present reconstructions of the past and visualizations of the future. Every scenario construction is therefore an intervention in history; it projects our present images of the future towards either self-fulfilling or self-negating prophecies. To critically understand scenarios, a deconstruction is therefore necessary in order to discover what lurks behind in the inarticulated interests and normative preferences. The following discussion will attempt to do this in terms of the above four scenarios of world development.

The continuity scenario projects past trends into the future to argue that a postindustrial information society will inevitably expand its domain from the world centers to the peripheries. This view of the future is well in keeping with some two centuries of the evolutionary "Idea of Progress" as the motor of history. It is based on a stage theory that suggests

---

[6]The Luddites refers to a working class movement that flourished around 1811–16—said to have been so called after Ned Lud—that countered the labor-saving effects of the new machineries by breaking them.

an inexorable transition from agricultural to industrial and information societies. It is a view largely held at the world capitalist centers of power who consider the transition to transnational capitalism as a progressive process toward increasing world economic, political, and cultural integration. There are, however, some dissenting notes on the concept of "information society." In a recent book, *Manufacturing Matters*, Cohen and Zysman (1987) have argued against that prevalent thesis to demonstrate that the standard of living in so-called postindustrial societies still vitally depends on industry.

Proponents of *the reform scenario* see some serious problems with the continuity scenario. Alarmed by the imbalances and dangers of the present trends in world development, the Reform Scenario has called for a New World Economic, Communication, and Information Order. It has also called for a continuing international dialogue between the North and South on the past and emerging problems of trade, development, and cultural relations. These perspectives and proposals have found their most comprehensive expression in the Brandt (1980, 1983) and MacBride (1980) reports. In the wake of the oil price revolution of 1970s, the North-South dialogue had opened up an important channel for the discussion of grievances. With the decline of OPEC, however, the pressures have subsided and the North-South dialogue has been put on a back burner. The liberal reformers in the First, Second, and Third Worlds have been thus frustrated in their efforts.

The collapse scenario thus emerges out of a more polarized world situation in which reformers have a declining influence. This scenario is largely held by frustrated reformers or committed revolutionaries who suggest that due to capitalism's internal contradictions and external failures, its collapse may be slow in coming but it is inevitable. The scenario points to the failures of such showcase peripheral capitalist countries as Iran, the Philippines, and South Korea to argue that the system will first break down at its weakest links. But it would also point to the uneven processes of economic growth in the sunshine and sunset industries and its disastrous social and political consequences—particularly in the United States during the Reagan Era—to argue that the economic collapse of the system might be imminent even at the centers. The stock market crash of October 19, 1987 in New York, Tokyo, and London has added a poignancy to such forecasts. Some believers in this scenario maintain, however, that the world capitalist system will continue to foment wars abroad and fascism at home in order to postpone or save itself from total collapse.

The transformation scenario stems from some 200 years of utopian thinking in response to the onslaught of world modernization and industrialization. These views have now crystalized into the perspectives and proposals of the Green movements around the world. Insofar as most of these movements would put the preservation of community and ecology at the center of their program, they might be also called "communitarian" democratic movements. The principles of the German Green Party, for instance, include ecology, nonviolence, social responsibility, and participatory democracy. Patterned after the American Revolution's Committee of Correspondents that linked a network of town meetings, a new Committee of Correspondents in the United States has enlarged these tenets into 10 "Politics of Principle," including Ecological Wisdom, Respect for Diversity, Personal and Social Responsibility, Nonviolence, Postpatriarchal Values, Decentralizaiton, Community Economics/Empowerment, Grassroots Democracy, Global Responsibility, and Future Focus. In Sri Lanka, the Sarvodaya Movement has captured on the fourfold Buddhist principles to arrive at a philosophy of development that proposes a "neither rich nor poor" society. In Poland, the Catholic Church has played a similar source of inspiration for the Solidarity Movement to challenge the authority of a Soviet-dominated, bureaucratic, and militarist regime. In Latin America, the Theology of Liberation has promised a liberation from both economic exploitation and spiritual poverty. Whatever its principles and political complexion, the transformation scenario is calling for a fundamental transformation of the institutions of the modern industrial societies to render them more human and humane.

CONCLUSION

The enormity of the topic at hand forbids any definitive conclusions. At the risk of oversimplication, however, let me conclude that information technologies can, in fact, serve a more democratic world development on at least the following three conditions: First, if they are made more interactive. Second, if they achieve more universality and accessibility. And third, if they are increasingly locked into participatory, democratic institutions and networks.

On all three counts, we have reasons for optimism as well as pessimism. The new information technologies possess all of the three potentials: interactivity, universality, and networking capability. But they also have the opposite potentials: unidirectionality by virtue of vertical one-way flows, privileged access by virtue of high cost and unavailability, and closed circuits by virtue of institutional and technological barriers to entry.

The new information technologies possess an additional trait that most other technologies of the past lacked. They feed on a renewable, self-regenerative, and exponentially growing resource. The more information we give, the more information we have. Information feeds on information and thus grows at an accelerating rate. Information sharing has a synergistic effect. This feature alone holds a high promise for the less developed countries trying to catch up with world development. But it is also a mixed blessing.

If the process of "catching up" imposes new privileged and exploitative elites on largely impoverished and ill-informed masses, we will continue to witness cultural and political backlashes. The revolutions in Iran, Nicaragua, and the Philippines present only the most dramatic examples in recent years. Since the current information revolution is global in scope, the backlash also assumes global dimensions. And since the gaps in information largely correspond to gaps in income and power, we may anticipate new populist revolts that may fall back on the certitudes of the past to face the uncertainties of the future.

However, the synergistic effects of information also present a challenge to the more developed countries to share their scientific and technological know-how with the less developed world. A more informed, developed, and equitable world will be a more peaceful world. The challenge before us is, therefore, not so much to foresee as to empower.

2

A Theoretical Framework

Democracy as it emerged originally in such places as Greece and Iceland was based on small communities with much direct, face-to-face interaction. No doubt the cornerstone of a large-scale democracy would be small-scale democracy, democracy at the local level. But the latter is only a necessary not a sufficient condition of a large-scale democracy to function. And we probably do not yet know how to make large-scale society function in the real sense of becoming a system effectively steered by the people, of the people and for the people. There is the old model based on building stones of small-scale democracy. And there is the challenge of a possible electronic large-scale democracy. Or a mixture of the two.

(Galtung, 1987)

The Chinese character for "crisis" also signifies "opportunity." Similarly, the crisis of democracy in the modern world seems to signify an opportunity. There are two main global forces at work that may be considered as both promising and perilous for democracy: (a) the rise to historical consciousness of over three-fourths of humankind at the peripheries of power (notably women, minorities, and the colonized peoples) promising liberation as well as threatening a "dictatorship of the proletariat," and (b) the simultaneous explosion in the technologies and sources of information providing both for expanding channels of political communication and mobilization, as well as for increasing centralized surveillance and control.

The linkage between communication and power is a well-established historical fact. As the examples of charismatic politicians in history demonstrate, effective communication often translates into political power. But on the other hand, a positive correlation between communication technologies and democratic politics is highly questionable. We could even argue along with Plato (1986) in *Phaedrus* that the invention of writing, and—by extension—all the subsequent mediated forms, have taken the "soul" out of human communication. In modern times, we could further argue that the centralized, unidirectional, homogenizing, and conformist mass media of communication have worked against the essential requirements of a democratic government for decentralized, interactive, pluralistic, and critical public discourse. We could also argue with equal justice that the invention of every successive media of communication has increased the capacity, efficiency, and interactivity of the channels of social and political communication.

Has the passage from oral to print "broadcasting" and increasingly interactive technologies of communication made a difference in the substance and style of politics? Can we reasonably speak of "modes of communication" as Marx spoke of "modes of production" to suggest transitions from one era or stage of history to another? Do the different media of communication "massage" our different sensory perceptions, as Innis (1950, 1951) and McLuhan (1964, 1969) argued? Can we persuasively speak, as they did, of oral as distinctly different from print and electronic civilizations? Has the transition from oral to print and electronic media signaled a commensurate shift from rural tribalism to urban pluralism and now back to another type of orality and tribalism that is global in scope?

What about the impact of the new interactive communication technologies on democratic participation? Will they lead to concentrations or dispersions of power? Can they bring back an era of direct democracy, lost with the Age of Pericles in Athens and the New England Town Meetings? Or will they usher in a new age of surveillance typified by an Orwellian nightmare? Alternatively, can we assume that the new technologies, like the old, simply lock into the institutional structures of society to amplify or abridge the existing and emerging social and political forces?

What is the fundamental nature of the current crisis of democracy? To what extent are conflicts among social systems and their corresponding ideologies (freedom, equality and community vs. responsibility, hierarchy and order) an essential part of the problem? Can these conflicting conceptions of democracy be reconciled at all? How do information and communication help or hinder the processes of democratization? In view of the contradictory impact of the new information technologies on democratic prospects, what choices and roads lie ahead?

This book is dedicated to the proposition that information technologies are a double-edged sword. They both concentrate and disperse information and power. By themselves, they are neither the technologies of freedom nor of tyranny. They should be considered technologies of power. But by "technology," I mean hardware and software as well as the underlying cognitive deep structures. As hardware technologies of communication, they are grafted into software and programmatic technologies of power—coercion, persuasion, manipulation, or cooptation—"hegemonic power," as Gramsci (1971) called it. Systematic distortions in communication are, however, achieved by the power of the modern mass media through administered silences that impose "black holes" on public consciousness. The modern mass media have the unique property of creating an illusion of knowledge and communication without its substance. But if used interactively in the context of a critical public discourse, they also have the power to inform and awaken. This "dual media effects" hypothesis seems largely to correspond to historical evidence, but it is also democratically expedient. It prompts vigilance in defense of democratic values.

The central argument of this chapter is threefold. First, democracy as an ideal of modern government grew out of the 18th-century Enlightenment philosophies of popular sovereignty and rational public discourse. This ideal has faced a dual crisis in the rise of popular dictatorships (Nazism, Fascism, theocratic regimes) and technocratic usurpations of power (corporate capitalism and state capitalism). Second, critical public discourse and power-free communication were the conditions for the original Enlightenment visions of democracy. But these conditions have been eroded by the systematic and ideological distortions of the mass media as well as by the persistent inequalities in communicative competence and access to the means of public communication. In the meantime, total world views such as those of liberalism and Marxism have lost much of their legitimacy as the twin ideologies of Enlightenment. Third, in part as a consequence of the fragmented nature of the modern means of public communication, a fragmented consciousness seems to have gained ascendency. As a result, it has proved nearly impossible to launch much democratic resistance against those abstract, invisible, and incomprehensible forces of domination in the modern world that colonize our minds. Democratic resistance has increasingly had to resort to a kind of "cognitive guerrilla warfare" in which fragmented resistance attempts to deconstruct the ideological pretensions of the existing power structures. This strategy, here labeled as a "communitarian democratic strategy," may also prove to be a most effective mode of resistance in an age of future shock and information overload. The new interactive media can play a useful, democratic role in this context.

This chapter presents the main threads of the above argument. I will begin with a brief diagnosis of the crisis of democracy, then move on to outline a general theory of communication, mediation, and democratization, to focus finally on the current debate on the dual effects of the traditional and emerging media.

THE GLOBAL CRISIS OF DEMOCRACY

The notion of "crisis" calls for some elucidation. As a medical metaphor, crisis suggests a stage in an illness in which most ordinary remedies have failed and the doctor has to decide whether extraordinary therapeutic procedures are now in order. As a dramaturgical metaphor, crisis signifies the turning point in a fateful process caught up in the person-

ality systems of the actors. "Fate is fulfilled in the revelation of conflicting norms against which the identities of the participants shatter, unless
they are able to summon up the strength to win back their freedom by
shattering the mythical power of fate through the formation of new
identities" (Habermas, 1975, p. 2).

In the social sciences, however, the concept of "crisis" often has been
employed to capture both the biological sense of an imbalance in the
body politic as well as to imply a social "steering" capacity denied to the
finite biological organisms. The capacity of social systems to monitor
their own activities (e.g., census reports) enables them to gain consciousness of the directions of change. However, due to the complexity
of factors and vested interests at work, social systems always lag in
responding to the requirements of social change. Crisis is thus endemic
to the developmental process of all social systems. In the Marxian metaphor, there is always a lag between changes in the forces of production
(determined by material forces), the relations of production (determined
by institutional structures), and the superstructure (determined by ideational factors). Crises occur whenever these imbalances between the
new material realities and their institutional and ideational fetters cannot be resolved by normal and well-established procedures. Reformist
or revolutionary measures are needed to resolve them.

What is the nature of the current crisis of democracy? If we judge by
the declining rates of electoral participation[1] and the rising tide of political violence, democracy is facing a serious crisis worldwide. We may
observe this crisis at three possible levels of analysis. Politically, a diminishing faith in the efficacy of democratic ideals and institutions has manifested itself primarily in the distortions of the electoral process, a concurrent decline in the rates of electoral participation, and an increasing
resort to political violence by governments and their oppositions. State
terrorism is increasingly matched by oppositionist terrorism in its feroc-
ity and pervasiveness. In advanced capitalist societies, professionalization of politics, expanding government bureaucracies, decline of political parties, and the rising costs of media campaigning have increasingly
divorced the public from the political process and led progressively to
higher levels of power without responsibility.[2] In socialist and developing countries, some of the same forces have combined with the heavy
hand of the state apparatus to repress the democratic forces from below.

Economically, the decline in resources, growth, employment, income
equality, and consumer sovereignty has further undermined the confidence in the democratic methods of conflict management and dis-

[1]President Reagan, for instance, won his 1984 "landslide" victory by the vote of merely
28 percent of the eligible American voters!
[2]Witness the Watergate scandal in the United States and the Tanaka scandal in Japan.

tributive justice. In advanced capitalist societies, the current technological revolution in robotics and informatics implies an increasing
exacerbation of social class conflicts. Labor-saving methods of production have already raised levels of *structural* unemployment. Tolerable
levels of unemployment used to be considered around 3–4 percent in
the 1950s and 1960s; they now have more than doubled to 7–8 percent.
In 1961, under 5 percent of the OECD workforce was unemployed; in
1985, 8½ percent. In the United States, historical evidence suggests that
to arrive at unemployment figures for black adults and youths, these
figures should be respectively doubled and quadrupled. If we add
cyclical unemployment rates to these figures, we arrive at a more realistic appreciation of the seriousness of the economic crisis facing advanced capitalist societies. Declining growth rates, rising public debts,
and diminishing public and welfare services—as exemplified by
Thatcherism in Britain and Reaganomics in the United States—are only
surface symptoms of a more profound legitimation crisis. Although both
regimes seemed for a while to have resolved the problems of capitalist
growth during the 1980s, by privatization in Britain and deregulation in
the United States, the stock market crash of 1987 has signaled the end of
an era of euphoric growth based on the quicksands of rising debts and
government defense spending.

In most developing countries, the declining prices of raw materials
vis-a-vis finished industrial goods, and a steady rise in indebtedness and
debt service as a percentage of export earnings, have spelled economic
disaster. According to *The Economist*, the poor countries contributed $65
billion to the growth of the rich countries through lower prices of their
raw material exports. The newly industrializing countries (NICs), which
have done best in terms of achieving high rates of growth, have lost
most with respect to their declining terms of trade. As exporters of raw
materials, they have lost 15–20 percent of their export earnings since
1980 while producing more. With the fall of crude oil prices in 1986, the
oil-exporting countries are expected to suffer more deteriorating terms
of trade. OPEC has some very rich members such as Saudi Arabia and
Kuwait, but it also includes some low-income countries such as Nigeria
and Indonesia. The income transfers from poor to rich countries constitute what *The Economist* (1985, pp. 75–76) has aptly called, "the poor
man's burden." The story of Southeast Asia is typical:

> The World Bank and others have long advised poor countries to diver-
> sify their commodity exports. But what happens when almost all raw-
> material prices are falling at once? South East Asia is now finding out. Few
> raw material producers have tried harder than Malaysia to follow the
> World Bank's advice. In the first five months of 1980, five commodities
> accounted for 72% of its exports: crude oil, palm oil, tin, rubber, timber. In

the first five months of this year [1985]—before prices of palm oil, rubber and tin began their sudden slump—those five commodities' share of total exports had fallen to 56%. Since then, the price of palm oil has fallen 57%. Tin price could soon halve. But the prices of goods that Malaysia has to import have risen steadily since 1983. The measure of this change in terms of trade, which is the ratio of export prices to import prices, Malaysia's terms of trade have fallen 19% since 1980. In other words, it has to export that much more this year than it did in 1980 to buy the same volume of imports. The terms of trade have fallen even more for Thailand and the Philippines. Only Indonesia, which gets 60% of its export dollars from oil, has improved its terms of trade, thanks to OPEC.

Culturally, the excessive polarization and dualism in many social contexts between the self-appointed modern, secular elites and their traditionalist constituencies have led to the rise of populist, nativist, and messianic movements fanning religious, tribal, racial, ethnic, or linguistic fanaticism. This is most evident in the developing countries where populations are the most heterogeneous and democratic institutions the weakest. But in the advanced, liberal, capitalist societies, too, the rise of fundamentalist religious movements has already reached alarming political proportions. In the United States, the electronic church, representing the views of the fundamentalist religious and political right, already captures nearly 50 percent of the television audiences. It represents a reaction against the cultural permissiveness celebrated by the profitable cultural industries. The incipient cultural cleavages thus generated could reach crisis proportions when and if combined with a major economic and political crisis.

The root cause of the crisis of democracy may be attributed to three fundamental processes of *depoliticization* taking place in the economic, political, and cultural spheres. All three processes find their common core in the rapid postwar penetration of a global capitalist economy throughout the world, including those parts of the world where the state still plays a dominant part in the economy (i.e., the communist and Third World economies). In most communist countries, the hegemonic political system may be more appropriately identified as "state capitalism." In these situations, the state rather than the corporate apparatus largely owns the means of production and makes the important saving and investment decisions. Rents, profits, and wages are distributed more through state planning than market mechanisms. Benefits are thus distributed largely through "political" rather than "economic" centers of gravity. But insofar as the "political" process is itself institutionalized into fairly rigid power bureaucracies and hierarchies of the state and the party, popular and democratic forces are locked out.

The *depoliticization of the economy* may be considered to be a fundamental feature of capitalism as a modern social formation. In a typology of three major sociohistorical formations into primitive, traditional, and liberal-capitalist (see Table 2.1), Habermas (1975) has argued persuasively that by institutionalizing the class relationships into the labor market, liberal-capitalism has delinked economic power from state power. In contrast to primitive societies in which most power relationships are a function of kinship, and traditional societies in which the landowning classes also directly control bureaucracy and state power, liberal capitalism decouples economic and political power. Through the creation of market mechanisms relatively free from the state, capitalism depoliticizes economic power and transforms class domination into anonymous forms. Through the creation of representative democratic institutions (parliaments, elections, etc.), voluntary associations (political parties, labor unions, etc.), and the mass media, liberal capitalism pluralizes political power into competing elite centers that enjoy some degree of *functional* autonomy. But in the meantime, the central function of the state becomes the protection of the market from external or internal disruptions. The state thus serves the fundamental interests of the capitalist class without being completely subservient to it; it provides a "political" barometer and a safety valve for gauging and releasing the pressures of the capitalist economic cycles of growth and stagnation.

As Habermas (1975, 1979) has argued, a permanent legitimation crisis is thus built into the structures of the modern capitalist state. By institutionalizing the opposition into the fabric of the modern constitutional state while releasing the economic forces to produce conditions of inequality, the capitalist state is constantly challenged on its fundamental principles and projects. The extraordinary achievement of capitalism in

Table 2.1.   Illustrations of Social Principles of Organization

Social formations	Principles of Organization	Social and System Integration	Type of Crisis
Primitive	kinship relations: primary roles (age, sex)	no differentiation between social and system integration	externally induced identity crisis
Traditional	political class rule: state power and socioeconomic classes	functional differentiation between social and system integration	internally determined identity crisis
Liberal-Capitalism	unpolitical class rule: wage labor and capital	system integrative economic system also takes over socially integrative tasks	system crisis

Source: Habermas, 1975, p. 24.

liberating the economic forces from their traditional institutional fetters and subjecting them to the rigorous rules of market competition is marred by an inherent instability of the system. The system is economically crisis-prone. Overproduction and underconsumption seem to be two sides of the same coin in the capitalist cycles of prosperity, crisis, and depression.

The economic crises of capitalism inevitably develop into political crises, focusing on problems of class, ethnic, or racial conflicts. In periods of prosperity, politics of *status* supersede *interest* politics (Bell, 1964). But in periods of recession and depression, social conflict manifests itself more starkly in the form of labor-management disputes, strikes, and open violence. But no matter what form they take, the fundamental issues at stake are those of distributive justice. State intervention in the economic system, via the Keynesian instruments of fiscal and monetary policies, has become an imperative in the salvation of liberal, competitive capitalism from its own powers of self-destruction. In the United States, for instance, the Keynesian Democrats have historically served capitalism far more effectively than the Republican monetarists. Periods of Republican prosperity (1920s and 1980s) have often led to excesses of income maldistribution, failure of effective demand, economic recession, or depression.

But an equally powerful means of resolving legitimation crisis is to resort to a totalitarian solution, that is, a mixture of extreme nationalism, populism, and statist policies. While liberal capitalism emphasizes individual liberty, social democratic capitalism stresses social equality, and totalitarian capitalism focuses on national solidarity at the expense of liberty and equality. Historically, periods of capitalist prosperity and liberal permissivess have been followed by economic depression to pave the way for the rise of totalitarian movements. But such periods have also historically led to leftist movements. The totalitarian right often employs a scapegoat psychology to focus on an external or internal national "enemy" to rally popular forces around its own cause. This provides the political justifications for repression at home and aggression abroad.

The rise of a global, corporate capitalism from the ashes of World War II has signaled a second set of crises rooted in the processes of *depoliticization of the state*. The increasing insularity of the state from the political process has been largely achieved through three fundamental mechanisms, including (a) separation of powers, (b) bureaucratization of the state apparatus, and (c) professionalization of the decision-making processes. Each of these forces has had a long history of development rooted in the making of modern industrial society—whether capitalist or communist. Together they represent an alarming degree of alienation of citizens from state power.

First, the doctrine of separation of powers—"discovered" by Montesquieu (1970/1978) in his analysis of the workings of the (unwritten)
English Constitution—has long been considered a key to the preservation of freedom under liberal capitalism. However, to the extent that it
still works, it could also be considered a key to the understanding of an
increasing dissolution of political responsibility and depoliticization of
the state. The doctrine finds its ultimate expression in the U.S. Constitution, in which the executive, legislative, and judiciary branches of government are differentiated by their forms of election/appointment,
terms of office, types of constituencies, and locus of power and responsibility. To the extent that the executive has grown in size, power, and
stature (representing an ever-growing bureaucratic state machinery),
the doctrine of separation of powers has declined in importance. The
doctrine, however, continues to serve as a fig leaf for political irrespon-
sibility in a state of affairs in which each branch of the government can
blame the other for the ills of democracy—mounting deficits, unemployment, crime, inflation, and so on. Under these circumstances, a "popular" president can be elected by a "landslide" (see footnote 1) while all of
these problems continue to smolder.

Second, the ever-growing bureaucratic machinery has depoliticized
the state in a variety of complex forms. By contrast to the Weberian
traditional and charismatic types of authority, rational-legal authority is
based on a series of universalized and depersonalized decisions. Bureaucratic justice is presumed to be blind. In a democracy, bureaucratic
authority is supposed to be subservient to the ultimate source of sovereignty—the people's will. However, state bureaucracies have come
under two distinctly different kinds of pressures that distort their presumed impartiality in the application of the law.

On the one hand, state bureaucracy faces a wide variety of larger,
more powerful and more pervasive private, corporate bureaucracies—
ever-watchful and protective of the decisions in their own spheres of
interest. In the United States, the oil lobby, the telecommunications
lobby, or the farmers' lobby, each provide abundant examples of the
kinds of pressures brought to bear continually on the legislative, judiciary, and executive decision-making processes. These pressures are
fueled more by the principle of one-dollar-one-vote than by the principle
of one-man-one vote. In their campaign contributions, armed with their
legions of lawyers and large pool of technical knowledge, these lobbies
often outweigh the power of the regulatory agencies and state bureaucracies charged with the defense of public interest.

On the other hand, the very insularity of state bureaucracies has
opened them to the pressures of careerism. Aimed at "protecting" bureaucracies from "undue" political pressures, their "neutrality" has
positioned them to coexist comfortably with the prevailing political

winds and the lures of post-retirement office seeking in private corporations. In the United States, following their retirement, former state officials from the president down often sell their political "know-how" to
the highest corporate bidders by sitting on their board of directors. This
is particularly true of the military personnel, whose technical and bureaucratic knowledge is vital for the procurement of defense contracts.

Third, the increasing professionalization of decision making in modern industrial societies has also contributed immensely to the processes
of depoliticization of the state. Ivan Illich (1971b, 1974, 1978; Illich et al.,
1977), among others, has provided a brilliant critique of the monopoly
power that goes with this phenomenon. The certification of the professions in the medical, legal, teaching, and counseling professions has
created monopoly markets based upon claims to scientific and technical
authority. To a certain extent, this is the inevitable result of an ever-
increasing division and specialization of labor characteristic of modern
industrial society. But the ensuing scientism and elitism subordinates
normative, and hence political, decisions to the dictates of narrow and
vested interests. If the power of big business were to match that of big
labor, as Galbraith (1956) has argued in his theory of countervailing
power, the resulting political balance may be considered somewhat
democratic. But when the organized sectors of the market collude, as
they often do, and restrict public discourse by agenda setting, public
opinion will be manipulated and distorted. This agenda-setting function
goes to the core of the constraints imposed upon public discourse by the
professional elites in almost every sphere—business, labor, medical,
educational, and military affairs. The administration of silence on vital
issues of public policy becomes, therefore, a more important task of
public and private bureaucracies than the encouragement of critical public discourse.

COMMUNICATION, MEDIATION, AND DEMOCRATIZATION

In the highly complex, differentiated, and bureaucratized industrial societies, the one last recourse of democratic will formation thus lies in
social movements and public communication. But culture and communication as the vehicles for the regeneration of new meanings and normative structures have themselves been increasingly routinized, bureaucratized, and industrialized. In advanced industrial societies, this
has been achieved fundamentally through the three processes of
distantiation, bureaucratization, and *homogenization* of culture and communication. All three processes have favored the centralizing and de-
politicizing tendencies in the modern industrial society. They have also

produced what Habermas (1975, 1979) calls systematic distortions in public communication and consciousness.

The processes of distantiation of communication began notably with the print technology, but they have accelerated by the pervasive presence of the electronic media. Interactive technologies, such as the telephone, have somewhat moderated the totally unidirectional character of modern media. But their effects have been thus far confined largely to interpersonal communication. The new technologies, such as computer networking and videotex, may change this by providing vehicles for interactive public communication. But due to prohibitive costs and required technological expertise, interactive uses of the new technologies have been largely limited to scientific and business elites. Smaller media, such as audiocassettes, mimeographing, photocopying, and—increasingly—desktop publishing have served some democratic movements. But distantiation of communication on the whole has served the interests and purposes of larger and more centralized organizations with greater financial and bureaucratic means at their command.

Bureaucratization of public communication has been an inexorable and accelerating trend in modern industrial societies. Mass communication as a new industry has called forth huge investments in equipment and personnel that only the state or large corporations can afford. The new cultural industries, from publishing to film, music, radio, and television have, in turn, had to follow the impersonal dictates of the state or the marketplace. In the heyday of liberalism, the publishing industry fought a valiant battle against government control and censorship. Keenly aware of its delicate dependence on credibility, the press insisted on the rights of free expression. The growth of the publishing industry also coincided with the development of capitalism and an industrial bourgeoisie keenly interested in the free flow of information and commodities. But the transition from competitive to monopoly capitalism has witnessed a transition from competitive to monopoly media (Bagdikian, 1983).

The new transnational media corporations have become, therefore, increasingly more interested in the free flow of commodities than of ideas. In the new cultural industries, ideas are indeed viewed primarily as commodities. As Marcuse (1964) has insightfully observed, even oppositionist ideas are treated as potentially lucrative sources of revenues. They are thus bought, transformed, newly packaged, mass produced, advertised, and sold to the mass markets with devastating effects on their original vitality and potency. Even the leading talents (actors, authors, conductors, painters, professors) are turned into commodities cum "stars" to capture the broadest possible markets. A great deal of marketing and advertising talent thus goes into the mass production of a new book, piece of music, or *object d'art* and their authors. The star system, first discovered by Hollywood in the 1930s, has now been extended to all genres of arts, letters, sciences, and politics. Bureaucratization of public communication in the socialist countries has taken fundamentally the same directions as under capitalism. However, robbed of the feedback mechanisms of the marketplace, the modern bureaucratic state has not developed as sophisticated techniques as the modern bureaucratic media corporations have. The central objective in both systems is the production of homogenized cultural products appealing to mass audiences. While under commercial media, economic objectives tend to predominate, in the state-run mass communication systems, political and ideological pursuits are the primary motive. In both cases, the manufacturing of consent along certain bureaucratically-contrived beliefs, values, and behavior is the ultimate political objective. Cultural currents from the grass roots are thus selected, transformed, and homogenized to fit the image that fits the needs of a narcotized, malleable, and abiding citizen-consumer. Mass communication systems also affect the socialization functions of the primary groups—the family, church, school, and peer groups. It may be hypothesized that in the absence of significant social movements, the other socializing institutions tend to merely replicate and reinforce the socialization effects of the mass media. A totally homogenized mass culture, produced by the mass media, may be thus viewed as the ultimate dream of a totalitarian regime.

Mass communication in its noninteractive modes clearly supports the powers-that-be, that is, the status quo. But a case can be made for the democratizing effects of the more interactive media. The new interactive information technologies (emerging from a convergence of print, telephony, broadcasting, cable, computer, satellite, and microprocessing technologies) are still in their infancy and therefore subject to speculation. Interactive public communication technologies, such as videotex, are just beginning to make their debut in history. We know little about their potential uses and effects. Thanks, however, to the increasing convergence, miniaturization, and accessibility of the interactive media, the new channels can be employed to achieve greater community access, participation, and self-management. For the first time in history, citizens can potentially vote not only with their feet (through representative democracy) but also with their voices (through direct democracy) and their collective will (through corporate democracy). Direct democracy, an ideal and partial practice of Athens in the Age of Pericles (which, by the way, excluded women and slaves from citizenship), can potentially complement representative or corporate forms of democracy.

This potential of the future, however, should be viewed in the light of a fundamental social reality—that the media are only one cog in the wheel of society, one institution among other institutions, dependent for their role on what is assigned to them by the more general, societal hierarchies of power. The central theoretical questions, therefore, may be posed as follows: Do the media mirror or mould the power structure? If they mirror the power structure, what functions do they serve? If they mould it, to what end and direction? Towards concentration or dispersion of power? Do different media entail different consequences for the power structure? What about the role of audiences? Are we to assume that they are dependent and passive, or autonomous and active? To reverse the traditional question of media effects on the audiences, what are the effects of audiences on the media? What uses and gratifications do audiences obtain from the media?

To raise these questions is tantamount to raising questions on the fundamental philosophical questions of freedom and necessity—of human agency and inexorable forces of social structure. Peterson (1976) and Rosengren (1981) have developed a useful fourfold typology of the different possible theoretical positions with respect to the mutual interactions of material and symbolic foundations of society, or "social structure" and "culture." The same four basic positions could apply equally well to the theoretical controversies surrounding the role of the media in power formations (see Table 2.2). In a matrix organized around two alternative propositions on relations between the media and the power structure, we may consider the following four possible theoretical positions: (a) Idealism, (b) materialism, (c) autonomy, and (d) Interdependency.

The theoretical literature on communication and social change has focused on the problems of "media effects" and "communication and democratization" to produce a variety of schools of thought, ranging from determinism to indeterminism, from idealism to materialism, and from empiricism to criticism. The debate has been largely between the proponents of the consensus and conflict models of society and, in the larger international context, between the modernization/growth para-

Table 2.2.   The Media and Power Structure:
Four Theoretical Positions

		Power Structure Influences Media	
		Yes:	No:
Media Influences	Yes:	Interdependence	Idealism
Power Structure	No:	Materialism	Autonomy

Source: Adapted from Peterson (1976) and Rosengren (1981).

digm and dependency/cultural imperialism paradigm. The theoretical challenge is, however, to go beyond this dichotomous and stale debate. Table 2.3 provides a conceptual map that points to the emergence of a third paradigm characterized by idealist/materialist interdependency, probabilistic indeterminacy, and the importance of human agency, structuration, and communicative action in the processes of social change. The discussion that follows, of necessity, has to be brief and presupposes some familiarity with the literature.

As in most conceptual maps, the boxes of this matrix should be interpreted liberally to allow also for the overlapping schools that result from the theoretical dialogue among contending schools. But the three dominant traditions delineated horizontally differ with respect to their views of determinacy/indeterminacy and idealism/materialism, while the three schools delineated vertically differ on the question of powerful/powerless media. We may also discern a historical evolution in the position of the various schools. The idealist positions have evolved from an earlier view of assigning a powerful role to the media in social change to views that consider the media only of marginal importance. In the earlier era, this school was characterized by the so-called "bullet theory" in the works of Lasswell (1927), Lerner (1958), Schramm (1964), Berlo (1960), and the source-message-channel-receiver (SMCR) models of communication that are heavily influenced by the engineering theories and systems models of information and communication (Shannon & Weaver, 1959). The diffusion, theories, beginning with Lazarsfeld, Berelson, and Gaudeh (1948), Katz and Lazarsfield (1964), and Rogers and Schoemaker (1971) viewed the media important only in conjunction

Table 2.3. Communication and Social Change: A Conceptual Map

Social Change:	Idealist Empiricist Consensus Modernization Liberal	Materialist Critical Conflict Dependency Marxist	Interdependency Structuration Communcative Action Another Development Communitarian
Communication:			
High Effects	Systems theory; bullet & boo- merang theo- ries	Semiotics & post- structuralism	Chicago & Toronto schools; symbolic interactionism; discourse theory
Medium Effects	Diffusion theories	Hegemonic theories; Frankfort School	Uses and gratification & structuration theories
Low Effects	Minimum effects theories	False consciousness theories	Communicative action & dialogical communica- tion theories

with the interpersonal channels of communication and the psychological dispositions (early adopters/late adopters, traditional/modern) of the audiences. One-step flow models (employing the bullet or hypodermic needle metaphors) thus gave their place to the two-step and multiple step-flows of communication. In the works of Joseph Klapper (1960) and George Comstock et al. (1972), however, this tradition of "media effects" theories is shown to have moved away from powerful media towards "the minimum effects theory" of communication that considers the influence of the media only in terms of the reinforcement of prior dispositions. Throughout, however, this tradition of communication research is committed to an Aristotelian and empiricist perspective on discrete causes and effects as applied to its studies of the effects of the media on the behavioral changes of the audience. This school thus tends to view communication primarily as a vertical flow process from source to receiver with the objectives of influence, persuasion, and behavior modification lurking behind.

The materialist, Marxist, and critical school is, by contrast, committed to a bottom-up approach to communication, that is, to discovering how ideology and communication serve to mystify the social relations of domination and exploitation and how to subvert those mystifications by "scientific" class analysis. The historic evolution of this school begins with theories of "false consciousness," as proposed in *The German Ideology* (Marx & Engels, 1970). In the orthodox Marxist view, ideology and communication are thus considered part of society's superstructure that is dependent upon its economic and technological base—forces and relations of production. Economic determinism and reductionism is, however, a position no longer entertained by most academic Marxists—who often refer to it as "vulgar" Marxism. The neo-Marxists (from Gramsci to the Frankfort School, the structuralists and post-structuralists, notably Althuser and Foucault) have assigned to "ideology" a more critical role in the processes of social and political change (Grossberg, 1985; Thompson, 1984). Gramsci's (1971) concept of "hegemony" departs from the classical Marxist views of ideology as false consciousness. It suggests that the ruling classes *co-opt* rather than *enforce* collaboration. The concept of hegemony has thus opened the theoretical door to various mixes of idealism and materialism, agency and determination. Nevertheless, the neo-Marxist theories of ideology continue to view the media as servants of the ruling classes—the owners and managers of the means of production and communication. With the rise of the electronic media and cultural industries, this relationship becomes increasingly more complex and mystified but no less real. The commercial media transform even the most revolutionary and popular cultural ideas and products into cultural commodities to advance their own profits while trivializing and sapping them of political power. At the same time, the consciousness industries propagate belief systems, values, and behaviors congenial to the continuity and prosperity of the capitalist system (Marcuse, 1964). Thus, in the works of the Frankfort School, the Marxist semioticians, and post-structuralists, we are back to the powerful media metaphors.

The third school is by far the most difficult to identify and situate. However, it clearly represents an emerging and powerful body of thought and literature. The school borrows from both the empirical and critical traditions to emphasize interdependency and to argue that idealism and materialism cannot be treated as mutually exclusive categories. In its methodology, the third school is critical of both the modernization and dependency paradigms for their determinism (Aristotelian causes and effects vs. Hegelian/Marxist dialectics), while emphasizing the importance of human agency and structuration (Giddens, 1984), communicative action (Habermas, 1983), and dialogical communication (Freire, 1978) in the processes of social change. The school has evolved from the Chicago School (the symbolic interactionism of George Mead and Herbert Blumer) to the Toronto School (Harold Innis and Marshall McLuhan), both emphasizing the centrality of the media, to the Habermas and Freirian perspectives on social change in which a hypothesized "Ideal Speech Community" and dialogical communication leave the media a secondary role to play. Concurrently, the school has also moved towards the uses and gratification (Blumler & Katz, 1974) and structuration (Giddens et al.) theories in which the media present themselves as part of a larger arena of consciousness and behavioral formation.

Clearly, the problematic of the effects of information technologies has not been addressed directly in all of the above theoretical traditions. Paradoxically enough, however, the idealist position may be viewed as closely identified with a kind of technological determinism. The proponents of this school have tended to argue that, through their impact on new cultural formations, communication technologies have also shaped human consciousness, social values, and power structures. By contrast, the materialists (notably the orthodox Marxists) have considered communication technologies as part of the larger cultural and ideological superstructure of a mode of production in which the forces and relations of production play the decisive role. The "autonomy" hypothesis assumes a high degree of institutional differentiation between the media and political institutions. For instance, Bell (1976) has argued that in modern capitalist societies, the economic, political, and cultural institutions are organized around different principles or axes of power and thus work rather autonomously. The "interdependency" hypothesis views society as a complex, interactive, open, and probablistic system in which few outcomes can be guaranteed.

In the theoretical schools associated with the names of Frankfort (Horkheimer, Adorno, Fromm, Marcuse, and Habermas), Chicago (Mead and Blumer) and Toronto (Innis and McLuhan), the interdependency hypothesis finds its best and most diverse expressions. But not all theorists address the question of mediated communication with equal directness. Innis and McLuhan are the notable exceptions. The Toronto School (Innis, 1950, 1951; McLuhan 1962, 1964) has argued that the introduction of each new technology of communication in history has brought about new sets of cognitive styles and belief systems characteristic of that technology's epoch of history. To use Innis's formulation, the media "bias" human communication. To use McLuhan's metaphor, the media "massage" the message.[3] The Age of Orality favors the immediacy and participatory power of tribalism. The Age of Print distantiates communication and imposes a linear rationality on the mind. The Age of Electronic Media partially brings back the tribalism of the Age of Orality. Radio is a "cool medium" in that it engages only one sensory perception, while television is a "hot medium" in that it involves two sensory perceptions. Neither Innis nor McLuhan had an opportunity to witness the Age of Personal Computers. But to extend their arguments, we may suggest that the more advanced, interactive computer work stations (via modems, telephone lines, printers, and facsimile machines) combine the characteristics of the print and electronic media into one. Computers have not as yet achieved the immediacy and full participatory power of face-to-face, oral communication, but when combined with videophones and three-dimensional pictures, they might approach it. The Media Lab at Massachusetts Institute of Technology (MIT) is currently engaged in active research on the creation of the next generation of media technologies of this genre (Brand, 1987). While the Innis-McLuhan perspectives have a great deal of intuitive appeal, their media-centric view of history borders on technological determinism.

As Rosengren (1981, p. 248) suggests, "it may well be that in coming years the discussion will concern the axis of interdependence-autonomy rather than of materialism-idealism, and that it will be moving from a holistic, overall perspective to a more differentiated one." Context-free theories of communication are, increasingly, losing their appeal and relevance. Communication and culture are inextricably tied together; theories of communication need to be, therefore culturally and historically specific to be relevant. From this perspective—a perspective that may be labeled "contextualism"—all of the above theoretical views may

---

[3]This is McLuhan's original formulation, later changed to "the medium is the message." While Innis's formulations are generally more tentative and scholarly, McLuhan's assertions tend to be more dramatic and dogmatic.

find some relevance to the understanding of some sociohistorical situations. But none of them can provide us with a general theory of communication relevant to all times and all places. It should be, however, possible to identify the main elements of a human communication process without asserting the preponderance of one. That question should be left to an empirical and historical analysis of the context at hand.

Similarly, the axis of debate seems to have shifted somewhat from the more simplistic technophilic and technophobic arguments to an emerging debate between the technoneutralists and technostructuralists. The neutralists tend to view information simply as a neutral commodity to be produced or consumed, bought or sold in the marketplace. The structuralists, by contrast, view information as fundamentally different from other commodities in that it *in-forms* the mind. Information thus embodies social values and imparts social power. In other words, there is no information without meaning. Stock market information, for example, suggests a high premium on wealth. Timely access to this perisherable information may impart socioeconomic power. From a technostructuralist and interdependency perspective—a view proposed here—the production of information, as indeed that of all intellectual production (music, painting, books, etc.), is profoundly interconnected with the production of wealth and income. Information and communication should thus be viewed as critical ideological factors in the legitimation of concentrations and dispersions of power.

A CONTEXTUALIST PERSPECTIVE

From a contextualist perspective, the idealist and materialist positions are not as irreconcilable as they seem at first sight. If we begin with the Weberian question of "why people obey," the response could provide us perhaps with a clue as to the role of communication in political life. People obey, Weber hypothesized, either because they are coerced or because they view the sources of command as legitimate. People obey, of course, often grudgingly or unknowingly due to both coercive and consensual factors–in terms of the elaborate structures of traditional, rational-legal, or charismatic authority. If we view "coercion" as the sum total of involuntary obedience enforced by hierarchies of power, and "consensus" as the sum total of voluntary obedience to social norms reached by genuine communication and democratic will formation, then society may be conceived to be based on these two indispensable pillars.

Figure 2.1 attempts to demonstrate the dialectics of this relationship and its consequences for social order or social anarchy. Society is held

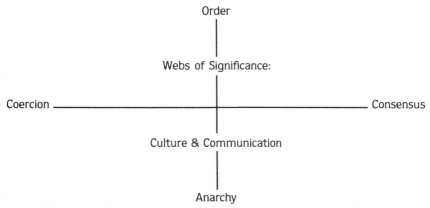

Figure 2.1.   The Webs of Significance: Communication and Social Order.

together within the tensions of this contradictory framework through its processes of cultural and communication exchange–or what Weber has most aptly called its "webs of significance."

This view of the role of coercion, communication, and consensus in social formations approximates the views of Habermas (1973, 1979, 1983), who has provided a useful synthesis of the Marxian, Weberian, Freudian, and Parsonian traditions in his theory of the "communicative action." In the words of his translator, Thomas McCarthy (Habermas, 1979, p. xvii), the theory

> might be best described as a three-tiered research program. The ground level consists of a general theory of communication—as Habermas calls it, a universal pragmatics—; at the next level this theory serves as the foundation for a general theory of socialization in the form of a theory of the acquisition of communicative competence; finally, at the highest level, which builds on those below it, Habermas sketches a theory of social evolution which he views as a reconstruction of historical materialism.

In his theory of ideology and communication, Habermas seems to have moved from methodological considerations to linguistic models and finally to a theory of fragmented consciousness (Servaes, 1987). In the first phase, he combines a Marxian critique of "false consciousness" with a Freudian theory of "repression" to arrive at a critical theory of ideology (Habermas, 1972). In the second phase, Habermas's interest shifts to the linguistic models of ideology in which he posits the notion of power-free dialogue (Habermas, 1975, 1979). In the third phase, represented by his magnum opus, *A Theory of Communicative Action*

(1983), Habermas arrives at a theory of fragmented consciousness. He argues here that a critique of ideology is no longer possible, because in a communicatively rationalized world, total world views are no longer trustworthy. People are no longer moved by ideological motives. Knowledge has become so fragmented that people can no longer observe the colonization of their life-world. Since there is no total world view, no critique of it is possible. We may conclude from this that we are in need of a theory of fragmented consciousness and intellectual guerrilla tactics in combating it. We need to develop a deconstruction strategy that gives, in Michel Foucault's apt phrase, "power no place to hide."

Despite their theoretical differences, Habermas and Foucault provide a framework for a symbolic structuralist perspective on communication and social change. To synthesize their contributions, it may be useful to begin with Table 2.4 that gives a schematic view of the three fundamental functions/processes of communication in society. The table couples these functions with the cultural, socioeconomic, and political institutions that perform them:

Habermas's complex arguments on communication and social evolution may be summarized as follows. First, Habermas conceptualizes "the ideal speech community" as one in which communication takes place without any external or internal constraints of force or domination. Deviations from this utopian ideal take place by systems of domination and systematic distortions in communication caused by the psychic and social repressions characteristic of existential and historical situations of domination. As in systematic distortions in communication at the psychic level, systematic distortions at the social level can best be corrected—to a degree—through the exercise of critical reason, emancipatory consciousness, and discursive, democratic will formation. Habermas's theory of communication is analogous to Freudian psychoanalysis in its emancipatory objectives. But Habermas attempts to unify a broader variety of theoretical endeavors usually assigned to disparate

Table 2.4.   Communication and Social Structure

Communication functions/ processes:	Signification	Socialization	Legitimation
Social structures of domination:			
Caste, status & class	Cultural institutions (language & the arts)	Socio-economic institutions (family, school, religion, work)	Political institutions (local, national, international)

and only occasionally related disciplines—from theories of knowledge and learning to theories of social action.

Second, Habermas provides a theory of socialization grounded in Freudian psychoanalysis, Marxian dialectical materialism, and Meadian symbolic interactionism. He starts from the interdependence of personality and social structures, forms of identity, and social integration, but goes beyond each of his sources of theoretical inspiration to provide a general theory of socialization, including communication, ego identity, and moral development. Communication can succeed or fail, he claims, on the basis of four validity claims: comprehensibility, truth, rightness, and truthfulness. Each of these represents a different dimension of reality—language, external nature, society, and internal nature. Human socialization and development may be viewed as a process of increasing critical autonomy of the subject with respect to these four domains. This means an interdependent process of increasing linguistic, cognitive, interactive, and ego competence (see Tables 2.5 and 2.6).

A key to the understanding of Habermas's argument is the distinction he makes between "communicative" and "strategic" actions. To provide a sharper distinction, I propose to call the latter "coercive" action. The following modified diagram (see Table 2.6) provides the main outlines of this distinction and their corresponding genres of communication, from artistic and religious to traditional/normative, scientific, ideological, and propagandistic.

The tensions between these types of action are represented by the tensions among different modes of communication. The tensions also represent their fundamentally different validity claims. To put it simply,

Table 2.5. Validity Claims and Domains of Reality in Communicative Action

Domain of Reality	Modes of Communication: Basic Attitudes	Validity Claims	General Functions of Speech
"The" world of external nature	Cognitive: objectivating attitude	Truth	Representation of facts
"Our" world of society	Interactive: conformative attitude	Rightness	Establishment of legitimate interpersonal relations
"My" world of internal nature	Expressive: expressive attitude	Truthfulness	Disclosure of speaker's subjectivity
Language	Practical: communicative attitude	Comprehensibility	Reproduction of meaning

Source: Adapted from Habermas, 1979, p. 68.

Table 2.6. Types of Social Action and Communication Strategies

Social Action			
Communicative Action: aimed at under- standing		Coercive Action: aimed at compliance	
Action oriented to reaching under- standing (artistic & religious com- munication)	Consensual action	Manifestly coercive action	Latently coercive action
Action (norms & tradi- tions)	Discourse (critical science)	Manipulation (propaganda)	Systematically distorted communication (ide- ology)

Source: Adapted from Habermas, 1979, p. 209.

coercive action assumes that "might is right," while communicative action presumes just the opposite. The points of tension among the two types of action and their subdivisions may be identified as follows (adapted from Habermas, 1979, pp. 209–210):

Communicative vs. Coercive Action

In communicative action, a basis for mutually recognized validity claims is presupposed; this is not the case in coercive action. By contrast, in coercive action, only an indirect understanding is possible—via use or threat of violence or psychological manipulations aimed at persuasion (e.g., advertising or systematic distortions of communication through ideological manipulations).

Action Oriented to Reaching Understanding vs. Consensual Action

In action oriented towards reaching understanding, such as in artistic or religious communication, an intersubjective leap of faith presupposes a common definition of situation and consensus. In consensual action, the rituals and procedures of traditions, norms, and scientific methods set the stage for a process of argumentation, interpretation, and final arrival at a tentative consensus.

Action vs. Discourse

In communicative action, it is naively supposed that implicitly raised validity claims can be vindicated (or made immediately plausible by way of question and answer). In discourse, on the other hand, the validity claims raised for statements and norms are hypothetically bracketed and thematically examined. As in communicative action, the participants in discourse retain a cooperative attitude.

Manipulative Action vs. Systematically Distorted Communication

In systematically distorted communication, at least one of the participants deceives *himself* about the fact that the basis of consensual action is only apparently being maintained. In other words, the manipulator deceives at least one of the *other* participants about his own coercive attitude. The difference is thus fundamentally one of operating at the unconscious versus conscious levels. While ideological distortions are often made unconsciously, drowning the ideologues in their own self-deceit, manipulative advertising and propaganda are consciously designed to reach and persuade particular target audiences.

Third, Habermas provides a theory of social evolution informed by his theories of communication and socialization. Three theoretical problems have traditionally confronted such an undertaking: idealism vs. materialism, individual vs. social development, social consensus vs. social conflict. In terms of the Marxian metaphor of base and superstructure, Habermas takes the position that "normative structures do not simply follow the path of development of reproductive processes but have an internal history" (Habermas, 1979, p. xxi). With respect to the problem of individual vs. social development, Habermas's strategy is to employ social structural comparisons with the developmental logic worked out for ontogenetic processes in the framework of his theory of communicative competence. Aware of the pitfalls of this strategy, he suggests three domains of comparison: rationality structures in ego development and in the evolution of worldviews; the development of ego and collective identities; the development of moral consciousness and the evolution of moral and religious representation. To make an effective linkage between the two sets of homologous structures of consciousness forming at the individual and social levels, Habermas turns to learning theory. But to explain the disjunctions between the two as well as to allow room for a theory of social conflict, Habermas makes a distinction between three types of human rationality, knowledge, interests, and learning processes.

Social evolution is conceived by Habermas as a tridimensional learning process, including cognitive/technical, moral/practical, and critical/emancipatory (see Table 2.7). As an "ideal type" distinction, this provides a useful analytical tool for the understanding of the different social and normative structures characteristic of different societies.

Table 2.7. Types of Rationality, Knowledge, Interests, and Learning

	Scientific/ Technical	Moral/Practical	Critical/Emancipatory
Type of Society	Modern	Traditional	Transitional/Revolutionary
Type of Learning	Cognitive/Additive	Affective/Regenerative	Behavioral/Transformative
Method	Science: empirico-analytical	Religion/Ideology: historical-hermeneutic	Discourse: critical
Action System	Instrumental	Communicative	Praxis
Domain	Subject-object relations	Subject-subject relations	Subject-self-society relations
Social Medium:	Work	Language	Power
Knowledge:	Law-like	Meanings & Interpretations	Self-Reflection
Function:	Technical Control	Mutual Understanding	Transformation of Dependency Relations

Sources: Developed from Habermas, 1972, and Bateson, 1975.

While traditional societies often emphasize moral/practical rationality and learning, modern industrial societies tend to emphasize the cognitive/technical. Transitions from one stage of social development to another takes place, however, through the exercise of critical/emancipatory rationality and learning aimed at the liberation of the individual and society from the fetters of social structures of domination as well as from their underpinning—hypothesized normative structures.

To conceive of development as progressive levels of learning and liberation suggests an 18th century, evolutionary bias that has proved excessively optimistic in the light of the bitter experiences of the 20th century. Habermas has been, in fact, critiqued for his strong rationalist bias—both in his conceptualization of society and his normative preferences for its reconstruction. While I consider Habermas's theoretical approach normatively useful for the development of democratic polities, the process of development as defined here is *not* guaranteed. In other words, contrary to what the 18th-century philosophers of Progress conceived, development does not appear to be a historically inevitable process. In the light of the increasing levels of environmental pollution, nuclear and space armaments, social and economic inequities and gaps, structural and spontaneous violence, and political repression, decay and dissolution of civil society seems as likely an outcome of the current world situation as "liberation" and "development."

The key to an understanding of why this is so lies in the differentiated nature and rates of progress of the three types of learning I have labeled here as "additive, regenerative, and transformative." Contrary to the Comtian stage theory of human learning, evolving from mythological to theological and scientific knowledge, I consider all three types of learning characteristic of the human species. As self-reflecting subjects, we are faced with the task of understanding not one but at least three interrelated worlds, including the world of objects (nature), our human relations (society), and our own inner selves (psyche). Each of these different domains of knowledge impose their own possibilities and constraints on human learning. Thus we are required to invent different epistemological and learning strategies toward an understanding of the intractable domains of nature, society, and the self. Mythological ambiguities do not necessarily contradict but complement theological certitudes and scientific skepticism. Myths, religions and sciences are all needed in the never-ending human search for meaning because they address fundamentally different domains and questions in the human condition. Myths, including modern ones, address the need for human solidarity, while religious dogmas provide the basis for categorical moral imperatives for which there is no adequate scientific proof. Science, on the other hand, is needed in the human struggle vis-á-vis the forces of nature—including human nature.

If there is any hierarchy of knowledge, it should perhaps be viewed in terms of a progressive movement from additive to regenerative and transformative. Additive (scientific and technological) knowledge and learning are relatively simple, because they are fundamentally logical and accumulative. Regenerative knowledge and learning, by contrast, engage the more complex psychosocial forces at work. Through its own experiences and sufferings, every generation has to relearn and regenerate the moral learning of all previous generations. Transformative knowledge and learning are even more complex in that they demand great spiritual and moral leaps in history; they may even require some biogenetic transformation. They are thus achieved within greater time lags and often when humankind faces great social and spiritual crises. Such great leaps as Hammurabi's code, Moses' Ten Commandments, Buddha's Four Paths, Jesus' Sermon on the Mount, and the Universal Declaration of Human Rights represent moral and spiritual transformations for human consciousness that dwarf and encompass the additive and regenerative learning processes.

In the developmental process, however, we face an "epistemological lag" perhaps as serious as the proverbial "cultural lag." Additive knowledge and learning grow exponentially, while regenerative knowledge and learning grow more slowly and only at the same institutional rate of change at which the socialization of the young advances. Transformative knowledge and learning come by, however, at greater historical intervals. While cultural lags suggest the institutional lags between changes in science and technology and those in our moral codes of behavior, epistemological lags involve the more profound changes necessary in human ways of perception which Thomas Kuhn (1962) calls "paradigms." While scientific paradigms change in response to the major breakthroughs in scientific knowledge, moral paradigms change only when faced with major spiritical crises. For more than a generation now, for example, the discovery of the atom and its weapons of total self-destruction have called for commensurate levels of human consciousness of its unity in diversity. But regenerative learning in most societies still emphasizes human differences and enmities, while transformative learning is still groping for a new breakthrough in our perceptions of global interdependence. The decay and dissolution of civil society at the local, national, and international levels thus seems to be an outgrowth of the cultural and epistemological lags.

The problems of communication, development, and democracy, therefore, have to be viewed in this larger, philosophical context—as the dialectics of historical necessity and human freedom. If development is viewed as progressive levels of learning and liberation, the democratic values of liberty, equality, and community are indispensable to its fulfillment. If communication is understood as discursive will formation, communicative action is the process by which those values can be ultimately realized in practice. As Habermas (1979, p. xxiii) puts it:

> Evolutionary statements about contemporary social formations have an immediately practical reference insofar as they serve to diagnose developmental problems. The restriction to retrospective explanations of historical material is dropped in favor of a *retrospective projected from the perspective of action;* the diagnostician of the present adopts the fictive standpoint of an evolutionary explanation of a future past. . . As a rule, Marxist explanations of developed capitalism also share this asymmetric position of the theoretician who analyzes developmental problems of the contemporary social system with a view to structural possibilities that are not yet—and perhaps never will be—institutionalized. It can be seen from this that the application of evolutionary theories to the present makes sense only in the framework of discursive formation of the will, that is, a practical argumentation dealing with reasons why specific actors in specific situations ought to choose specific strategies of action over others.

This conception of communication and democracy does not presuppose any particular political, social, or economic system. As Habermas (1979, p. 186) puts it, "the attempt to arrange a society democratically

[is] only as a self-controlled learning process. It is a question of finding arrangements which ground the presumption that the basic institutions of the society and the basic political decisions would meet with the unforced agreement of all those involved, if they could participate, as free and equal, in discursive will-formation. Democratization cannot mean a priori preference for a specific type of organization, for example, for so-called direct democracy."

Habermas's somewhat evolutionary perspective, however, calls for an injection of some Foucaultian skepticism. For Foucault, technologies of power provide an ever-present web of domination and dependency in society that are best revealed in discourse/practice. And discursive practices always entail ideological distortions. While this skeptical perspective deprives us of entertaining utopian schemes for a "power-free" discourse, it encourages us to adopt a critical and deconstructionist strategy for unmasking power. Giving power no place to hide from its own ideological mystifications of domination and dependency, then, becomes the essential task of social and political criticism. The construction and defense of democracies depend as much on free, equal, and fraternal social relations as on a critical public discourse. From this perspective, then, we would have to focus on the production of meaning in society—whether through mediated or unmediated messages. The media cannot be divorced from the other processes of discourse/practice in society that contribute to the social constructions of reality.

THE DUAL-EFFECTS HYPOTHESIS

The role of communication technologies in the processes of political coercion and communication seems to have been historically twofold and contradictory. On the one hand, by a growing distantiation between the sources and receivers of messages, the media of modern communication have led to increasing bureaucratization and centralization of message production and distribution systems. On the other hand, the proliferation of communication technologies has provided an increasing diversity of and accessibility to channels. The chief constraints to this have been, of course, the concentrations of ownership and control and inequalities of access, so prevalent between and within nations. Procedural pluralism provides an abundance of channels airing fundamentally the same set of views and values. Substansive pluralism, by contrast, can be viewed only as the consequence of democratic and discursive will formation and not of technological abundance.

But we make our tools, and our tools make us. What Marx asserted about human freedom is perhaps no less applicable to technologies. Technologies shape history, however, not so much in an arbitrary fashion as within the confines of the institutional arrangements with which they come. The open-ended and probablistic dialectics of man, machine, and society is thus at the root of much of the controversy on the role of the new communication technologies in the processes of democratization. In this process, consciousness of the limits of human freedom plays a central part.

The controversies surrounding the new technologies are thus not so much about their inherent qualities as the interests and values they ought to serve. The two elements converge when certain technologies can be shown to serve certain clusters of interests and values particularly well. Denis McQuail (1984) has provided a useful typology of the images of the media and the values they seem to serve primarily. Table 2.8 modifies McQuail's typology to present them along a continuum of authoritarian to democratic potentials, clustered on the left and right columns. New technologies, such as personal computers (PCs), are also added to the list.

Table 2.8 provides a taxonomy that can be vigorously debated. Two observations are, however, in order. First, generally speaking, the "big media" appear mostly on the authoritarian side while the "small media" locate mostly on the democratic side. Low cost, accessibility, and simplicity of the small media as opposed to high cost, inaccessibility, and complexity of the big media seem to be chiefly responsible for this fact. Second, aside from this observation, there appears to be no direct cor-

Table 2.8. Images of the Media: Locating the Media on the Authoritarian-Democratic Continuum

Authoritarian Potentials					Democratic Potentials
I. Conditions of Content, Distribution, and Use					
Unitary Content	Book, Film Music	Press RTV	Videotex Teletext	PC* Databases Facsimile	Multiple Content
Use Time and Space Bound	TV Film Videotex Teletext	Press	Radio PC Music	Book Facsimile	Use Time and Space Free
Supply Managed	Videotex Teletext Databases	Press, Film TV, Radio, Music	Book	Facsimile	Supply Not Managed
Content Time & Space Bound	Videotex Teletext Databases	Press Film TV Radio	Book	Music Facsimile	Content Time & Space Free

Table 2.8. (Continued)

Authoritarian Potentials					Democratic Potentials

II. POLITICAL

Central To State	Databases Videotex Teletext	Press	Book, RTV	Film Music Facsimile	Peripheral To State
Control & Conformity	Databases DBS	TV,Film	Press, Book, Small Media** Radio, Music, Computer- Videotex, teletext Networking Facsimile		Freedom & Resistance

III. Social and Cultural Values

Fantasy- Oriented	Video Games Pay TV	Film Music	Book, Press Radio TV	Databases Facsimile	Reality- Oriented
Moral/ Serious	Book	Press TV Radio	Film Music	Video Games Pay TV	Nonmoral/ Fun
Non- Art	Press	Radio, TV, Music	Film	Computer Design Book	Art

IV. Social Relationships

Solitary	Book, Press PC, Radio, Music	Film Facsimile TV	Computer Networking	Group
Involvement Low	Radio, Press	TV Video Games, PC, Computer	Book Networking Facsimile	Involvement High
Distant or Unlocated	Databases	Film Facsimile	Book	Press PC	Location Close

V. Organizational

Message Central	Book, Film Production Music Central		Press Databases Radio TV, Videotape	Distribution Central
Technology High	Computer Satellite	Film TV	Facsimile Press Music	Book Radio Small Media	Technology Low
Profession Defined	Book	Press Film Music, TV, Radio, Electronic Journalist Electronic Publisher		Profession Ill-Defined

*Personal Computer
**Including mimeographing, audio and video-cassettes, copying machines, citizen's band radio, photography, mail
Source: Adapted from Denis McQuail, 1984, pp. 32–33.

relation between types of technologies and types of values they serve. For example, videotex, teletext, and data bases appear both on the authoritarian side as well as the democratic side of the continua. Some media have a long history with fairly well-established institutions and patterns of social influence; others are just beginning to make their appearance only in the most advanced industrial societies. We cannot be equally assertive about their role. Moreover, the current telecommunication revolution is fundamentally altering some old patterns of intermedia structures and functions. Newspapers, for instance, have already changed their role several times during the course of their history. They started out as organs of news. Subsequently, they also turned into agents of opinion, propaganda, and political struggle in the form of the elite and party press. With the advent of the penny press, they developed further into the urban mass circulation organs of an emerging mass culture—focusing particularly on sensationalist news of sex, scandal, and violence. Electronic publishing promises yet another transformation of the newspapers—from their traditional roles into a general information utility function.

There is, however, no general consensus on the emerging structures, functions, and effects of the new media. The accelerating technological innovations in information and communication industries have revived the old debates between the technophiles and technophobes. To recapitulate the main outlines of this debate, only some of its chief contenders will be cited here. Enzenberger (1974, pp. 96–97), for example, has argued that "the open secret of the new media, the decisive political factor, which has been waiting, suppressed or crippled, for its moment to come, is their mobilizing power. When I say *mobilize*, I mean *mobilize*, make men more mobile than they are. As free as dancers, as aware as football players, as surprising as guerrillas. . . . For the first time in history, the media are making possible mass participation in a social and socialized productive process, the practical means of which are in the hands of the masses themselves." (Emphasis in the original.)

By sharp contrast, Wicklein (1981, p. 27) has pointed to the enormous potentials of the new information technologies for political and commercial mischief: "Two-way cable is *fun*. Playing the system, subscribers are only vaguely aware that the preferences they state, the products they select, the personal opinions they express can all be stored in the computer's memory and tallied, analyzed, and cross-referenced with the demographic and financial information that is known about them."

In an analysis of the impact of the new technologies on public policy, Pool (1983) has taken a libertarian position to argue that the new information technologies can serve freedom only if government regulation could be held at bay. But he further argues that the convergence of the

print, common carrier, broadcasting, satellite, and computer technologies is creating such vast opportunities for government intervention that
traditional First Amendment restraints, mainly applicable to print in the
United States, may be swept aside. Pool thus underestimates the danger
that emanates from business monopolies. Nonetheless, his warnings on
excessive government regulation, often exercised to protect monopolies,
is well-taken.

In a provocative essay on the impact of computers, Ivan Illich (1983)
has argued that "computers are doing to communication what fences
did to pastures and cars did to streets"[4] In the same way that in 18-
century England, common pastures were "enclosed" for private use to
raise sheep and to produce wool, common pathways have been turned
into commercial highways, and the common cultural heritage of man-
kind is being privatized into large-scale information data bases for sale to
the highest bidders. In all three cases, common properties have been
turned into privatized uses for commercial or political gain. Illich warns,

> As enclosure by the lords increased national productivity by denying the
> individual peasant to keep a few sheep, so the encroachment of the loud-
> speaker [read the mass media] has destroyed that silence which so far had
> given each man and woman his or her proper and equal voice. . . . Just as
> the commons of space are vulnerable, and can be destroyed by the
> motorization of traffic, so the commons of speech are vulnerable, and can
> be destroyed by the encroachment of modern means of communication.

The contradictory views expressed above by four thoughtful analysts
of the impact of information technologies on democratic prospects reveal, if anything, a profound ambiguity. For every argument that can be
made on the democratic effects of information technologies, from hiero-
glyphics to fifth-generation computers, an equally powerful argument
can be marshalled to suggest their counterdemocratic consequences. A
technological determinist view of history would focus on the unique
properties of the new technological developments and their implications
for society, economy, and polity. But technologies come in institutional
packages; they generally augment the existing systems of domination.
They could also provide the means at the disposal of certain repressed
cultural or political groups to voice their grievances or amplify their
social or political deviations. That is why new technologies can have
certain intuitive as well as counterintuitive effects. The print technology
facilitated centralized bureaucracies, but it also created a modern secular
priesthood—the modern intelligentsia—challenging the traditional au-

---

[4]Illich's forthcoming book will appear under the title *The History of Scarcity*.

thorities of the monarchy and the church. The small media (mimeographing and copying machines, transistor radio and tapes), have created an immense consumer market for commercial products, but they have also put the means at the disposal of revolutionary groups to reach out a vaster audience despite the domination of the big media (the national press and broadcasting). An increasingly mechanized world, driven by information technologies, has brought about greater efficiency and productivity, but at the same time a yearning for the lost community, manifested in a renaissance of ethnicity and cultural identity. The dual effects of information technologies need no further belaboring.

The study of electronic democracy thus faces more questions than answers: In what way, if any, have the electronic media of communication shaped our democratic institutions? In style, as in the rise of celebrities to political power? In substance, as in the decline of political parties? In both style and substance, as in the rise of political advertising and the emergence of special interest groups (known, in the United States, as political action committees) that pay for them? In what way, if any, have the electronic media of communication shaped our political consciousness? In the rise of mass culture and totalitarian regimes in full control of the minds of their audiences? In the rise of "public" opinion as a new force in democratic self-governance? In other words, in homogenizing or pluralizing, informing or stupefying, encouraging or suppressing opinion?

Contextualism, or symbolic structuralism, presupposes an interdependency between the material structures (technologies and the economic forms of ownership and control) and the symbolic formations (intellectual and artistic content of the programs). The structure is the message, but in the longer run the message also determines the structuration process. This assumes that the audiences are creative in their resistance against structures of oppression and their ideological forms of repression. From this viewpoint, the chain of interactions in authoritarian and democratic systems may be hypothesized as in Figures 2.2 and 2.3.[5] In an authoritarian model, government or the state may be viewed as the executive committee of the ruling caste, class, or elite. Feedforward channels are thus largely one-way—from the rulers to government, communication institutions, and—finally—the people, who are placed at the bottom of the social pyramid. The only feedback government might receive from the people is channeled through pockets of resistance— erupting sometimes into spontaneous or organized violence.

In the democratic model, people stand at the apex of the system; they

---

[5]In the development of these two models, I am indebted to Johan Galtung's stimulating paper, "Democracy and Development," unpublished manuscript, January 1987.

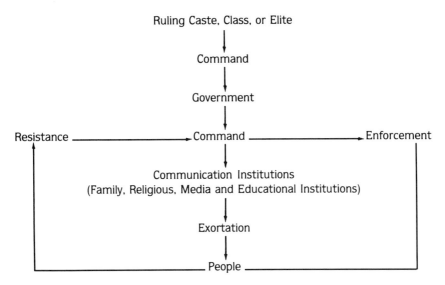

Figure 2.2.   An Authoritarian Model

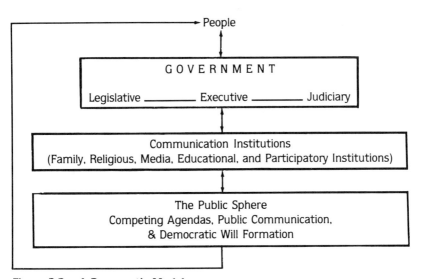

Figure 2.3.   A Democratic Model

participate in the government through voluntary and corporate associations (political parties, trade unions, etc.), representative institutions
(legislatures), or direct democracy (plebiscites, referendums, demonstrations, etc.) The structure of government is differentiated into the
legislative, executive, and judiciary branches with a system of checks
and balances. In addition to the traditional communication institutions
(the family, religious, media, and educational institutions), participatory
institutions (trade unions, professional and voluntary associations) are
now in full operation. These institutions have access to the government,
and in return they provide reports to the government on their views,
activities, and decisions. Moreover, with their competing agendas, they
engage in public discussions on public issues. Democratic will formation
results in a process of deliberation in the public arena in which people
become better informed and are, therefore, ready to signal their informed opinions to the government through direct or indirect channels
of communication.

This communication model of democracy assumes a cybernetic, interactive, multiple-loop, feedback system. However, no democratic system is totally open. Established social structures of domination and the
emerging structures of popular resistance work their way through their
own respective channels of communication, including the big media
(the national press, radio, and television) and the small media (graffiti,
wall posters, pamphleteering, audio and videocassettes, xerocracy, underground radio!). The small media may escape surveillance and control. But most media are more or less regulated by the government in all
social systems. This, in turn, determines the shape of the dominant
media institutions, which together with the government and other social
institutions set the competing agendas for public discourse. In this
model, the greater the plurality of the channels and interactivity of communication, the greater are the possibilities for democratic will formation. The fewer the channels and voices, the lesser are the possibilities
for genuine public discourse and democratic participation.

The degree of democracy in a communication system therefore
hinges on at least the following six conditions outlined in Chapter One:
interactivity, universality, channel capacity, content variety, low noise,
and speedy transmission. First, interactivity in the form of multiple
feedback systems assumes autonomous centers of power engaged in a
system of checks and balances. Second, universality means both penetration and access to the means of communication. Third, channel capacity depends on technological abundance as well as how equally it is
shared. Fourth, content variety is the outcome of true access and active
participation in the production of messages. While a democratic communication system reflects the symbolic variety in the social structure, an
authoritarian system represses it and reflects only those messages privi-

leged by the authorities. Fifth, low noise is a technical as well as a political condition of rational and intelligible discourse. To the extent that democratic rules and procedures of discourse have been internalized as the dominant social norms, to that extent the level of political noise can be minimized. Finally, speedy transmission may be also considered both as a technical as well political requirement. The time it takes between the transmission of a message, its reception, and the response to it reflects the technological as well as institutional capacities for speedy communication.

The symbolic structuralist view thus focuses on the production of meaning in all spheres of life rather than on media technologies alone. People's beliefs, legends, myths and, yes, even superstitions, are reproduced through the interpersonal and telecommunication networks. Ultimately, of course, the dominant structures of society determine our lives and our consciousness, but since change is the only permanent "law" of history, we are also confronted with choices between competing structures and ideologies. Symbolic structuralism thus believes in human agency under the conditions of necessity imposed by the prevailing social structures of domination and meaning. As Anthony Giddens (1984) has argued in his theory of "structuration," no social structure is completely static. In our choices of communication technologies, institutions and strategies from an existing and emerging menu of possibilities, we also create new options and configurations.

CONCLUSION

This chapter has presented four contending perspectives on communication and democratization, but it has argued for an interdependency position—labeled here as a contextualist perspective. While rejecting the traditional dichotomies between the technophilic vs. technophobic and idealist vs. materialist perspectives, the chapter has argued for a theoretical position that argues for an interactionist view of social structure and symbolic production. From this perspective, the chapter has also argued for a dual-effects hypothesis on the historical impact of information technologies. Information technologies have historically played a dual role in the service of centralization and dispersion of power. Democratic formations ultimately depend on a set of at least six cybernetic conditions in the development of their communication systems: interactivity, universality, channel capacity, content variety, low noise, and speedy transmission. As argued in Chapter One, these requirements should be considered both technical and institutional. The social and historical context ultimately determines the impact of technologies; it is the context rather than the technologies that should be therefore problematized.

3

Totems and Technologies

Indeed the Idols I have loved so long
Have done my credit in this World much wrong:
Have drown'd my Glory in a Shallow Cup
And sold my Reputation for a song.

Omar Khayyam

Where is the life we have lost in living?
Where is the wisdom we have lost in knowledge?
Where is the knowledge we have lost in information?

T. S. Eliot

Totems and technologies seem worlds apart—as far apart as the so-called "primitive" and "advanced" societies.[1] Yet, if we look carefully at the history of communication technologies, we may discern an interesting connection between the rise of certain technologies and the emergence of certain communication elites and social systems. Totemism is a primitive religious belief that systematically associates groups of persons with species of animals (occasionally plants or inanimate objects) and a certain element of social organization (Freud, 1919; Malinovski, 1927; Levi-Strauss, 1966). Communication technologies, from the invention of writing to informatics, also seem to have occasioned social, political, and cultural formations peculiar to their own biases (Innis, 1950, 1951). As a form of identity fetishism, totemism has occasioned belief in the magic of certain totemic objects, plants, or animals as representatives of tribal power. Has technological fetishism similarly led to idolatrous beliefs in the power and magic of certain communication technologies as signs of superiority of certain social systems?

The celebration of the Age of Information in recent years in both scholarly and popular literature calls for a critical reexamination of the concept's underlying myths and realities. Has the advanced capitalist world really entered a new historical stage known as the "post-industrial information society"? Are the new information technologies creating new possibilities of "technological leapfrogging" for the less developed countries? Can the global spread of the new technologies narrow

---

[1]This is a revised version of an article originally published in *InterMedia*, 14(3), May 1986.

the information gaps among and within nations? Will they bring about world integration on the basis of a universal secular-scientific civilization? Or will they exacerbate the existing inequalities and lead to a cultural backlash against the onslaught of modernization? Will they foster democratic equity and participation or totalitarian efficiency and tyranny?

This chapter will attempt to provide a historical retrospective in order to shed some light on the contradictory potentials of information technologies in our own particular era. It will begin with the current theoretical controversy regarding "information society," then provide a conceptual framework that relates the evolution of communication technologies (from prespeech to fifth generation computers) with their corresponding cultural/epistemological paradigms (from magic to ecology), communication elites in society (from soothsayers to futurologists), and communication institutions and networks (from primitive bands to the emerging global Integrated Services Digital Network—ISDN). In the light of this framework, the chapter will then examine the two distinctly different potentialities of the new information technologies, and conclude with a vision of a future "communitarian democracy." This is a vision in the great tradition of communitarian criticisms of modern industrial society. Such critics have included Jean-Jacques Rousseau, the European utopian socialists, the American transcendentalists, and countermodernists such as John Ruskin, Goethe, Tolstoy, and Gandhi. In more recent years, E. F. Schumacher, Ivan Illich, Paulo Freire, Johan Galtung, Fritjof Capra, Ariyaratne, and an increasing number of communitarian and "Green" writers have also offered parallel visions in their writings.

INFORMATION OR INFOGLUT SOCIETY?

The explosion of a great diversity of information technologies and their diffusion around the world during the past two decades have given rise to hopes for accelerating global development and democratization. However, what some liberal theorists have considered as the dawn of a new postindustrial, information society, Marxist theorists have generally viewed as the increasing commodification and privatization of information in the worldwide expansion of monopoly capitalism. By contrast, a third and emerging school of thought, to be labeled here "communitarian," considers the same processes as an example of the dual effects of information technologies—the harbinger of new possibilities for increasing levels of participatory democracy as well as new possible threats to individual freedom, social and information equality, and cultural autonomy and identity.

The liberal theorists have taken their cue largely from a tradition of research focusing on the technologically-propelled changes of social structure. The transition from natural sources of energy (muscle power, wind, water) to the steam engine and internal combustion clearly marks the beginnings of the First Industrial Revolution. The liberal theorists have considered the new information society as the harbinger of a Second Industrial Revolution, characterized by the application of information technologies to production, distribution, and consumption processes, transforming thereby the old industrial social and economic structures, eliminating the need for routine and repetitive jobs, providing greater opportunities for leisure and cultural creativity, and breaking down sociocultural differences and inequalities. Others in the liberal school of thought are urging the developing countries, which missed out on the First Industrial Revolution, to make efforts to bridge the widening gap between themselves and the more technologically advanced by "leapfrogging" in order to take part in this Second Industrial Revolution (Olsen, 1986).

The literature of "information society" is vast and expanding, but the origins of the concept date back to Colin Clarke's celebrated analysis (Clarke, 1940) which said that, due to sectoral differences in productivity and the increasing demand for social services (health, education, recreation, consulting, etc.), the labor force in the industrial societies will move increasingly from manufacturing to service sectors. This observation has been born out by the historical trends, elaborated upon later by Fritz Machlup (1962, 1980–84), Daniel Bell (1973), and Marc Porat (1977). While Machlup has focused on the production and distribution of knowledge as a key to the understanding of the new economic structures and processes, Bell provides a broader historical view to suggest a new stage theory of development, a movement from agrarian to industrial and information societies (see Table 3.1). Porat examines these transitions in terms of the U.S. economy where massive statistical evidence suggests a clear shift from predominantly agricultural to manufacturing, service, and information occupations and employment (see Table 3.2 and Figure 3.1). To quote Porat: "In Stage I (1860–1906), the largest group in the labor force was agricultural. By the turn of the century, industrial occupations began to grow rapidly, and became predominant during Stage II (1906–1954). In the current period, Stage III, information occupations comprise the largest group" (Porat, 1978, p. 7).

The theories of "information society" have also given rise to a pop sociology serving as a new ideology to legitimate global capitalism. Alvin Toffler (1970, 1980) and John Naisbett (1982) have provided perhaps the most daring of such popular visions of "information society," focusing particularly on the democratization effects of the new information

Table 3.1. The Postindustrial Society: A Comparative Scheme

Modes	Preindustrial	Industrial	Postindustrial
Mode of production	Extractive	Fabrication	Processing & recycling services
Economic sector	Primary Agriculture Mining Fishing Timber Oil & gas	Secondary Goods producing Durables Nondurables Heavy construction	Tertiary Transportation Utilities Quaternary Trade Finance Insurance Real estate Quinary Health Research Recreation Education Government
Transforming resource	Natural power: wind, water, draft animal- human muscle	Created energy: electricity, oil, gas, coal, nuclear power	Information*: computer & data transmission systems
Strategic resource	Raw materials	Financial capital	Knowledge†
Technology	Craft	Machine technology	Intellectual technology
Skill base	Artisan, farmer, manual worker	Engineer, semi- skilled worker	Scientist, technical, & professional occupations
Methodology	Common sense, trial & error, experience	Empiricism, experimentation	Abstract theory: models, simulations, decision theory, systems analysis
Time perspective	Orientation to the past	Ad hoc adaptiveness, experimentation	Future orientation: forecasting & planning
Design	Game against nature	Game against fabricated nature	Game between persons
Axial principle	Traditionalism	Economic growth	Codification of theoretical knowledge

*Broadly, data processing. The storing, retrieval, and processing of data become the essential resource for all economic and social exchanges.

†An organized set of statements of facts or ideas, presenting a reasoned judgement or experimental result, that is transmitted to others through some communication medium in some systematic form.

Source: Bell, 1973.

Table 3.2. Typology of Information Workers
and 1967 Compensation*

	Employee Compensation ($ Millions)
Markets for information	
Knowledge producers	46,964
Scientific and technical workers	18,777
Private information services	28,187
Knowledge distributors	28,265
Educators	23,680
Public information disseminators	1,264
Communication workers	3,321
Information in markets	
Market search and coordination specialists	93,370
Information gatherers	6,132
Search and coordination specialists	28,252
Planning and control workers	58,986
Information processors	61,340
Nonelectronic based	34,317
Electronic based	27,023
Information infrastructure	
Information machine workers	13,167
Nonelectronic machine operators	4,219
Electronic machine operators	3,660
Telecommunication workers	5,288
Total information	243,106
Total employee compensation	**454,259**
Information as percentage of total	*53.52%*

Note: (a) Based on 440 occupational types in 201 industries. Employee compensation includes wages and salaries and supplements.
Source: Computed using BLS Occupation by Industry matrix and Census of Population average wages. Parat, 1978, p. 5.

technologies. While Toffler is somewhat ambivalent about the prospects such a society might hold for democracy and human happiness, Naisbitt is unabashedly enthusiastic. The corporate world of telecommunication and computer industries have, in turn, found these concepts congenial to their own interests and views. It is not surprising, therefore, that Toffler and Naisbitt have been adopted as corporate futurologists while attaining public fame and fortune as best-selling authors and business consultants.

Figure 3.1. Four Sector Aggregation of the U.S. Work Force by Percent, 1860–1980.

(Using median estimates of information workers)

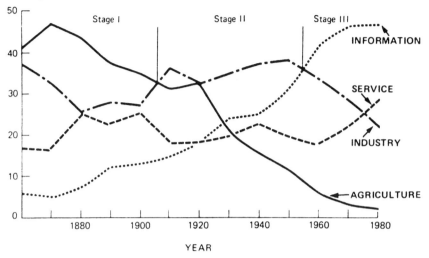

YEAR

Source: Porat, 1978, p.7.

Theories of information society have thus rapidly evolved from simple statistical observations—demonstrating a shift in occupations from agriculture to industry and services—to a neo-evolutionary theory of historical development. In their simplicity and sweep, these theories bear a striking resemblance to their 18-century antecedent—the Idea of Progress. The fundamental assumptions are the same: inevitability, linearity, universality, and technological determinism. Information society is presumed to be an inevitable stage in a universal pattern of progressive evolution from industrial to postindustrial society—propelled by the invention and diffusion of the new information technologies.

In contrast to the liberal theorists, however, the Marxist critics of "information society" and its corporate futurologists have generally pointed to the rising tide of dualism at national and global levels, creating islands of riches and information abundance in a global ocean of poverty and information scarcity (Schiller, 1981, 1985; Mosco, 1982; Slack & Fejes, 1987). They have suggested that the new technologies have generally widened the existing gaps, mainly through the privatization, concentration, and exploitation of information resources by the transnational corporations (TNCs). To avoid increasing dependence and vulnerability, they have argued that the developing world is well-advised to pursue a strategy of dissociation, national self-sufficiency, and collective self-reliance.

The two schools clearly represent the increasing stratification of the world into centers of wealth, power, and information against the peripheries of poverty, dependency, and revolt. But the communication technologies that have contributed to this stratification have also created a global interdependence whose future depends vitally on cooperation rather than confrontation. Furthermore, international trade and cooperation in the field of information—perhaps more than any other field—depends on a clear understanding of the nature of this unique "commodity" and its role in the historical transformations of our own era. The following critical questions might therefore be well worth considering:

- Does the increasing abundance of raw data also mean increasing levels of *information* (contextualized data), *knowledge* (contextualized information), and *wisdom* (contextualized knowledge)?
- Or, conversely, is the explosion in the sources and varieties of information leading to information overload, future shock, and intellectual confusion?
- Are the technological and socioeconomic advances of the information age creating greater information equality or information gaps and dualisms between the information rich and poor?
- Does the phenomenal growth in channel capacity, brought about by the introduction of cable television, direct broadcasting satellite (DBS), teletext, videotex, and fiber optics imply greater political freedom and participation, cultural pluralism, and enrichment *or* centralization, political surveillance, cultural domination, and impoverishment?
- Are the processes of automation, implied by the application of robotics and computer-integrated manufacturing, computer-assisted design and manufacturing (CIM-CAD-CAM), leading to greater leisure and cultural creativity, *or* increasing levels of structural unemployment and waste of human resources?
- Will the worldwide extension of the new technologies lead to the diffusion of a universal, modern, scientific, and technological civilization, *or* cultural backlash against the onslaught of modernization?

A more balanced view of the possible impact of information technologies on society than those offered by liberal and Marxist theorists would have to begin perhaps with a critique of the concept of "information society" itself. I will present here the beginnings of such a critique in terms of three fundamental points:

First, in a profound sense, all human societies may be considered to have been "information" societies. No human society can be, in fact,

conceived without a system of signs, meanings, and communication—
however "primitive"–that vitally binds it together. Peter Berger (1967,
p. 22ff) has put the central argument of this position rather poignantly:

> The most important function of society is nomization. The an-
> thropological presupposition for this is a human craving for meaning that
> appears to have the force of instinct. Men are congenitally compelled to
> impose a meaningful order upon reality. This order, however, presup-
> poses the social enterprise of ordering world construction. To be separated
> from society exposes the individual to a multiplicity of dangers with which
> he is unable to cope by himself, in the extreme case to the danger of
> immanent extinction. Separation from society also inflicts unbearable psy-
> chological tensions upon the individual, tensions that are grounded in the
> most anthropological fact of sociality. The ultimate danger of such separa-
> tion, however, is the danger of meaninglessness. This danger is the night-
> mare par excellence, in which the individual is submerged in a world of
> disorder, senselessness and madness. Reality and identity are malignantly
> transformed into meaningless figures of horror. To be in society is to be
> 'sane' precisely in the sense of being shielded from the ultimate 'insanity'
> of such anomic terror. Anomie is unbearable to the point where the indi-
> vidual may seek death in preference to it. Conversely, existence within a
> nomic world may be sought at the cost of all sorts of sacrifice and suffer-
> ing—and even at the cost of life itself, if the individual believes that this
> ultimate sacrifice has nomic significance.

Second, to proclaim the dawn of a new "information society" as the
unique hallmark of our own age is to confuse information with commodification of information. In the advanced capitalist societies, information has been increasingly commodified to provide an expanding
infostructure (i.e., information infrastructure) of online information networks and transborder news, data, sound, and images. This suggests
the historical development of capitalism from its earliest stages of primitive accumulation within the national boundaries (national capitalism),
to the expansion of national capital to the colonies (international capitalism), and increasingly towards a global capitalist system (transnational capitalism) in which production and distribution decisions are
made on the basis of the strategic interests of the global corporations. To
arrive at the presently emerging transnational capitalist stage, there is a
vital need for a fully global transportation and information infrastructure. The new information technologies are clearly providing that infostructure, while creating the conditions for a new international division of labor.

Under international capitalism, the world division of labor relegated
the production of raw materials to the peripheries, while manufacturing

was concentrated at the centers of industrial production. With the rise of land, labor, and residual costs (including the costs of environmental protection imposed by the new antipollution measures in the industrial countries), manufacturing (the so-called sunset industries) has increasingly moved from the centers to the peripheries. Such peripheries as the southern states in the United States and the new industrializing countries (the so-called NICS, including Brazil, Argentina, Mexico, South Korea, Taiwan, India, Singapore, Malaysia, and the Philippines) have been the main beneficiaries of this trend. Their textile, steel, and automobile industries have thus shown considerable growth in exports during the last two decades. In the meantime, the sunrise industries (including telecommunication, computer, aerospace, and weapons industries) and the services associated with them (investment banking, value-added networks, electronic publishing, etc.) have shown remarkable growth in the advanced capitalist countries at the expense of the manufacturing activities.

Porat's four-sector workforce aggregation (see Figure 3.1) bears out this argument rather dramatically in the case of the United States. U.S. manufacturing takes a downward turn in 1945, precisely at the moment that the United States assumes the role of a dominant superpower in world affairs. Subsequent to that, U.S. manufacturing industries began to invest massively abroad wherever economic conditions proved more favorable (i.e., lower land, labor, and residual costs) and political conditions more secure (in allied or client states). The Marshall Plan in Europe and Point Four in the Third World were, in fact, efforts towards the reconstruction of war-torn economies as well as conduits for the encouragement of American investment abroad. They succeeded particularly well in Western Europe and in a number of other U.S. client states in Africa, Asia, and Latin America, where U.S. corporations became a dominant force in the national economies. A commensurate rise in the services and information sectors during the same period suggests not only a rise of demand for the activities (as Colin Clarke had predicted) but also the transformation of the United States from an exporter of mainly manufactured goods to an exporter of primarily banking, insurance, shipping, high technology, and information services.

In this respect, the United States followed a pattern the British economy had traversed before, that is, the transformation of an imperial economy from manufacturing to service industries in which the capitalist class begins to clip coupons on their investments abroad through their shipping, banking, and consulting activities. In the meantime, other capitalist economies (such as the "defeated" Germany and Japan) moved into the manufacturing fields in which the United States was losing its competitive edge. "Coupon clipping imperialism," to borrow a phrase from Stuart Hall, has thus had deleterious effects not only for the United States as an industrial power but also for the work ethics and motivational forces that sustain an industrial society. Although the United States is a greater economic and political power than Britain ever was, one cannot escape the conclusion that economic decline awaits any imperial power that depends too heavily on the insecure hinterlands for its vital resources.

To appreciate the significance of the differences in employment structure between the imperial and nonimperial industrial powers, it would be instructive to compare and contrast the service and information sectors in the United States and Britain with those of Japan and Germany. As holders of world financial centers (London, New York, San Francisco), United States and Britain provide a great complex of banking and investment services. As the world's most advanced commercial societies with the most elaborate legal structures, both countries employ legions of lawyers at the service of TNCs. In the United States, for example, the number will soon surpass one million as compared to about 1,000 in Japan! As the world's two leading Great Powers of the twentieth century, the size of government (both civilian and military) has been large and growing in the former two countries. Despite an ideology of *laissez faire*, Britain and the United States currently lead West Germany and Japan both in the size and wages of central government employees (*The Economist*, December 17, 1983; IMF, Government employment and pay. Occasional paper 24). As the world's leading exporters of media commodities (Tunstall, 1977; Head, 1985), both countries outpace Germany and Japan in the size and composition of their cultural production and exports. For all of these reasons, it is not surprising that their information sectors are large and growing, suggesting their preeminent position in the world cultural and communication industries.

Some other factors have also contributed to the growth of the service sectors in the United States. Increase in productive possibilities has historically run ahead of rise in consumer purchasing power, necessitating ever-expanding marketing, advertising, and promotional activities to induce demand. The U.S. system of adjudication of social conflict through litigation has also necessitated a complex legal system and a huge legal establishment to operate it. By contrast, in Japan, where production and exports are far more important than domestic sales and where conflict is often adjudicated through the informal processes of interpersonal mediation, the relevant "information" professions are largely unnecessary to the operations of the industrial system.

The situation in the less developed countries is even more confounded. Caught in the fusions and con-fusions of living simultaneously at several different stages of technological evolution and in different socioeconomic systems, the solutions they have adopted are often as inappropriate as the problems are felt and pressing. Before having fully reached the age of print and literacy, for example, most developing countries have had to face the age of satellites and computers. High levels of illiteracy among the masses are thus combined with high levels of education for elites tied to the global information and power networks. The contradictions of combined and uneven development have thus affected them more than the more developed countries. Technological and social leapfrogging are theoretically possible, but so are the intellectual confusions and social dislocations of having to deal with too much social imbalance and complexity too soon.

This new international division of labor in the world capitalist system and its consequences for the changing structure of employment should not be taken, therefore, as conclusive evidence for the rise of a new social system. The fundamental features of the world capitalist system have clearly remained unchanged. These include the legal rights of private property, the corporate domination of the economy, a social class structure flowing from the inequalities in the ownership of the means of production, a liberal political system that intervenes in the economy only at times of crisis to correct the economic imbalances, and a cultural environment supportive of the motivational patterns of capitalist growth and inequality. These fundamental features have continued to operate successfully at the centers and have even expanded into some metropolitan centers of the Third World.

Cohen and Zysman (1987) have carried the critique of theories of postindustrial society a step further by arguing that the decline of manufacturing in the United States has already led to a loss of its international competitiveness. Services are sources of economic strength so long as they serve manufacturing. Without the manufacturing backbone, an economy will be subjected to an inevitable decline demonstrated by the cases of Britain and the United States. To regain its economic preeminence, therefore, Cohen and Zysman argue that the United States should ignore the myths propagated by the postindustrial theorists and begin to modernize its traditional manufacturing sectors while strengthening those services that support manufacturing. This is going back to those economic basics that have been largely ignored by the information society theories. It provides a necessary distinction between research, development, and educational services that directly support manufacturing and those such as government, insurance, legal and entertainment services that are, if at all, tenuously related to increasing productivity.

Third and last, despite the foregoing, the growth of the information sector has meant increasing automation through robotics, reduction of repetitive and routine jobs, a commensurate rise in total leisure time available to society as a whole, greater social networking possibilities, and immense potentials for a new cultural effervescence and political participation. These opportunities have coincided with a complex variety of worldwide grass-root movements, new democratic ideologies and countercultural theories well articulated in the works of Schumacher, Illich, Freire, Ariyaratne, Galtung, Habermas, Berger, Capra, Roszak, Sale, and many others. I have called this third school of thought "communitarian," in that they all focus, more or less, on the need for the reconstruction of community, identity, and solidarity in the face of the atomizing, disintegrating, and anomic effects of modern industrial society. In contrast to the liberals and Marxists, whose central emphases are respectively on freedom and equality, the communitarians' primary concern is with fraternity and community. In the face of the threats of nuclear war, bureaucratic domination (of both the capitalist and communist varieties), and cultural and environmental disintegration, the peace movement, populist revolts, and the struggles for indigenous cultural identity have all converged in a variety of Green and Rainbow coalitions. These movements have found a new ally in the smaller, less costly, more accessible, less surveillable, and more interactive media.

THE SEVEN AGES OF HUMAN COMMUNICATION

Historically, however, information technologies have always shown a Janus face—they have served centralizing as well as devolutionary trends, unifying as well as disintegrating forces, homogenizing as well as pluralizing values. To provide a historical perspective on the contradictory potentialities of our own current situation, I will now focus on a conceptual framework that points to the interactions of information technologies and their corresponding social systems. Despite some correspondence, however, it will be argued that there are no necessary historical stages at work. Agricultural societies are not necessarily followed by industrial and information societies. As noted above, in a real sense, all human societies are information societies. The increasing diversification of information technologies and professions simply point to an increasing productivity of the industrial system and its cultural and epistemological lags in channeling this productivity into higher levels of democratic achievements—of political freedom, social justice, and human solidarity.

The following conceptual framework should be considered only as a preliminary effort towards an understanding of the interactions of communication technologies, overlapping cultural paradigms, emergence of new communication elites in society, and their corresponding institutional origins (see Table 3.3).[2]

In considering Table 3.3, three important caveats are in order. First, this schematic view of thousands of years of historical evolution does not presume any deterministic, stage theory of history. It merely suggests a series of *possible* correspondences between emerging communication technologies, cultural paradigms, communication elites, and communication institutions. The seventh social system, characterized here as "communitarian society," clearly represents a historical potential rather than a historical reality.

Second, the table should not be interpreted as a technological determinist view of history. In the ongoing debate on the causal links between technologies, social institutions, and cultural values, an interactionist rather than a materialist, idealist, or autonomist view is presented here (see Chapter 2.) It is argued that no causal links can be universally established unless we consider each case on its own merits and in a given historical context. In historically specific situations, however, we are likely to find strong multilinear and interactive, rather than linear and unidirectional, causation.

Third, in a global situation characterized by combined and uneven development, we often encounter overlapping and interlocking communication technologies, paradigms, elites, and institutions. In other words, magic is as present in postindustrial, technocratic societies as it is in hunting, band societies. It only appears in different forms; the magic of technology replaces the magic of the supernatural. But the dominant paradigm in technocratic societies is clearly "technology" and its programmatic imperatives, while the dominant paradigm in prespeech societies seems to have been the anthropomorphic convergence of the human and nonhuman into a unified worldview. But the emerging unity of mysticism and science, as in quantum physics (Capra, 1976), is leading us back once again to an understanding of the delicate balance between humans and nature, which we have largely lost in industrial civilization.

Each of the following ages of human consciousness could be the subject of a separate chapter or, preferably, a separate book. Here I will only provide brief and suggestive characterizations, which of necessity will be schematic. I hope what is lost in historical depth is gained by historical breadth.

---

[2]See particularly Innis (1950, 1951), McLuhan (1964, 1969), Gouldner (1982a,b, & c), Thompson (1971, 1985), and Eisenstein (1979). For an extensive and annotated bibliography on Culture, Technology and Communication, see Carey, 1981.

**Table 3.3.   The Seven Ages of Human Communication:
Communication Revolutions and Historical Change**

Social System	Communication Technologies	Cultural Paradigms	Communication Elites	Communication Institutions
Band	Prespeech	Magic: super-natural	Shaman	Hunting Bands
Tribal	Speech	Mythology: Magic	Poets & sooth-sayers	Tribe
Agrarian feudalism	Writing	Religion: reve-lation	Priesthood	Temple
Commercial capitalism	Print	Science: reason	Intellectuals	University
Industrial capitalism	Film & broad-casting	Ideology: action	Ideologues & persuaders	Mass media & movements
Technocratic capitalism	Computers Satellites	Technology: program	Technologues	National/global technocracies
Communitarian society	Informatics: ISDN	Ecology/com-munity: hu-man agency	Communologues	Global/local net-works

The Age of Magic is characterized primarily by hunting, "band" so-cial organizations, epistemological unity of the objective and the subjec-tive in human consciousness, a prespeech language of signs, and the leadership of what the anthropologists call "the Big Man" with the Shamans as his conduits to the world of magic and supernatural.

The Age of Mythology, by contrast, represents the gradual evolution of speech, beginnings of mobile settlements in tribal forms, an epis-temological dualism between the objective and the subjective, and the unity of the temporal and spiritual authorities in the figure of Divine Chiefs or Kings, advised and guided by the poets, soothsayers, and astrologers (Frankfort et al., 1964).

The Age of Religion corresponds to the invention of writing, the preservation of revelation in the Holy Books, the emergence of the "scribes" and priests as custodians and interpreters of revelations, re-sulting in the separation of temporal and spiritual authorities, and the emergence of the temple, the church, or the mosque as the institutional bases for this social differentiation.

The Age of Science dawns upon us primarily with the European scientific revolution of the 17th century, propelled by the invention and spread of printing technology. Its pioneering institutions are the emerg-ing modern European cities and universities. Its communication leaders are the new scientist/humanist intellectuals (e.g., Galileo, Newton, Bacon). Its epistemology is grounded in empiricism and a careful separation of the objective and subjective categories, while its "culture of critical discourse" (Gouldner, 1982a) presents a scientific outlook on social and philosophical issues.

The Age of Ideology is led by the American, French, and other European bourgeois revolutions, but it reaches its peak with the rise of the mass movements in the 20th century. It is characterized by the emergence of a new communication elite of "ideologues," addressing a "public" created by the extension of literacy and the newly emerging institutions of the mass media, mass movements, and mass organization (chiefly political parties and trade unions). In contrast to the cultural orientation of the intellectuals, which is scientific and reflective, the ideologues tend to be oriented towards politics and action.

TECHNOCRATIC VS. COMMUNITARIAN SOCIETY

Finally, our own Age of Technology clearly exhibits two contradictory tendencies—here identified as "technocratic" and "communitarian" societies. The technocratic society has been led by the cybernetic revolution and it is developing further by an accelerating technological revolution in robotics and computer-integrated manufacturing (CIM). The convergence of telecommunications and computers has led to the creation of databases and networks that serve as the infostructure of the new Technocratic Society. The progressive introduction of ISDN will only increase the level of sophistication of existing networks into a simultaneous transmission of sound, vision, and data linking global and local networks. At present, the new technologies serve primarily the purposes of the highly centralized, global, and national technocracies such as the giant transnational corporations and the national military and civilian bureaucracies. They also serve a new communication elite which we call "the technologues." This elite is acting as the custodians and managers of the large bureaucratic machines that dominate our world today. The preponderance of the engineers, programmers, and efficiency managers has in turn resulted in the dominance of a new cultural paradigm that puts technology above ideology, means over ends, and programming efficiency over spontaneity and participation.

The "Technological System," as Jacques Ellul (1983) calls this social order, has also bred its own institutions of research and instruction outside of the traditional liberal arts universities. The R & D establishments such as the Bell Labs, Rand Corporation, Arthur D. Little, or Battle Memorial Institute (all in the United States) serve the defense and corporate sectors without much of the moral and material constraints of traditional universities. Numerous "corporate universities" have also emerged as degree-granting institutions to overtake the tasks of training in the industrial arts without the constraints of teaching the liberal arts. In the United States, these alternative institutions of higher training and applied, industrial research spend over twice as much as the traditional institutions of higher education.[3]

The Technocratic Society is first and foremost a global system. It is characterized by an international communication regime of information networking indispensable to the operation of its global transportation, banking, finance, and marketing activities. This global information network connects the corporate and government headquarters with their respective localized branches in a vast and complex network of centralized nodes of decision making. It provides services in airline reservation, electronic fund transfers, remote sensing and intelligence, marketing, advertising, transborder news and data flows, and so on (Dordick, Bradley, & Manus, 1981; Ganley & Ganley, 1982). The Information Society discourages, however, spontaneity and participation by its routinized systems of communication and control, innovation and production, reduction of decisions to their technical component, and fragmentation and delegation of decision-making powers to the technocratic elites (Galbraith, 1978; Kumar, 1978; Ellul, 1983).

Are we embarking upon a new, seventh age of human communication, a posttechnocratic Age of Communitarian Democracy, that could reap the benefits of information technologies without their dulling and enslaving effects? The distinction made here between "technocratic" and "communitarian" societies entertains some measure of cautious optimism on this question. In the debate outlined above between the liberal and Marxist theorists, I am taking a middle ground by granting to the former that some fundamental changes are occurring in the technological and social structures of what might be considered a "hyperindustrial" information society, but the sum total of these changes has not as yet manifested itself in the capitalist political and economic institutions. It is hypothesized, however, that the potentials for fundamental cultural, political, and economic changes are ever growing and will no doubt manifest themselves sooner or later. These changes could be observed particularly in the cultural spheres, but a variety of "green" political movements in Western Europe and the United States have also made their impact on the ecological and nuclear issues. In the socialist and Third World countries, the same set of antitechnocratic sentiments

---

[3]See the recent report published by Princeton University Press on "the Corporate Universities."

are expressing themselves in movements calling for political decentralization and participation as well as self-reliant development.[4]

A "communitarian society" is, of course, a far more difficult entity to define.[5] There are clearly no historical precedents for it. With the possible exception of modern democracies, all human societies in the past have been based primarily on coercive rather than communicative methods of rule. The idea represents therefore merely a potential—a hope. But this is a hope that is not altogether utopian; it is a historically-grounded hope. Its central concept—communication—suggests an interactive process sharply in contrast to what goes on in the mass communication systems of the world today. It further suggests "communication" against "coercion" as a procedure for discursive will formation for developing genuine "consensus" rather than manufacturing "consent." The new interactive technologies of communication are making this more and more possible. Direct democracy as distinct from representative democracy appears therefore as a viable alternative or a complementary institution. Moreover, the centralized and bureaucratic institutions of both capitalism and communism have produced such a degree of economic exploitation, political alienation, and cultural depersonalization that each system currently faces its own particular brand of legitimation crises (witness Poland alongside the advanced capitalist societies).

But history does not move in a new direction simply because of the presence of some new technological or social possibilities; it takes human consciousness and will to reshape institutions. Such movements as the Green Party in Germany, the Solidarity Movement in Poland, and the Sarvodaya Movement in Sri Lanka suggest that the ideals of a "communitarian" democracy have spread worldwide.[6] These ideals call for peaceful, cooperative, and antitechnocratic strategies of social change, including nuclear and general disarmament, conservation and ecological balance, decentralization and devolution of power, direct democracy, soft and intermediate technologies, smallness, self-reliance and self-management, cultural pluralism and identity, community media, and an economic growth based on intrinsic human needs rather than extrinsic appetites artificially induced by market or bureaucratic forces.

These ideals represent human aspirations against a disturbing situa-

---

[4]For early accounts of the counterculture movement, see Roszak (1969, 1972). For its further developments, see Toffler (1970, 1980); Naisbitt (1982); Ferguson (1981). For the Green Movement, see Capra (1984).

[5]See Voge (1983, 1985) for similar distinctions and views.

[6]For the Green Movements, see Capra (1984). For the Sarvodaya Movement, see Ariyaratne (1986).

tion—replete with the conflicts of a nuclear race, enormous and widening inequalities among and within nations, and cultural homogenization and depersonalization. If these ideals fail to materialize, we might face serious political problems and tragedies. The rise of a variety of dogmatic and fundamentalist movements around the world, in both developed and developing countries, are currently giving vent to the frustrations of the common people against an incomprehensible and unjust world system. If these movements continue to gain momentum, they could once again turn the world into an arena of uncompromising racial, religious, and political prejudices and conflicts.[7]

An "escape from freedom" (Fromm, 1963) and a regression to the sanctity and security of tribal solidarity thus seems to be as likely an outcome of our own age of transition as the realization of its great democratic potentialities. The new information technologies thus present a double-edged sword. On the one hand, they can eliminate the routine and repetitive tasks in production and administration, create greater leisure for cultural and political pluralism, facilitate access and participation in a new direct, electronic democracy, foster open learning systems through tele-education, and extend a variety of other social services (telemedicine, teleshopping, telebanking, telelibrary, etc.) to the remotest and most deprived sectors of the population. But on the other hand, they can also serve as instruments of a new totalitarian hegemony by reinforcing the surveillance powers of the state, expanding the gap between the information-rich and-poor, creating unemployment and underemployment through automation and robotics, and fostering excessive reliance on high technology in the problems of human conflict. The outcome clearly depends not on our stars but on our choices.

In a provocative article, Anthony Smith (1984) calls for a cultural transformation to match the technological upheavals of recent decades. "The advent of computer intelligence," he argues (p. 25), "certainly drives us towards a new attempt to define ourselves as cultural beings operating in time and space. It obliges us to grasp some definition of human totality in order to locate the self. . . . We have today to find a way to be defined as something other than particularly sensitive computers. It seems to me that this wholeness must lie somewhere in the historical sense, the sense of our own interconnections in time and space, in the shadow of which the computer's intelligence is but a copy, a representation, an intelligent picture, a piece of reality, but still object rather than subject." This means nothing less than a recapturing of the

---

[7]For the Islamic fundamentalist movements, see Mortimer (1982) and Tehranian (1980a & b). For the Christian fundamentalist movements, see Armstrong (1979).

human spirit and agency in the face of the technical and organizational monstrosity of technocratic societies.

CONCLUSION

The current debate on "information society" represents a recurrent pattern in the history of major technological breakthroughs. The second Industrial Revolution, as the First, has found its celebrants among those who tend to assume technological determinist views of history. They tend therefore to underestimate the institutional fetters that stand in the way of spreading the full social benefits of the new technologies. They are the technological optimists. At the other extreme, however, we have the technological pessimists—the Luddites (see chapter 1, footnote 6).

It would be salutary to remind ourselves that modern societies have proved themselves as prone to the powers of magic and myth as their so-called primitive counterparts. Modern political myths have operated as powerfully as any technology to bring about untold human tragedies in this century. Modern technologies have only put mightier means at the disposal of those myths. Such myths as the "white man's burden" in imperial Europe, "manifest destiny" in imperial America, "Aryan supremacy" in imperial Germany, "historical mission of the proletariat" in the imperial Soviet Union, the "chosen people" in an expansionist Israel, and the "Islamic empire" in the fundamentalist movements of the Muslim world provide telling examples. These myths have combined the eschatological promises of a religious zeal with the mundane, political hopes of this world-worldly gain. This tonic has proved enormously powerful both in developed and developing countries. Political religions as well as religious politics fuse temporal and spiritual authorities into a single state apparatus.

The deification of the state on the basis of extremist secular or religious ideologies emanates from a single, inexorable source of power in modern society—the totalization of the means of social control: in production under the auspices of state or corporate capitalism, in surveillance under the authority of totalitarian ideologies, in culture under the auspices of mass communication, and in ecology under the awesome power of modern technologies. But technologies have no will of their own; they are developed by society in response to human needs as defined by our cultural values and institutional arrangements. They produce some intended but also many unintended consequences. They amplify certain power configurations but also set into motion certain powerful countercultural and antisystemic forces. They can be thus understood and tamed only through a reconstruction of our human traditions of civility.

But the new information technologies possess an additional trait that was lacking from most other technologies of the past. They feed on a renewable, self-regenerative, and exponentially-growing resource. The more information we give, the more information we have. Information feeds on information and thus grows at an accelerating rate. But that is also a mixed blessing. The cultural backlash against "information overload" has led, in many parts of the world, to powerful social movements representing escapes from information. These movements recoil from complexity and call for simpler models and choices in facing reality. Since the current information revolution is global in scope, the backlash is also of global dimensions. And since the gaps in information largely correspond to gaps in income and power, we may anticipate a new populist revolt that falls back on the certitudes of the past to face the uncertainties of the future.

4

Technologies of Democracy and Development

History, Leon Trotsky wrote, is the natural selection of accidents. Democracy may be, quite simply, an accident of history—an exotic social variety heady with possibilities but with questionable survival capacity. The question the democrat must face is simply this: What conditions contribute to democracy's survival power, and how may our understanding of these conditions allow us to extend and deepen democratic culture and institutions.

(Bowles & Gintis, 1986, p. 210)

To recapitulate, Chapter 1 has argued that the global processes of democratization have faced countertrends in the transnationalization of the world economy at the centers, tribalization of politics at the peripheries, and increasing potentials for totalitarianization of power and surveillance throughout the world. Chapter 2 has provided a theoretical framework for the understanding of the dual role of information technologies in these concurrent trends, while Chapter 3 has focused on the contradictory potentialities of what has come to be known as the Age of Information. In this chapter, I propose to review the four dominant, competing models and strategies of communication and democratization in the modern world. In keeping with our conception of technology as hardware and software, as well as those deep cognitive structures that uphold a technological system, this discussion of technologies of democracy will consider the entire grid of power that has sustained or undermined democratic systems.

It will be argued here that the linkages between information technologies and democratic formations can best be understood in terms of four competing models of communication and democracy that have gained currency in different national contexts, that is, (a) the capitalist democratic, (b) the communist democratic, (c) the communitarian democratic, and (d) the authoritarian-totalitarian counterdemocratic models that are generally prevalent in the so-called First, Second, and Third Worlds of development. Each of these models has emerged out of a different set of historical circumstances reflecting radically different conceptions of democracy, but their historical development may reveal an evolution in democratic concepts and practices. This evolution has extended the concept from "political democracy," including civil liberties often written into constitutional Bill of Rights documents, to concepts of "social democracy" emphasizing the rights of employment and social security, to concepts of "cultural democracy" focusing on the rights of human collectivities to autonomy, self-determination, and identity. But all three schools have emerged out of the same common democratic tradition that gave birth to the modern world in a series of successive democratic revolutions—the bourgeois democratic revolutions of the 18th and 19th centuries in North America and Western Europe, the communist democratic revolutions of the twentieth century, notably in Russia and China, and the national liberation movements of the Third World in Africa, Asia, and Latin America.

However, each model of communication and democracy has also contained within itself the seeds of its own self-destruction. The counterdemocratic forces unleashed by the processes of industrialization have historically managed to undermine the institutions of liberal capitalism into Nazism and Fascism, revolutionary communism into Stalinism, and Third World Communitarianism into a variety of military or populist dictatorships. Each school clearly focuses on the maximization of a different set of values in the democratic trinity of liberty, equality, and community. Here, I will briefly discuss the main features of each model in theory and practice and touch on the challenges and opportunities they face with respect to the new technological and social developments in information and communication.

COMPETING STRATEGIES OF COMMUNICATION AND DEMOCRACY

Table 4.1 identifies the four prevailing models in a matrix that combines the repressive and participatory strategies of development with the corporatist, collectivist, representative, and direct concepts of democracy. The totalitarian model represents those strategies that combine high capital accumulation with unequal income distribution, political repression, and negative peace. The capitalist model typifies those strategies that combine high capital accumulation and growth with trickle-down income distribution mechanisms and civil liberties. The communist model represents those strategies that combine the "great leap forward" and "big push" strategies in development with high mobilization, restraints on mass consumption, and civil liberties. Finally, the communitarian model suggests an emerging type of development philosophy that calls for ecologically and culturally sensitive strategies combined with decentralized power structures and participatory democracy (see Tables 4.1 and 4.2 and Figure 4.1).

The four models roughly correspond to the four major historical

Table 4.1.   Competing Models of Democracy and Development

	Repressive Development/ Growth/Modernization: Negative Peace	Participatory Development/ Another Development: Positive Peace
Corporatist/Collectivist Democracy: Vertical Communication Flows	Totalitarianism: High Repression	Communism: High Mobilization
Representative/Direct Democracy: Horizontal Communication Flows	Capitalism: High Accumulation	Communitarianism: High Integration

Source: Adopted from Hettne (1983).

KEY:

Symbolic Color:
Social System:
Axial Principle:
Leadership:
Psychic Energy:
Ideology:
Development Strategy:

THE GREENS
Communitarian Democracy
Community
Intelligentsia
Super-Ego
Enviromentalism
High Integration

Fundamentalist Greens   Pragmatic Greens

THE REDS
Communist Democracy
Equality
Proletariat
Alter-Ego
Marxism
High Mobilization

Revolutionary Socialists   Social Democrats

THE BLUES
Capitalist Democracy
Freedom
Bourgeoisie
Ego
Liberalism
High Accumulation

Left Populism:
Khomeini & Qadhafi

Right Populism:
Reagan & Thatcher

THE BLACKS
Totalitarian Dictatorship
order
Big & Petty Bourgeoisie
Id
Fascism
High Repression

Figure 4.1.   A Conceptual Map of Modern Political Ideologies

Table 4.2. Communication, Development, Democracy, and Dictatorship: Four Historical Paths/Strategies

	Capitalism	Communism	Communitarianism	Totalitarianism
Value Tensions	Freedom/Property	Equality/Bureaucracy	Community/Conformity	Order/Tyranny
Leaderships	Intellectuals	Ideologues	Communologues	Marginals
	Bourgeoisie	Proletariat	Middle Classes	Big and Petty Bourgeoisie
Development Strategy	High Accumulation	High Mobilization	High Integration	High Repression
Ideology	Liberalism	Marxism	Populism	Fascism
Power Organization	Industrial Organization	Party Organization	Grass-Roots Organization	Conspiratorial Organization
Communication Strategy	Multichannel Flows	Single-Channel Flows	Networking Flows	Monolithic Flows
Media Organization	Commercial	State	Community	Statist
Methods/Tactics	Electoral, Incremental Change	Class struggle, Party leadership, Macro-Revolution	Nonviolent Civil disobedience, Micro-Revolution	Racism Coup, Putsch
Epistemology/Worldview	Mechanical Positivist Science	Organic Dialectical Science	Cybernetic Mystical Science	Dogmatic Racist Pseudoscience of Eugenics

paths to development, including capitalism, communism, communitarianism, and totalitarianism. The ranges from repressive to participatory development, from corportist to direct conceptions of democracy, and from vertical to horizontal flows of communication should be considered as a series of continua. These models represent the Weberian "ideal types" and heuristic categories for analysis. Historical examples are always far more complex and richer in diversity and meaning. They combine elements from different social systems as well as from their own traditional cultures and polities. Scandinavian capitalism, for example, is so radically different from American capitalism that it is often referred to as socialism. For a time, Soviet communism served as a model for the rest of the communist world, but increasingly, communist countries in eastern Europe, China, Vietnam, and Cuba have assumed their own unique features, adopting different strategies of development. In the face of changing material and ideological circumstances, no system can afford to stand still and remain loyal to its own purist ideals.

To account for these systemic gradations, Figure 4.1 redraws the political map of the world around the four paths. Instead of the conventional half-circle showing the political spectrum from right to left, the map proposes a full circle that demonstrates four distinct political polarities (the Blues, Greens, Reds, and Blacks) with their respective axial principles and socio-psychological-ideological tendencies. The Blues—the liberal capitalists—have historically put freedom (including individual liberty and property rights) above all other social values. They represent the ego-rationality of the modern world calling for an "efficient" allocation of resources through the market mechanism. The Communists—the Reds—represent the opposite polarity by their dual emphasis on social equality and the alter-ego rationality of state planning. The Communitarians, although never fully in power anywhere, have been represented in a variety of populist, countermodernist, democratic, and utopian movements consistently calling for the primacy of community and ecology. As such, they have served as the nagging conscience of the modern world—a superego—reminding it of the heavy costs of industrialization in the destruction of traditional communities and ecological balance. The Blacks—the totalitarian regimes typified by Nazi Germany, Fascist Italy, and racist South Africa—represent the "id" forces of aggression and domination unleashed by class, ethnic, and racial conflicts of the modern world. Their axial principle is "law and order" in the name of a higher civilization represented by doctrines of racial or cultural superiority. As shown by the examples of Social Democrats, neoconservatives, fundamentalist Greens, Christians, and Muslims, we should have no difficulty in placing the different ideological and political groups on this map.

Table 4.2 provides a schematic view of the three paths to development. In each of the four strategies of communication and democracy, the table proposes a fundamental tension between two competing values and leaderships. In capitalist democracies, the tension focuses on the civil liberties and the rights of property. These two competing/complementary values are, in turn, championed by the two different leaderships of liberal capitalist democracies, that is, the intellectuals and the industrial bourgeoisie. In communist democracies, the tension manifests itself primarily between the democratic values of social equality and the centralizing forces of state and party bureaucracy. The readerships that champion these values are, in turn, represented by the revolutionary ideologues (e.g., Lenin and Trotsky) and the emerging party and state bureaucratic bosses (e.g., Stalin and his henchmen). In communitarian democracies, the tension focuses on the needs for a sense of community undermined by the structures of foreign or domestic domination and an equally strong urge to seek those trappings of power that have eluded the colonized and the powerless. Communitarian leadership, in turn, comes primarily from the "communologues," the communication leaders closest to the cultural and communal ethos of a society, and the middle-class elements created by the processes of modernization and industrialization. Finally, the totalitarian strategies are torn between the need for law and order in the class conflicts of industrial societies and the opportunities this creates for the tyranny of the majority. The leaderships here come primarily from the marginalized intellectuals and ideologues (witness the biographies of Hitler and Mussolini), while the threatened bourgeoisie and the dislocated lower-middle-classes provide the political following.

THE CAPITALIST DEMOCRATIC MODELS

The liberal models of development, communication, and democracy originated with the birth of Western capitalism but have now been extended to all parts of the world.[1] They are based on the fundamental concepts of popular sovereignty, universal rights of suffrage, representation through elections, checks and balances through a separation of executive, legislative, and judiciary powers, and a Bill of Rights to guarantee the individual rights to speech, assembly, and religion. By extension, the development of voluntary associations such as political parties and trade unions and the Fourth Estate (the media) has also become a

---

[1]For thoughtful critiques of these models, see Macpherson (1973), and Bowles and Gintis (1986).

vital feature of this model of democracy. Their function consists of acting as watchdogs to the elected or appointed officials, shaping public opinion, and bringing pressure on the government on behalf of special interest groups.

The bourgeois democratic revolutions of the 18th and 19th centuries that gave birth to liberal, parliamentary regimes in the West owed much of their origins to the advent of print technology. The new technology of public communication had by then created a new communication elite (the secular intellectuals), a new communication institution (the modern university), and a new cultural paradigm (the modern scientific worldview). The predominance of secular intellectuals in the revolutionary leaderships of France and the United States (e.g., the Encyclopaedists, Montesquieu, Rousseau, Jefferson, Hamilton, Jay, Madison) is an eloquent testament to this fact. But even in England where there was no violent overthrow of established order, the intellectuals had taken the lead in paving the way for the new, evolving parliamentary democracy. The classical economists and political theorists of liberalism in England and Scotland (Adam Smith, David Ricardo, Thomas Malthus, John Stuart Mill, John Locke, Thomas Hobbes) all came out of the intellectual ranks. The Federalist Papers were written by pamphleteers and publicists. It is not necessary to be a technological determinist to recognize the critical importance of the print technology in the diffusion of the new scientific knowledge and breakdown of the traditional authorities of the church and the monarchies. Other factors such as the Crusades, the discovery of the New World and its riches, the rise of modern cities, and so on had already paved the way for the emergence of modern capitalism and liberalism, but the advent of print technology clearly played a central part in the publication and dissemination of the new democratic ideas and values (Eisenstein, 1979).

The liberal/pluralist school has viewed democracy essentially in terms of the expansion of individual *liberty* through the processes of *pluralization* of economy, society, and polity. The liberal political economists and their theoretical contemporaries and descendants have identified democracy with individual liberty, including freedom of enterprise and the rights of private property. They have also considered the safest guarantee of freedom in the processes of pluralization that followed the transition from agrarian to industrial capitalist societies. The economists viewed pluralization primarily in terms of increasing levels of division of labor and competition among numerous buyers and sellers, presumably leading to the most efficient allocation of resources and talents. the sociologists (notably August Comte and the positivists) viewed the differentiation of society into distinctive structures and functions as the chief mechanism for achieving higher orders of complexity, rationality and freedom. The political scientists (notably Montesquieu, Locke, and the Federalists) saw in the separation of powers and the diversification of autonomous interest groups the key to the preservation of liberty from tyranny and arbitrary government.

All liberal theorists and ideologues, however, saw in the diversification of markets, interest groups, and channels the sources of competition, growth (both material and intellectual), and a dynamic social balance. For classical and neoclassical economists and political theorists, the free dissemination of knowledge and information in the marketplace of ideas was thus the *sine qua non* of economic growth and political liberty. Freedom of speech, assembly, and association—as guaranteed by the First Amendment to the U.S. Constitution—was thus considered the backbone of a free society. The advent of the mass media simply transferred the same rights and privileges to the new channels of public communication.

Ithiel de Sola Pool (1983) has provided an analysis of this historical process in the United States. He has also pointed out the variety of factors that have threatened this freedom. From time to time, technological innovation, economic concentration, and political censorship have limited the diversity and autonomy of the channels of public communication. In liberal democracies, the media have thus attempted to act as a "Fourth Estate" to check and balance the three main branches of government, but in reality they have faltered and have sometimes been subjugated to the increasing levels of concentration of technological, economic, and political power. Paradoxically enough, the media have also been accused of the tyranny of "mediacracy," including the power to make and unmake politicians through both positive and negative political advertising. Russell Neuman (1986) has alarmingly argued that the size of the holders of informed opinion in the U.S. is no larger than 5 percent of the population.

Buckminister Fuller (1983, p. xxiii) has observed that the Reagan Administration in the United States was elected by the votes of only one-sevenths of the U.S. population. The Republicans spent $170 million—more than five times the money raised by their opponents—to buy their victory. Conscious of the facts that a U.S. presidency costs $50 million, a senatorship $10 million, and a representative's seat $5 million in media advertising, the American people have come to distrust government officials that owe their loyalties more to their corporate sponsors of media campaigns. They have thus increasingly abstained from participation in the electoral process—a phenomenon that has been aptly called by one author, "the empty voting booth." Such media power, linked with property power, also suggests a power that is unrepresentative and arbitrary, subject to the vagaries of commercial advantage and political influence.

The theory and practice of liberal democratic models have also been

subverted by a number of other historical developments. The most serious of these include concentrations of economic and political power,
bureaucratic power without representation, tyrannies of majorities, and
mind management and manipulation through mass media propaganda.
The long-term tendency of capitalist growth towards economic concentration is a well-established historical fact. This tendency towards the
development of big business has been, to some extent, checked by the
development of countervailing powers in big government, big labor
unions, and big media (Galbraith, 1956). However, all four institutional
structures are, in fact, expressions of the same general trend in modern
capitalist societies toward concentrations of economic and political
power in the hands of technostructures (fused technologies and bureaucracies) that represent no one in particular but themselves (Galbraith,
1978). These structures have become increasingly divorced from their
original constituencies (the stockholders, the general electorate, the labor union members, and the mass media audiences), self-perpetuating,
and often democratically unaccountable (Murdock, 1982).

The first two subversions of democracy emanate from above; the last
two originate from below. The "tyranny of majority" seems to be a
weakness of democratic societies diagnosed first by Tocqueville (1835–
40). Ever since his predictions, the world has witnessed several different
mass movements in the forms of Fascism, Nazism, and McCarthyism
prevailing in the Western democracies for at least short periods of time.
For Germany, this lasted from Hitler's ascendency to power in 1933 to
the conclusion of World War II in 1945. In Italy, Mussolini's fascist
regime lasted even longer—from 1922 to 1945. In Spain, Franco's regime
ruled that country from 1939 to 1975. In the United States, senator
Joseph McCarthy's anticommunist witch hunt lasted from 1951 to 1954.
The historic conditions which gave rise to these movements are still with
us. Economic depression, the potential rise of radical movements from
the left, and an alliance of the propertied classes with the lower-middle
classes to exploit class interests and status anxieties, can still ignite repressive, right-wing mass movements that have little regard for civil
liberties. Such movements would gleefully sacrifice liberty at the altar of
domestic repression and foreign expansion.

Despite these criticisms, however, Western capitalist democracies
and their media have so far survived the technological and political
shocks of the twentieth century. Given the nature of the challenges to
democratic freedoms, this is no small achievement. Representative democracy has been preserved primarily through the vigilance of the public, the courts, and the media. The doctrines of social responsibility,
equal time and fairness have been developed over time by the judicial
systems in Western democracies to correct the abuses of an unfettered

freedom of speech (Siebert et al., 1956; Gross, 1983, chapter 12; Pool, 1983). The media's role in this process has been pivotal insofar as a free media's survival depends on its credibility with its audiences. Traditional civil liberties have combined with a supporting public and judicial system to safeguard the media's rights in probing and questioning established policies and procedures. The role of the BBC in the Suez Crisis of 1956 and the Falklands Crisis of 1983 in Britain provides an excellent example of the public system's role in this respect. The role of the U.S. media in the Vietnam War (1954–75) and Watergate Crisis (1972–74) provides another example of a mixed system's vital interest in maintaining credibility with its audiences by responding to public outcries. Media responsibility and vigilance thus continue to be a legacy of liberal capitalism. It can be thwarted, however, under the extraordinary circumstance of a putsch by fascist and totalitarian elements.

Grass-root democratic movements also continue to reemerge periodically, some would argue cyclically, to revitalize the democratic traditions. In the United States, it appears that a new cycle is at work every 30 years. Arthur Schlesinger, Jr. (1984) has argued that this cycle goes all the way back to early American history and was first identified by Henry Adams. However, the length of the cycle seems to have increased from 25 to 30 years, due perhaps to increasing life expectancy. In the 20th century, the cycle could be conceived as swinging from *privatization* to *tribalization*, or from the pursuit of private gain to that of community solidarity. In each cycle, as the enthusiasm of the younger generation for "tribal" solidarity dissipates within a decade or so, the forces of individualism and private pursuit of individual gain and professional advancement overtake. This process goes on until a sense of social malaise sets in once again to pave the way for another round of a grass-roots movement attempting to correct the social inequities of the earlier era. The cycles correspond to what I have identified as *high accumulation* and *high mobilization* strategies of development. Periods of relative economic growth (e.g., the 1980s) often lead to lopsided income distribution and mobilized social movements calling for government intervention on behalf of social justice and welfare.

The cycles also seem to coincide with the U.S. presidential elections. The progressive Era was inaugurated by the election of Theodore Roosevelt in 1901, lasting until World War I and the subsequent failure of Woodrow Wilson's efforts to enlist the United States in the League of Nations (1918–1946). The decade of the 1920 was characterized by a privatization of American life and the gathering crisis that led to the Crash of 1929, the election of Franklin D. Roosevelt in 1933, and the inauguration of the New Deal. The tribalization movement of the 1930s was consummated by the U.S. entry into World War II, but the postwar period witnessed another period of privatization stretching into the 1950s. The election of John F. Kennedy in 1960, however, inaugurated yet another era of grass-root movements for democracy in the civil rights, women's rights, and anti-Vietnam War movements. With university revolts peaking in 1968 and the election of Richard M. Nixon in the same year, the polarization of American politics had reached a new peak. But with the conclusion of the war in Vietnam, and the disillusionments with the presidencies of Nixon and Carter, another period of privatization set in firmly in the 1980s. If this cyclical view of U.S. history holds true, we should be expecting another round of a grass-roots movement by the early 1990s after the mounting social inequalities of the 1980s have reached their peak. The stock market crash of October 19, 1987 might be considered as a harbinger of these developments.

If we compare these theories of short cycles with the theories of long cycles such as those proposed by Toynbee (1972), Kondrieff (Vask, 1988) and Batra (1987), it appears that such factors as civilizational life cycles, generational changes in leadership, cycles of scientific and technological innovation, business cycles, and shifts in political leadership (as Batra argues, from business leaders to soldiers or intellectuals), each have played their part in producing discernable cyclical patterns in history.

THE COMMUNIST DEMOCRATIC MODELS

The communist democratic revolutions, no less than the liberal democratic ones, owe much of their origins and spread to the advent of the new communication technologies. In this case, however, a combination of the print and radio broadcasting spread the revolutionary messages to the literate, semiliterate, and illiterate target audiences. By the mid-19th century, the advent of the mass circulation newspapers had already provided a vehicle and an organ for the working class movements. In the twentieth century, radio broadcasting provided an even more powerful vehicle to reach the semiliterate or illiterate, peasant populations.

In the meantime, the emerging mass movements and mass parties also gave rise to a new communication elite—the *ideologues*—who used the new mass media as their chief channel of communication to large audiences. In many respects, the new elite was different from the intellectuals of the liberal democratic leadership. They were recruited from journalistic, labor union, and political party as well as academic and publicist ranks. It was inclined more toward action than reflection, more toward agitation than legislation. The ideologues depended for their sources of social support on what the liberal and more elitist intellectuals have disdainfully called "the mob" or "the multitude." In the language of the American Federalists (Hamilton, Jay, and Madison), it was against the "multitude" that they wished to protect the rights of private property and individual liberty. It was also against the Tocquevillian "tyranny of the majority" that a whole generation of liberal elitist theories (such as Walter Lippmann) wished to protect public philosophy and public opinion. The liberal intellectuals prized the rationality of public opinion and abhorred the emotionality of mob agitation. By contrast, the radical ideologues—whether of the right or of the left—reveled in the charged power of the masses and call to action. The differences in outlook are best revealed in the pejorative and glorifying attitudes towards the "masses" in the lexicons, respectively, of liberals and radicals.

Communist democratic revolutions and doctrines presented to the world a second alternative model of communication and democracy. Although the principles of representation were still maintained, the theory of socialist democracy went beyond it to focus on problems of social inequality. Representative democracy, Marxists have critically argued, presumes a state of social and economic equality among the citizens that, in fact, does not exist. The principle of one-man-one-vote runs counter to the principle of one-dollar-one-vote dictated by the capitalist marketplace. Representative democracy is thus often distorted to the extent that it is manipulated by the dominant corporate interests in society to achieve their own special interests. Orthodox Marxist critics consider government as "the executive committee of the ruling class" and the so-called public media (such as the BBC) ultimately as agents of government. By contrast, the privately-owned media are held to have a dual interest in the maintenance of systems of privilege. As corporate entities they need to defend the capitalist system of privilege, but as entities dependent for survival on the size of audiences and commercial revenues, they also appeal to the lowest common denominator in their audiences' tastes and preferences. The content of the media is thus largely determined by the profit motive and tends to be sensationalist and manipulative.

The solution of orthodox Marxism to this problem has been, of course, the collective ownership of the means of production—including the means of public communication. The concentration of ownership and management of all means of public communication in the hands of the Party and the State is predicated upon the notion that, for a transitional period, all power should belong to the proletariat. However, "the dictatorship of the proletariat" is considered as only a transitional stage to the final stage of "the withering away of the state" (Marx & Engels, 1848). True freedom of communication will be thus established once social and economic inequities are completely eradicated, the class system is abolished, and when the state as an instrument of oppression of one class by another ceases to serve any useful purpose.

Liberal Marxism demonstrates a passionate love of both freedom and equality. But Marxism is also the pursuit of rationality. This is rooted in the Hegelian tradition with its emphasis on the role of reason in the process of historical development and the State as the ultimate embodiment of that rationality. Marxist views of history are thus centered on the key role of technological advances in the progressive unfolding of history, the increasing rationalization of the processes of production at successively higher levels, the proletariat as the vanguard of socialist rationalization, and the communist state as the ultimate embodiment of that rationality.

The deification of the State (writ large) as the ultimate source of all authority and legitimacy thus has often led to the corruptions of both liberalism and Marxism. In Fascism and Stalinism, we find the devotion to the State and the disregard of civil liberties and social justice as two sides of the same totalitarian coin. In practice, too, socialist democracies have shown themselves no less vulnerable to technocratic pressures than capitalist democracies. The state has not withered away, and the dictatorship of the proletariat has taken the shape of dictatorship of the Party led by an elite within it and, under Stalinist circumstances, a system of terror controlled by one strongman. The "iron law of oligarchy" (Michels, 1966) has been thus at work in the socialist parties no less than in the large capitalist corporation. It is, in fact, in the socialist parties of late 19th century that Michels recognized of the machinations of this oligarchic "law." The Party leaders, like the corporate managers, have often succeeded in seizing power from their constituencies and exercising it, but without much accountability. Communication under these models of socialism has been dubbed as "democratic centralism." Following a period of free discussion within the party ranks, the center is expected to issue the commands that must be faithfully carried out by party discipline. This principle has worked rather well in the earlier periods of revolutionary enthusiasm, but as power is consolidated in the new state and party, the bureaucracies have ossified and the parameters of freedom narrowed.

A variety of different attempts have been made in the communist democracies to correct the rigidities inherent in such a centralized system—inimical both to political democracy (freedom) as well as social (equality) and cultural democracy (fraternity). The de-Stalinization reforms following the 20th Congress of the Soviet Communist Party opened the door to a number of other reforms in the rest of the Soviet camp. Outside of the Soviet camp, however, even more daring attempts have been made to guard against concentrations of power. The

Yugoslav model of market socialism and self-management and the Chinese Cultural Revolution suggest two such efforts with diametrically opposite purposes and consequences. Following the uprising of 1956, the Hungarian political reforms and economic liberalization seem to have also produced some progressive results attracting the attention of the rest of the Soviet camp[2]. However, the postwar development of Eastern European socialist democracies has brought them increasingly into the orbit of world transnational forces. Their dependence on the major sources of world technology and capital has opened them up to pressures now global in scope. We have discussed some of these pressures in the preceding section; we will now focus specifically on the pressures for direct democracy that are present in the First, Second, and Third Worlds.

THE COMMUNITARIAN DEMOCRATIC MODELS

In contrast to the liberal democratic and communist democratic models that stress liberty and equality, the communitarian models of communication and democracy tend to underscore the primacy of fraternity and community. The social and psychological dislocations of industrial society in both the First and Second Worlds and their devastating effects in the Third World in the form of colonial and neocolonial domination have led to the emergence of a variety of neotraditionalist movements, from the United States to Poland to Iran, that insistently demand direct community participation in decision making. The common ethos of these movements consists of a skeptical attitude towards all authority, whether representative or corporate, an emphasis on cultural democracy (identity and ethnicity), and a desire for the assertion of the community will in matters of social concern.[3]

There is a linkage between the countercultural movements in the First and Second Worlds and the countermodernization, communitarian trends in the Third World. That linkage can be perhaps best understood in terms of the concepts of direct democracy. Western ideals of democracy have been shaped to a large extent by the Greek ideals of direct democracy. In the Age of Pericles, the citizens of Athens (excluding the slaves and women!) participated directly in the discussion and resolution of public issues. Our modern democracies have fallen short of that ideal on at least three counts. First, modern democracies are, at best,

---

[2]See "Hungary: The Lessons for Mr. Andropov," 1983.

[3]For a review of the main ideas and trends of these movements in a diversity of historical contexts, see Roszak, 1969, Ferguson, 1981; Sale, 1980; McRobie, 1981; Toffler, 1970, 1980; Feather, 1980; Naisbitt, 1982; Capra, 1984; Friberg and Hettne, 1983.

representative democracies. The views and interests of citizens are thus channeled and inevitably distorted through representation.

Second, as modern industrial society grows more and more complex, ordinary citizens are further removed from the decision-making processes affecting their fate by technostructures that are neither representative, nor accountable, nor responsive. The increasing concentration of economic and political power in the hands of the modern private corporations and state bureaucracies and their technomanagerial elites is a universal phenomenon.

Third, the Fourth Estate and the voluntary associations which—in democratic theory—were supposed to check and balance any concentration and abuse of power, have themselves fallen victim to the same technostructural forces they are supposed to correct. Communication in modern industrial societies is largely mediated; social reality is constructed by "manufacturing news" and by setting agendas in accordance with the views and interests of the dominant corporate or state managers. Public opinion polls test these agenda items to the neglect of other agenda items. Opinions are thus shaped, doctored, manipulated, interpreted, and reported not through interactive discussions in the public arena but by a communication elite at the service of the same media, corporate, or state technostructures they are charged to check and correct. However, the drama and theater of public debate and public hearings of media events (such as the Iran-Contra Hearings in the summer of 1987) tend to obscure the fundamentally constrained and circumspect nature of this method of public discourse.

What then are the prospects for direct democracy under these circumstances? Some of the current technological and social developments seem to suggest grounds for cautious optimism. For the first time in 2,000 years following the Athenian experiment, direct democracy seems to have become a viable complement to representative and collectivist models of democracy. However, certain conditions would have to be met beforehand.[4] First, in direct democracy, small size is imperative. The bigger the size of a political community, the greater would be the need for representation and the higher the level of distortion and manipulation of the electoral process. That is why citizens often feel more politically efficacious at the local than at the regional or national levels (Margolis, 1979).

Second, public office should be considered more as a public trust than as a social privilege. If public office is stripped of its many privileges

---

[4]Thanks are due to Johan Galtung for some of the following points raised at the Conference of the World Future Studies Federation, University of Hawaii at Manoa, March 1983.

(higher salaries, bonuses, expense accounts, and all the other trappings of power), it would tend to attract people who posses a greater commitment to public service than to personal gain. Power, nevertheless, corrupts and absolute power corrupts absolutely. Some of the world's worst dictators have been also the world's greatest ascetics. Stalin, for example, slept on a wooden bed, frequently changed his bedroom in the Kremlin, left most of his paychecks unopened, and never amassed a personal fortune for himself or his family. But his jealousies of power and office knew no bounds. Long tenures of office breed corruptions of power worse than financial corruption.

Third, rotation of public office should be radically redesigned to guarantee that no professional class of self-perpetuating politicians is made possible. Periodic, mandatory rotation of office holding would result not only in more responsible and responsive office holders but also in a more experienced pool of citizens.

Fourth, the right to information and communication should be considered as an inalienable right with a minimum degree of necessary constraints to protect the equally important rights of privacy and collective security (Margolis, 1979).

In the meantime, the technologies of information and communication have evolved in the direction of miniaturization, mobility, and widespread accessibility. The transistor radios and cassette tape recorders, videocassette recorders and players, the printing and copying machines, the long-distance telephone facilities, citizens' bands (CB) and cellular radio, low-powered radio and television transmission, personal computers, modems, and an increasing variety of electronic networks are the chief examples among such technologies. These technologies are clearly not available equally or universally, but they have made considerable inroad into even the remotest areas of the world. If present trends continue, they also promise to become increasingly more available at progressively lower costs and smaller sizes. They can be operated by a minimum of technical expertise, elude the government censors and regulators, and are mobile and maneuverable. They have been grafted more easily into the traditional networks of social and interpersonal communication than the big media (the national press, broadcasting, cable, telecommunications, and mainframe computers) that tend to become the power instruments of the modern state and corporation.

The small media have thus already provided new ammunition in the hands of a new communication elite, who—for want of any better terminology—may be called *the communologues*. This emerging group should be distinguished from the intellectuals, ideologues, and technologues of the earlier eras. The new communication elite is closer and far more sensitive to the realities of the community life and includes the religious leaders, community workers, teachers, and the alternative media people. A new worldview and cultural paradigm is also emerging worldwide that is attempting to reconstruct our traditional concepts of democracy. Alvin Toffler (1980) has suggested the concept of "the Third Wave" to underline its long-range historical significance, Marilyn Ferguson (1981) calls the phenomenon "the Aquarian Conspiracy"; Buckminister Fuller (1983) has called it "the Network People," and others (Becker, 1987; Arterton, 1987) have proposed "Teledemocracy" as a more appropriate description. But by whatever name we call it, the phenomenon should not be considered limited to the First World. In Iran and Poland, for instance, similar cultural and political sentiments against the heavy hand of the state have produced movements employing small media. The audio and video cassettes, copying machines, and small printing presses have mobilized traditional social and communication networks (the Mosque and the Church), undermined established authority, and asserted new perspectives on the age-old democratic ideals (Lewis, 1984).

The hardware and software technological requirements for direct democracy are thus already with us. The challenge is to create the cognitive technologies by generating the appropriate values and norms, political consciousness and will, and institutional arrangements. The global integrated system digital network (ISDN) is making it increasingly possible to switch ordinary citizens into interactive systems of communication carrying voice, data, text, and images. One such experiment in Britain dubbed "Project Universe," undertaken jointly between industry, government, and universities, is among the world's first attempts to meet the challenge ("Casting light on super fast computing," 1983). It will tie into the global telecommunications network with six local networks, including over 150 computers of different types. The technology is available, but it will take considerable economic and political resources to put it to democratic uses.

To insure citizen participation, however, at least two conditions must be met. The services must be made universally available and the price must become affordable. On both counts, the performance of telecommunications industries has been encouraging. On the whole, the rapid growth of these industries has been counterinflationary. Since 1965, the price index of INTELSAT unit service charge has dropped from 100 to 5, while cost of living has risen beyond 250 (Pelton, 1981). Developments in fiber optics and optical computing rather than electronic computing promise further cuts in cost, greater speed in transmission, breakthroughs in robotics, higher artificial intelligence, and more universal availability ("Britain has a go at linking telecom and computing," 1983c). Obstacles to direct democracy do not seem to be so much technological as institutional (Wicklein, 1981). Nevertheless, there is some room for cautious optimism on this score as well. There are now some political movements afoot around the world that have made direct democracy their cause. The most notable of these showing some political success at the polls is, of course, the Green Party in Germany (Capra, 1984). In March 1983 parliamentary elections, the Greens won 5.6 percent of the vote and 27 seats. Although critical of representative democracy, the voice of the Greens in the German parliament has been against traditional politics and for a nuclear freeze, devolution of power from central to local government, and rejuvenation of democracy by rotation of their own office holders and direct citizen participation (Galtung, lecture notes, 1983). The political ethos of the Greens has been in the air since the countercultural movements of the 1960s, but its transformation into political movements with a political philosophy and program for the transformation of our democratic institutions is a relatively new development.

The strength of the ideals upheld by the communitarians can be perhaps best gauged not so much by the proportion of votes they have received as by the espousal of those ideals in the rhetorics of the more well-established parties. A nuclear freeze resolution, for example, passed the U.S. House of Representatives in 1983. The devolution of power from federal to state governments has been part of the campaign rhetoric of the Republican Party in the United States. Legislation for the establishment of government-sponsored peace academies or institutes have now passed in the United States, Canada, and Australia. In the United States, the bill could not be vetoed by President Reagan because it was attached to the defense appropriation bill! None of these developments necessarily suggest any structural changes. The Greens are having their own difficulties and squabbles and may ossify into yet another established party;[5] the peace legislations and academies may be overwhelmed with the power of the military-industrial complex and its continuing interest in nuclear armament. But the seeds of a powerful idea have been already planted in the minds of citizens of democracies.

In the Third World where most models of communication and democracy have been adopted from the industrial world, demands for direct democracy have taken another shape. The psychological wounds of colonialism have combined with the pressing needs for grass-roots mobilization to underscore the primacy of fraternity and community vis-á-vis liberty and equality. President Julius Nyerere's call for *ujama* in the

---

[5]For a report on the evolution of the Green Party since its inception, see "Have West Germany's Greens Found a Future," *The Economist*, August 11, 1984, pp. 37–43.

development of Tanzanian society, the prominence of the concept of an Islamic *umma* in the neotraditionalist movements of the Islamic world, Pauolo Freire's central preoccupation with "conscientization" (*conscientizacao* in Portuguese) in the process of self-awakening of the oppressed are all suggestive of the same fundamental trends of thought and social action for a revitalization of community and communal rights and responsibilities. Small media as opposed to big media are increasingly providing channels of public communication hitherto denied to the people. These media have already made a difference in social movements such as the one that brought about the fall of the Shah in Iran (Tehranian, 1979, 1980a). With some imagination and inventiveness, they may also make a difference in the reconstruction of the democratic institutions along more accessible lines.

THE TOTALITARIAN COUNTERDEMOCRATIC MODELS

All of the above four democratic models have shown themselves historically vulnerable to the totalitarian temptation. Table 4.2 attempts to compare and contrast the major features of the totalitarian model with those of the three models of communication and democracy discussed above. Instead of freedom, equality, or fraternity, the totalitarian model typically chooses "order" defined in terms of an exclusionary identity as its central value to promote. Identity is clearly as defensible a value as any of the other three democratic values, particularly when and if a majority's cultural identity has been denied or oppressed by colonial or semicolonial domination. But after assumption of power, the racial, ethnic, or religious identity of the new rulers can also take a sinister aspect when imposed with impunity upon the rest of the population. Such were the racist doctrines of white or Aryan superiority that provided the ideological springboard for much of modern imperialism and fascism. A fetish of identity seems to be the road to a political tyranny far more potent than traditional dictatorships.

The sources of leadership and social support for the totalitarian formations often come from "the marginal" social classes. Industrialization has historically created some definite new class formations, such as those of the industrial bourgeoisie and the working class. But it has also created social classes that stand at the margins of clear-cut class formations. The newly-arrived peasants in search of employment in the large industrial cities, the small shopkeepers and tradesmen threatened by the encroachments of the larger and more powerful industrial and retail organizations, and the unemployed intellectuals who have failed to gain steady, gainful employment in government or industry are well-known examples of such marginals prone to extremist ideologies. The shift of modern capitalism increasingly from labor-intensive to capital-intensive techniques of production—including automation and robotics—has turned marginalization into an acute problem particularly in the Third World countries. But the cyclical patterns of capitalist development, from growth to stagnation and back, have also produced their own economic and political crises of marginalization. It was in such a period of European history during the 1930s that the Nazi and Fascist regimes came to power in Germany and Italy.

However, totalitarian temptations do not seem to be a prerogative of capitalism alone. It was the marginalized petty bourgeoisie of the socialist state (the petty state or party officials) who seem to have provided the main social support for Stalinism in the Soviet Union. The Green movement, although young and idealistic at this stage in history, is no less vulnerable to the same temptations. The Iranian revolution transformed quickly from a communitarian revolt into a theocratic dictatorship. The stories of the Charles Manson murders in the United States and the James Jones collective suicide in Jonestown also demonstrate the contradictory potentials of communitarian movements.

The totalitarian development strategy has historically combined a high degree of political repression with a high degree of capital accumulation. However, in the Third World—where population pressures and resource constraints are serious impediments to economic growth—that need not be the case. High capital accumulation is not therefore necessarily a concomitant of high political repression. Stagnation and repression can go together and often do. In the first situation, the totalitarian communication strategy justifies repression in terms of some economic efforts to build the state. In the second situation, repression is justified largely in terms of some external or internal enemies threatening the security of the state. The media are centrally controlled in both models and devoted to the propagation of the official dogmas and worldviews, including racist and xenophobic doctrines. In the meantime, the monolithic, ideological, and political apparatus of the state allows a full suppression of the democratic values of freedom, equality, and community.

CONCLUSION

This and the previous chapter have examined the global and national contexts of the current technological revolution in information and communication. I have argued that information technologies have had contradictory effects on the processes of democratization in the past,and will probably continue to do so in the future. They have, on the one hand, led to a broadening and deepening of public participation in the processes of decision making at the local, national, and international levels. On the other hand, they have also facilitated a level of concentration of information, power, and decision making within complex technobureaucratic organizations (notably the modern state and corporation) unprecedented in human history. In view of the perennial problems of cultural and epistemological lags, we may anticipate that the short-run effects of the present technological revolution in information management will lead to further concentrations of power, privilege, and dualism between the information-rich and information-poor.

I have also identified in these two chapters some global and national trends that suggest both concentrations and dispersions of power. The transnationalization of the world economy at the centers of power is undermined by the tribalization of world politics at the peripheries, while the processes of democratization of political values throughout the world are slowly building up the requisites of a more free, egalitarian, and united world. At the national level, the processes of democratization are reaching the local levels of power where demands for direct community participation are beginning to break through the institutional rigidities imposed by representative and corporate models of communication and democracy. The new abundance of channels, accessibility in price and quantity, and interactivity in modes of communication—made possible by the new information technologies—promise unprecedented levels of access, participation, and community media experimentation.

There is clearly no single road to democracy. I have identified here at least three faces of democracy in the modern world as revealed in the capitalist democratic, communist democratic, and communitarian democratic traditions. Each tradition has focused on a different configuration of democratic values, maximizing some at the cost of others. But each one has also broadened and enriched the concept of democracy. Liberalism's love of individual freedom through plurality of centers of power, communism's passionate pursuit of social equality through class struggle, and the communitarian faith in social solidarity through revival of traditional ties of community and direct participation have complemented each other in many ways. Each also stands to benefit from the critiques provided by the other competing and complementary perspectives. Democracy like other human ideals should be viewed, therefore, more as a process than an end in itself. Democratic processes lose momentum, in fact, precisely at the moment that we assume we have achieved the final goals of democracy. Countries that conceive of themselves as democratic have historically proved themselves the most vulnerable to totalitarian temptations, because the struggle for democracy and the public discourse that safeguards it have often ceased to live as strongly in public life as in public memory.

II

Promises, Perils, Prospects

5

The Promises of Teledemocracy

The open secret of the new electronic media, the decisive political factor, which has been waiting, suppressed or crippled, for its moment to come, is their mobilizing power. When I say *mobilize*, I mean *mobilize*, make men more mobile than they are. As free as dancers, as aware as football players, as surprising as guerrillas. . . . For the first time in history, the media are making possible mass participation in a social and socialized productive process, the practical means of which are in the hands of the masses themselves.

(Enzenberger, 1974, pp. 96–97)

Enzenberger's (1974) rhapsodic anticipation of teledemocracy is not an isolated view. It is, rather, a perspective that has been shared by many scholars of the media over a long period of time. Lasswell (1927), Lazarsfeld, Berelson, and Gaudet (1948), Pool et al. (1973), Schramm (1964), Lerner and Pevsner (1958), and Katz and Lazarsfeld (1964) have generally considered the electronic media as powerful democratizing forces. The effects of the media might be somewhat modified by two-step or multiple-step flows of communication through complex interpersonal networks (Rogers & Shoemaker, 1983), but their democratic impact has largely been taken for granted.

In fact, Enzenberger's poetics had earlier been presented as a scientific model by Lerner's influential theory of modernization. The model suggested that urbanization, literacy, mass media exposure, and political participation were positively correlated in the historical experience of transition from preindustrial to industrial societies. Indeed, the mass media were considered by Lerner as a kind of "mobility multiplier" (Lerner, 1958). This model was extremely influential in shaping a whole generation of empirical research on problems of communication and modernization (Frey, 1973; Inkeles & Smith, 1974). The premises of the model were questioned only after the historical experiences of the 1960s and 1970s revealed that the phenomenal growth in mass media exposure had not necessarily led to the emergence of democratic regimes (Rogers, 1976; Tehranian, 1979). Historical developments did not match the media scholars' expectations, but it could be reasonably argued that political and commercial interests have not allowed the technological possibilities to serve democratic ends.

The new interactive information technologies have prompted another era of optimism. The new optimism, like the old, has also been accompanied by a flurry of media activism. In contrast to the old "development support communication" programs that were largely government financed, flowing vertically from the top to the bottom of power structures, the new media activism has been community-centered, popularly supported, and bottom up. The community media movement, as documented by Berrigan (1977; 1981), Lewis (1984), O'Sullivan-Ryan and Kaplar (n.d.), Jankowski (1982), Ito (1980), Teicher (1984), and others suggests a social movement of worldwide proportions. The survey conducted by the author for this study suggests the same.

This chapter will examine the teledemocracy movement in terms of its historic evolution from telecommunity to televoting and teledemocracy. To follow in the footsteps of Harold Innis (1951), the distinction here suggests an evolution from time-biased to space-biased communication. Whereas the earliest experiments with interactive media have focused on their organizing and mobilizing functions at the local community where interpersonal communication networks are already strong, later experiments have attempted to broaden their scope to include large cities, regions, or even countries (Dutton, Blumler, & Kraemer, 1987). It may be generally argued that the movement from time- to space-biased networks has also entailed greater expense, organization, and hierarchy—and, by the same token, less participation. This chapter will provide an account of the origins, technological parameters, and institutional frameworks of each of the three movements. It will also try to show the linkages between telecommunity, televoting, and teledemocracy experiments.

THE TELECOMMUNITY MOVEMENT

The telecommunity movement may be considered from at least three different perspectives: historical origins, technological parameters, and institutional frameworks. Although the growth and diffusion of interactive information technologies have served as vehicles to the movement, it is clearly the democratic impulses behind them that provide the fuel. The historic drives for liberty, equality, and fraternity have found in the new information technologies a new ally and multiple channels for expression. The crucial test of the movement will be in whether or not this new combination of forces will be able to overcome the present technostructures of domination. The movement may do so by giving a new lease on life to the representative and corporate institutions of democracy as well as by creating some new institutions for *direct* democratic expression.

Historical Origins

The idea of community media is perhaps as old as the media itself. The media have been used to serve community needs in at least six different ways: to inform, to educate, to entertain, to react, to mobilize, and to organize. The first three functions are what David Webster, formerly of the BBC, once characterized as the illuminating, elevating, and ventilating roles of broadcasting. These are fundamentally no different from the functions telecommunity can also fulfill. However, the last three functions are more community-action-oriented, demanding the media to be differently organized from the presently dominant state, commercial, or public media systems. And that is where community media have come into the picture.

Since the latter three media functions are not as well known as the former three, it might be useful to illustrate them with some definitions and examples:

To React. This function of the media is well served in letters to the editors, phone-ins to radio and television stations, group petitioning from telegraphic houses, and so on.[1] It is an attempt to turn the one-way mass media systems (the press and broadcasting) into a partially interactive system serving audience and community views and needs. From the community point of view, however, this is a fundamentally reactive mode of operation. In other words, the media are still controlled from the center while the community reacts to the messages on an ad hoc basis.

To Mobilize. This function of the media—according to many scholars, including Enzenberger and Lerner—is central to modern mass media. However, revolutionaries from Lenin to Freire and Khomeini have also recognized and utilized the print and electronic media effectively in conjunction with interpersonal networks and political, educational, or religious organizations to mobilize public opinion on behalf of certain revolutionary objectives. According to Lerner (1958), the most significant role of the modern media lies in offering new role models to their audiences. This has a positive effect on their "psychic mobility," "empathy," or the ability to think and feel as others do—psychological characteristics considered vital to modernity and modernization. While Paulo Freire's (1972) concept of "conscientization" has an entirely different cast, it still highlights another dimension of psychological mobilization,

---

[1]To cite an example of this latter, the introduction of telegraphic lines in Iran towards the end of the 19th century led to the practice of public protest meetings at the telegraphic houses for the people to send their grievances and petitions directly to the Shah in the capital (see Browne, 1966).

that is, the process of self-awakening to one's own social conditions and needs. We may, therefore, argue that the "mobilization" function of the media has objective as well as subjective dimensions, consisting of the dialectics of awakening to the "objective" social structures and one's "subjective" position in it. This may be considered as a process of, in Freire's words (1973), "education for critical consciousness."

To Organize. This function of the media goes beyond the earlier two. It suggests that the media can serve as channels for reaction and mobilization as well as community organization. Some revolutionaries and media activists have recognized this function rather explicitly by using "community media" as an instrument for organizing certain social classes or interest groups for common action. For instance, Lenin's explicit objective in the publication of *Iskra* was to organize the Russian social democrats around a common ideological organ (Lenin, 1969). Many of the telecommunity projects I will review in this study are those primarily oriented towards reformist community action.

The telecommunity movement as a whole seems to have served all of the above six functions. However, some experiments have been designed to serve primarily one or a specific combination of the six functions better than others. The movement clearly owes its origins to the introduction of certain new information technologies that have made two-way, interactive, and community-oriented and community-controlled communication progressively more possible. But the pressure of social needs for access, participation, community mobilization, and organization has been an equally important factor. In industrial countries, this pressure has expressed itself primarily in the form of increasing trends towards local rather than network programing. In developing countries, the pressures for economic growth and social mobilization have revealed community participation to be an imperative. It is, therefore, not surprising that the movement receives its inspiration both from social critics—such as Freire—and media activists. The unity of theory and practice has been an underlying tenet of the movement in developed as well as developing countries.

The dual origins of the movement come together at about the same time in the early 1970s. The Community Media and the Freirian movements originated from two different worlds, the First and the Third, but they shared in common antiauthoritarian and direct democratic impulses. Freire's ideas were shaped in the social context of one of the poorest regions of the world, the Brazilian Northeast. Born in Brazil in 1921, he grew up knowing hunger and beginning to understand "the hunger of others." One biography of him suggests that "it was here, at the age of 10, that Freire first realized the many wrong things . . . in this world of men" and asked himself how he could help those who lived in continuous deprivation. Freire's work originated in confronting that question as he conducted his initial adult literacy programs during the late 1950s. By 1963, he had become coordinator of the federal government's national adult education campaign. After the 1964 military coup d'etat in Brazil, Freire was forced into political exile. He moved to Chile where he continued to apply his method to peasants, working for both the federal government and UNESCO. Finally, as a member of the World Council of Churches and of the Institute for Cultural Action, Freire has been working with the Commission on Education of the Guinea-Bissau government since 1975. Brazil in the early 1960s, Chile in the late 1960s, and Guinea-Bissau in the middle 1970s generated the "political-pedagogical activity" from which Freire's ideas have emerged and developed" (Lima & Christians, 1979, pp. 135–136).

By contrast, the community media movement emerged out of the turbulence of the 1960s in the United States and Western Europe. The countercultural movement known as the "Flower Revolution" was anti-war, antiauthoritarian, and radically democratic (Roszak, 1969). It also had a strong pedagogical dimension that could be characterized, as in the Freirian case, by a call for "dialogical communication" (Lima & Christians, 1979). It led to the student revolts of the 1960s throughout the United States and Western Europe, resulting in some educational reforms in the universities. The Port Huron Manifesto of the Students for Democratic Society eloquently expressed these sentiments and social objectives for participatory democracy (Jacob & Landau, 1966).

By the 1970s, the movement had petered out and had been, in part, coopted by the establishment. It continued however to express itself in cultural rather than political forms. It was at about the same time that individuals and groups in North America and Western Europe discovered a new communication tool: the portable video camera. As recounted by Jankowski (1982, p. 33), "armed with these 'portapaks,' people began making their own television programs. Some of these productions circulated not farther than the editing and viewing rooms; others reached a wider audience through transmission on cable television systems."

This combination of festering sentiments and new technological possibilities has led to a series of unceasing experimentations around the world, some spontaneous and some planned, to bridge the gap between people and the media. In Western Europe and North America, the combination of portable video, cable television, telematics (convergence of satellites, computers, telephones, cable, and broadcasting) has created virtually unlimited possibilities for interactive communication. The appearance of personal computers on the scene during the 1980s has extended the horizons of the users beyond their local communities to wider networks. Local community media are thus fast becoming "tele-communities" through electronic bulletin boards and teleconferencing in their three distinct varieties of audio, video, and computer communication. Much of this work has been done through trial and error without much organization or large-scale financing. But in a few countries— notably the United States, England, the Scandinavian countries, the Netherlands, and West Germany—nationally authorized experiments have been sponsored and monitored through social science research. Organizations like the Cable Television Information Service and the Public Interest Computer Association in Washington, DC, the National Film Board in Ontario, the Council of Europe in Strasbourg and UNES-CO in Paris have taken it upon themselves to document these efforts and to promote exchange of experiences.

In the Third World, demands for participatory development and dialogical communication have been the result of several different factors, including the anticolonial revolutionary movements, the failure of development projects adopting top-down communication support systems, the rapid expansion of macromedia (the national press and broadcasting) often propagating government-controlled messages and imported foreign films and television programs, and an equally rapid diffusion of micromedia (transistor radio and cassettes, mimeographing, xeroxing in conjunction with the availability of telephones). The intractable problems of poverty and mass apathy have led Third World governments to pay more attention to the communication components of their development plans, but it has also become increasingly clear that without fundamental changes in social and political power structures, not much can be accomplished. Demands for "another development" (Nerfin, 1977), calling for more equitable income distribution, access, and participation, open planning, and appropriate technologies have become increasingly insistent. In some countries, such as Tanzania, the new style of development became part of official government policy and ideology (Nyererre, 1968). But in some others, where the structures of power have been too entrenched and insensitive to give way to popular demands for greater participation, revolutionary movements have assumed greater momentum. The new micromedia, available at low cost and eluding government censors, have served to mobilize mass discontent into organized opposition. The Islamic Revolution in Iran provides the most dramatic example of such uses of the new media (Tehranian, 1979, 1981), but there is evidence to suggest that such "illicit" telecommunity media are also playing a part in the social and political fermentations under the repressive regimes in Poland, Chile, South Africa, Saudi Arabia, and the Philippines.

In a worldwide environment of technological revolution and institutional resistance, telecommunities represent an "underground" movement. For an understanding of the variety of the telecommunity movements, it would be useful now to turn to an examination of the technological parameters and institutional frameworks of this movement.

Technological Parameters

The current revolution in information technologies may be characterized by three major trends: (a) from scarcity to abundance of channels; (b) from analogue to digital signals; and (c) from media divergence to media convergence. Each of these technological transitions is having— and will continue to have—profound consequences for the society's communication institutions. The monopoly of airwaves by governments and government regulatory agencies, justified by the scarcity of channels, has had to give way now to deregulation in an industry that is increasing its channel capacity through the cable and fiber optic technologies. The increasing digitization of communications signals, capable of carrying audio, visual, and data messages over the same channels, will provide an Integrated System Digital Network (ISDN) that can link up the remotest world communities to any other spot on the globe (*Inter-Media*, March 1983). And finally, these developments are increasingly blurring the boundaries between the point-to-point telecommunication and the mass media as well as among the mass media (print, radio, and television) themselves. Electronic publishing, for example, can provide information in any variety of multimedia forms through rapid digital transformation and transmission of signals.

These revolutionary developments have enhanced interactive communication in three fundamentally different ways, including human-machine, human-machine-human, and human-machine-community interactions. To provide a bird's-eye view of the variety of the new information technologies and their interactive applications, Table 5.1 classifies the most well-known technological systems with respect to the above three types of interactive applications.

It is not my purpose here to go into any detailed explanation of the technical aspects of the above systems. Bretz (1983) has provided one such clear explanation of the interactive information technologies, classifying them into fully-interactive and partially-interactive systems. By "interactive," Bretz (1983, p. 137) means systems

in which each of the two (or more) communicants receives and responds to messages originated by the other(s). This means that the system is functionally symmetrical; the roles of the communicants are interchange-

Table 5.1. Interactive Information Technologies and Their Applications

Technologies	Human-Machine	Human-Machine-Human	Human-Machine-Community
Teletext (Ceefax, Antiope) Over the Air System	Database, Computer-Assisted Instruction/Entertainment		Newsletter, Narrowcasting
Videotex (Prestel, Telidon, Viewdata) Over the Wire System	Database, Computer time-sharing, Notebook, Personal Calendar, CAI/Entertainment	Mail, Shopping, Reservations of any kind	Video-conferencing Newsletter Narrowcasting
Computer Conferencing (EIES, Confer, CBBS)	Computer time-sharing Personal Notebook, CAI/Entertainment	Mail	Newsletter, Computer Bulletin Boards, Conferencing
Value Added Networks (Telenet, Tymnet, Arpa)		Mail Code Translation	Narrowcast
Two-Way Cable	Video	Shopping Education, Entertainment Narrowcast	
Enhanced Database Brokers (Source, Develop)	Database Notebook, Personal Calendar, Education, Entertainment	Mail, Shopping, Reservations	Newsletter, Conferencing, Narrowcast
Subscription Television (Over-the-air)	Video		Education, Narrowcast
Regular Brokers (Lockheed, SDC)	Database		Newsletter
Facsimile		Mail	Newsletter

Sources: Bretz, 1983; National Citizens Committee for Broadcasting (NCCB), 1979.

able; each may alternately be sender and receiver. A 'communicant' may either be a human or a sophisticated machine, such as an elaborately programmed computer.

An example of the latter is a computer program, the Eliza, that acts as a psychiatrist, processing the information received from the patient to provide appropriately-phrased questions, comments, and positive reinforcements at appropriate junctures in the therapeutic dialogue. However, this is not a substitute for human interaction. In fact, Joseph Weizenbaum—the author of Eliza—was shocked when his program was reviewed as a major step in artificial intelligence and a possible substitute for psychotherapy which the program was designed to simulate! (Weizenbaum, 1976).

The term "artificial intelligence" itself also may be considered somewhat of a misnomer in that it suggests levels of human learning in machines that are unlikely to be achieved. Rote learning (memorization) and feedback learning (trial and error) have already been achieved by sophisticated computers, but pattern recognition (analogical learning) and pattern creation (innovation and creativity) are something that has proved to be far beyond the reach. In terms of Bloom's taxonomy (Bloom, 1956), computers have shown until now "intelligence" only in the knowledge category of the cognitive domain. Science fiction to the contrary, there is no evidence to suggest that they will be able to learn in the affective and psychomotor domains.

Among the more familiar fully-interactive systems, Bretz makes a distinction among the following: television systems, audio systems, augmented audio systems, alphameric media systems, data response, and slow scan TV. Among the less familiar, quasi-interactive media systems, he counts the teletext and videotex systems. The distinction between the latter two systems is a technical one. The first, teletext, is an auxiliary broadcasting service that is fed into the home as part of a standard television signal, without affecting the TV broadcast. The second service, videotex, is not broadcast but comes into the home via the existing telephone line, using the television set only as display screen (Bretz, 1983, p. 141).

Of the fully-interactive systems, television combines both audio and visual signals and is most familiar and ubiquitous. In 1970, the British Post Office pioneered its first video-conferencing service under the name of Contravision. Many other post, telephone, and telegraphic (PTT) services in several countries have developed teleconferencing systems by means of which joint meetings may be held with participants located in two or more cities. Next best-known teleconferencing systems are the so-called audio systems, both the simple and augmented varieties. Audio systems are, however, as fully audiovisual as television systems, except that the visual portion is not in full and realistic motion (Bretz, 1983, p. 31). In addition, some audio systems are augmented by two-way audio or by automated means of speaker identification and automatic switching. The various nodes (locations) of teleconferencing systems may be interconnected by a variety of different network configurations. That is why it would be misleading to generalize across all audio systems, or all television systems, or all alphameric systems. Computer conferencing and electronic mail currently present the least expensive and most available of the fully-interactive media.

The last two fully-interactive systems discussed by Bretz are Data Response and Slow Scan TV. The Qube in Ohio provided an example of Data Response (see Chapter 6). The system represents a convergence of the cable and computer technologies. Recognizing the potential of data response in increasing the usefulness of cable TV to the public, the U.S. Federal Communications Commission (FCC) currently requires that all cable systems larger than 3,500 subscribers should have such "potential capability" (Bretz, 1983, p. 115).

By contrast, Slow Scan TV is a technology available to anywhere that the worldwide networks of telephone wires, microwave beams, and satellite channels can carry the human voice. Slow Scan carries still pictures, and that is why it has also been called phone-line or narrow-band video. Because it transmits still pictures, Slow Scan has also been referred to as "freeze-frame" video. Furthermore, as Bretz (1983, p. 118) points out, any device that can record and play back audio signals, can record and play back Slow Scan TV. It can also be sent over standard narrow-bandwidth radio channels. It is estimated that between 3,000 and 10,000 radio amateurs in over 100 countries now communicate visually as well as audially via inexpensive slow scan." Because its cost is equivalent to the cost of using the telephone lines to send still pictures electronically, Slow Scan TV is frequently used by universities across the United States (e.g., at University of Wisconsin's Center for Interactive Programs and University of Hawaii at Manoa's Social Science Research Institute).

Institutional Frameworks

The increasing diversity in available types and possible configurations of interactive technologies should be encouraging to the variety of institutional arrangements and purposes for which they can be used. As often is the case, however, institutional lags have greatly slowed down the possible benefits that interactive technologies could bring to the fulfillment of the democratic ideals of free flow of information, equality of access, and full participation in the decision-making processes. Four dominant media systems in the world are identified here; state, commercial, public, and community. Each system has its own unique ownership, management, financing, regulation, programming, access, and participation features. National media systems are often a mix of these models with one or a combination of models dominating the total system. Interactive technologies come with institutional packages and are subject to the objectives or constraints of the system they serve. State systems primarily serve the objectives of the central political powers; commercial systems frequently bow to the profit motive above all; public systems tend to be culturally elitist serving their own sources of "public" support. As a plularizing system, therefore, community media come closest to the democratic ideals. Although this system is still in its infancy, the new interactive communication technologies tend to favor its growth.

Table 5.2 provides a highly schematic, comparative view of the four systems with respect to their characteristics of ownership/management, financing, regulation, programming, and access/participation. Prevalent in the communist and Third World countries, the state system is synonymous with government monopoly of the means of public communication. The system is typically managed by such government ministries as the Ministry of Information and Communication or government agencies such as the radio and television organization. Although many state systems derive a portion of their revenues from advertising, the system depends mostly on direct budgetary allocations from the government. Regulation of the media is often centralized, but in communist and Third World countries where a single political party is often in power, this regulation is jointly undertaken by the government and party bureaucracies. Programming is similarly official and directive, while feedback is limited to the officially sanctioned letters to the editors and broadcasters.

The commercial media system is characteristic of most capitalist democracies, most notably of the United States. However, it is also heavily represented in Western Europe, Japan, and Latin America where it is supplemented by an equally strong public system. Although media management is relegated to a professional cast of journalists and broadcasters, the commercial media system is ultimately beholden to the rules of the market. Dallas Smythe (1977) has aptly characterized the main activity of the commercial system as that of "selling audiences to advertisers," who in turn look to program ratings as their chief barometer. Regulation of the commercial media considerably varies from one country and medium to another. Broadly speaking, however, regulation is

Table 5.2. Four Models of Media Systems: A Schematic View

	Ownership/Management	Financing
State	Government monopoly ownership and management through Ministry of Information or similar bureaucracies	Direct state budgetary allocations
Commercial	Private ownership through proprietorship, partnership, or corporate control. In corporate systems, the separation of ownership from management creates symbiotic relations between private stockholders and professional managers	Through selling audiences to advertisers, commercial rates depending on ratings
Public	Ownership and management in public trust through a publicly owned and managed corporation under the authority of a publicly appointed and autonomous board of trustees or directors, e.g., BBC, PBS or NHK	Through license fees, private donations, government subsidies, or limited advertising
Community	Community ownership and management through duly elected representatives or direct and voluntary community participation. Ideally, a media of the people, by the people, and for the people	Mix of the above

Regulation	Programming	Access and Participation
Centralized and direct	Official and directive	Limited to officially sanctioned "reactions"
Centralized at the level of state regulatory authority (e.g., FCC) and decentralized at the level of market mechanisms of monopoly and competition	Controlled in news and public affairs; responsive to audience preferences in entertainment and cultural programming	Limited to legal requirements
Subject to general regulatory rules and political and cultural preferences of the trustees	Generally reflective, subject to the degree of autonomy enjoyed from government and need to compete with commercial system	More open than state and commercial systems still subject to government regulations and public propriety
Subject to general regulatory rules and their own ownership and management structures	Community-oriented programming, produced by the community members for community members	Highly responsive to highly targetted audiences, using interactive methods as much as possible

often centralized for purposes of allocation of broadcasting frequencies, licensing and codes of conduct, while decentralized at the level of market competition. In the United States, for instance, the FCC primarily regulates common carriers and broadcasting while the state regulatory agencies mainly oversee cable and publishing industries. A trend towards deregulation has been in force both at the federal and state levels. Programming in the commercial system primarily follows the dictates of the market while looking for approval to the regulatory authorities. Where regulatory procedures are weak, the natural tendency is to bid for the highest ratings by sinking to the lowest common denominator of taste. Access and participation is similarly limited to what the regulatory and licensing procedures require.

The public system, of which the BBC and NHK are prime examples, represents a compromise between government monopoly and commercial competition. Ideally, the system is removed from direct government control by means of trusting its management to an autonomous public corporation whose directors are appointed as trustees of public interest. But the notion of public trust is as fragile as the politics of the media, and public systems often find themselves at the center of controversies in which their divided loyalties to government authority and audience credibility are severely tested. Their courage to face their detractors, therefore, depends on the strength of the democratic traditions of media autonomy. A subtle but powerful way that governments try to influence the public systems is through mechanisms of financing. Although most public systems in western Europe and Japan are financed through license fees, giving them a measure of autonomy vis-á-vis their governments, the rates depend on legislative approval. This gives government an opportunity to influence the broadcasters during inflationary times. Only Japan's NHK is responsible for the collection of its own license fees, which gives it a further measure of autonomy and self-reliance. Other sources of financing such as government subsidies, private donations, and limited advertising clearly open the door to further influence peddling.

In view of its recent origins and diversity of forms, the community media system is perhaps the most difficult of the four systems to define. The system has been called by many names, including "community media," "rural press," "alternative media," "local origination programming," "localism," "guerrilla media," "community broadcasting," "electronic bulletin boards," "electronic town meetings," and so on (Lewis, 1984, pp. 61–62; Jankowski, 1982). But most of the experiments share in their common democratic ethos an attempt to build a media of the people, by the people, and for the people. These efforts run against considerable institutional odds imposed by national and international media systems reflecting existing and entrenched power structures. A useful distinction introduced by Peter Lewis (1984) is to differentiate between access, participation, and self-management. Access programs are those offered by existing state, commercial, and public systems to community groups to reach their own audiences. They often provide little opportunity for the community to gain experience in the message production process. Participation constitutes the next higher level of community media. It allows the community group to participate and control the production process. This may be achieved by providing public or private funding for production facilities and programming. However, genuine community media are those that are community planned, managed, and operated. Self-management is an ideal towards which community media are currently striving, but the realization of that ideal is still facing considerable obstacles in the hostile environments dominated by state, commercial, or public systems.

Ownership patterns in the world currently reflect a dominance of the state and commercial systems. Table 5.3 provides some information on the ownership of world broadcasting systems. It shows that, while about 50 percent of the world's radio and televisions systems are government-owned and -operated, public and commercial systems follow that lead by sharing fairly equally in the other half. This is a misleading picture, however, if we take the content of programming rather than formal ownership into account. In fact, as Tunstall (1977) has persuasively argued, the world media are still mainly Anglo-American and commercial. Economies of scale, scope, and status favor the commer-

Table 5.3.   Ownership of World Broadcasting Systems

Type of Ownership	Radio		Television	
	Number	Percent	Number	Percent
Government	91	49	63	48
Public corporation	38	21	29	22
Private, commercial	36	21	21	16
Combinations of the above	19	10	18	14

Commentary: Percentages rounded to nearest whole number. "Public corporation" refers to ownership by a nonprofit corporation. The largest percentage, nearly half, of both radio and television systems are entirely government-owned. The proportions of public corporate and private ownerships are about equal. Television has a lower percentage of commercial systems but a higher percentage of combination systems. Note that the number of commercially owned systems does not reveal the full number that sell advertisements, as many government and public systems depend on advertising for part of their income.
Source: Adapted from late 1970s data in UNESCO, *Statistical Yearbook, 1982,* tables 11.1 and 11.3. ©UNESCO 1982. Used by permission. The tables omit some countries and count the Panama Canal Zone, the U.S. Virgin Islands, and Puerto Rico as separate systems. (Head, 1985, p. 60).

cially produced Anglo-American products. Lower costs per unit of production resulting from catering to massive English-speaking audiences make the Anglo-American cultural products cheaper than those of others. The large scope of production of Anglo-American companies, engaged in a variety of multimedia markets, gives them another edge. Finally, Anglo-American media productions enjoy a high level of prestige worldwide not only because of their superior production techniques but also because they portray what is perceived to be the world's highest standards of living, taste, and culture!

FROM TELECOMMUNITY TO TELEVOTING

The community media movement has largely been a localist phenomenon. It has rarely attempted to project its democratic ideals of media access, participation, and management into the larger, national scene. By contrast, televoting experiments attempt to move beyond the local scene to employ the communication technologies for encouraging informed participation at urban, regional, or national levels.

Televote is a novel method of public opinion polling originally designed by Vincent Campbell as a new public communication system for the San Jose Unified School District in California.[2] The experimental program was funded by the National Science Foundation (Campbell & Santos, 1975). Campbell's method was not a public opinion poll in the traditional sense. It was, instead, a two-way decision-making process in which official policies and plans were submitted to the public ·for its consideration and direct feedback.

Televoters were sent factual information, balanced arguments, and a wide range of policy alternatives. This material was mailed to them in brochure form. The televoters had a week or so to think about the issues. Then they relayed their opinion by telephone to the central televote office where the data were collated, analyzed, and distributed. This method of televote was based on self-selective participation. It was consequently unrepresentative of the population-at-large. Campbell (1974) notes that "the largest minority group in the area is Mexican-American and they participated at a lower rate than Anglo-Whites." Nevertheless, approximately 6,000 respondents took considerable time and care to ponder over local educational policy issues and transmit their opinions and ideas to administrators interested in them.

---

[2]I am grateful to my friends Ted Becker and Christa Slaton for permitting me to use their extensive writings on "televote" in this section.

In 1978, Ted Becker, Richard Chadwick, and Christa Slaton of the University of Hawaii revised the San Jose Televote in order to turn it into a scientific random public opinion sample of a population. In contrast to conventional public opinion polls, however, the new Televote method attempts to *inform* the public before sampling their opinions. Following a random selection of Televoters, they were provided with brochures on the issues at stake. Ample time is allowed for the reading of these materials before the Televote staff calls up the voters to ask for their responses.

Televote has been implemented in Hawaii, New Zealand, and Los Angeles. In Hawaii, where it has been conducted several times, the topics have ranged wide and far, including citizens' initiatives, the public's legislative priorities, mandatory sentencing of criminals, competency testing for high school graduation, public transportation system, and Reaganomics (Becker & Slaton, 1981).

Transferring the experience of Hawaii Televote to New Zealand in 1981, Ted Becker (since 1988 of Auburn University) and Brian Murphy (of Auckland University) coordinated the work in three university centers (Christ Church, Wellington, and Auckland). This was a national survey on "The Future of New Zealand." It consisted of several "games" to encourage Televoters to make some difficult choices among four different futures for their country.

The Los Angeles Televote was conducted in 1982, sponsored by the Southern California Association of Governments (SCAG) and coordinated by Kirk Bergstrom and David Grannis. It was divided into two parts. The first part involved four major initiatives on the November 1982 ballot, including such issues as beverage containers, nuclear weapons freeze, water resources, and a handgun ban. The second part was called "Your Future in Los Angeles" and covered such emerging issues as flexible work hours during the 1984 Olympic Games, computer training as an educational requirement, tax breaks for high-tech industries, and limits on new housing in the LA area (SCAG, 1983).

Although televoting has not become a routine method of public opinion polling, it has shown its potential to serve the dual purpose of public education and public feedback on questions of important public policy. An evaluation of this method has to address at least the following three questions: (a) Is televote a valid method of polling? (b) How does televote compare with conventional polling? and (c) How do people react to the televote method?

Becker and Slaton (1981) have responded to these three questions in the following manner. First, in evaluating the validity of televote as a new method of public opinion polling, it must be recognized that two groups of respondents tend to get lost along the way—those who refuse to participate in the first place, and those who lose heart after signing up. Although the original sample can be carefully randomized, this raises a problem as to the final outcome. But Becker and Slaton report that, both in Hawaii and New Zealand televotes, they have managed to end up with a group of respondents who roughly represent the population-at-large with respect to such factors as age, sex, income, education, racial, or ethnic background. To achieve this kind of representation, however, a televote project would have to be well-publicized in order to receive a balanced participation from all sectors of the population. This, in turn, raises the problems of good organization and financing.

Second, how does televote compare to conventional public opinion polling? The quick answer is that it reduces the percentage of "I don't knows!" Becker and Slaton report that in comparing the results of two experiments, called Telepoll and Televote, with a sample of approximately 400 persons in each, the difference in outcome was significant. In Televote, the respondents were provided with a good deal of information on two different transportation systems proposed for Honolulu (a new rapid transit system vs. a major expansion of the public bus system). Only 4 percent of Televoters said I "don't know" as compared with 18.3 percent in Telepoll.

Finally, what are the reactions toward Televote? The mass media institutions and professionals seem to have received it as another method to engage their readers and audiences. Both the print and electronic media have voluntarily publicized televote projects and have reported on the findings. The impact of televote on policy makers and officials also seems positive. Televote provides officials with feedback. But the impact on policies is unknown or minimal. Campbell (1974, p.45) reports that of the 14 major recommendations made by the Televoters in San Jose, four were substantially adopted as policy. Nevertheless, the attitude of the Televoters themselves seems to have been overwhelmingly positive. Becker and Slaton report that in the nine Televote polls, some 85–95 percent of Televoters expressed a willingness to participate in another televote in the future.

Televote can thus be viewed as another arsenal in the never-ending task of gauging public opinion. In contrast to conventional polling, however, televote combines public education with public opinion polling. But that may be where the problem lies. No public opinion polling, whether conventional or televote, can avoid biases in framing the questions, packaging the accompanying information, and interpreting the results. Framing questions is often tantamount to eliciting certain kinds of answers. "Are you for an increase in U.S. *defense* spending?" would probably elicit a different answer from some respondents than "Are you for an increase in U.S. *military* spending?" The words "defense" and "military" in these two questions provide different built-in biases. Similarly, the information that accompanies the televote questionnaire cannot be completely neutral. Furthermore, the interpretation of the findings would take us one more step away from "objective" opinions and their *representation*. To say this, however, is tantamount to acknowledging the dual role of public opinion and televote polling—in *shaping* as well as *measuring* social phenomena.

FROM TELEVOTING TO TELEDEMOCRACY

Teledemocracy as a concept suggests the efforts to go beyond telecommunity and televoting to overcome their spatial and temporal limitations. Telecommunity is mostly limited by *space* to a locality, while televoting is primarily limited by *time* to a one-shot affair in public opinion polling. Teledemocracy could be considered as a more generalized and institutionalized use of telecommunication technologies (a) to achieve greater *direct* democracy, (b) to improve the feedback channels of *representative* democracy, and (c) to facilitate *corporate* democracy by raising the consciousness and participation of the oppressed and periphery groups. This definition broadens those provided by Becker and Scarce (1987) and Arterton (1987). While Becker and Scarce emphasize teledemocracy as a means for achieving direct democracy, Arterton sees it primarily as a way to reinforce representative democracy.

By contrast, the above more inclusive definition views teledemocracy in the context of all three fundamental purposes of democracy to enhancing freedom, equality, and community. While direct democratic participation is the ultimate test of *freedom,* representative democracy gains its legitimacy to the extent that it manages to provide *equality* of access to the decision-making process. The term "corporate democracy," however, may give rise to some misunderstanding because it has had an unfortunate historical career. It was used by the Nazi and Fascist movements to define their own conception of democracy against the liberal and Marxist perspectives. Here I wish to disassociate the term from that historical past and reserve it for a more legitimate use recognizing that apart from human individuals, human collectivities also have their own democratic rights. In fact, individuals live in collectivities from whom they derive their sense of identity and belongingness. Corporate democracy, therefore, begins with an acknowledgement within society of the diversity of cultural and political groups (e.g., MexAmericans, AmerAsians, etc.). The corporate identity, cultural integrity, and sense of community of these groups must be enhanced in order to enable them to pursue their legitimate interests. This is especially true of the oppressed minorities or majorities (e.g., women almost everywhere and the blacks in south Africa) whose sense of identity and community has been systematically undermined by the disintegrating effects of their oppression. In other words, genuine democracy is a process of pluralization rather than homogenization.

However, the means for reaching these different modalities of democracy might be significantly different. Direct democracy includes such phenomena as town meetings, initiatives, referendums, and recalls. By contrast, representative democratic participation operates primarily through duly elected legislative, executive, or judiciary officials who plan, execute, and adjudicate public policy on behalf of the electorate. By further contrast, corporate democratic participation requires a higher level of societal commitment to the well-being and political participation of such oppressed groups as women, ethnic or religious minorities, and remote or low-income populations. It calls for consciousness raising through fully interactive, dialogical communication. Distantiated communication may not, therefore, be an equally effective channel for all three modalities.

Although there is considerable tension between them, the three forms of democracy need not be considered as mutually exclusive. On the contrary, they could be considered as complementary and corrective of each other. They correspond also to what has been more commonly called political, economic, and cultural democracy. Corporate democracy is the oldest form of democracy; it springs from the natural solidarity of a family, a neighborhood, a tribe, a village, a nation or, ultimately, any culturally cohesive group. Corporate democracy assumes a high-context culture (Hall, 1977), including common historical memories and explicit or implicit worldviews, norms, and attitudes. Representative democracy is an invention of the modern, large-scale, industrial society to meet its needs for legitimation and hegemonic power under conditions of heterogeneity of population. Electoral politics also serves the need of the industrial society for high levels of social and economic participation. However, it only allows for a *controlled* measure of political participation, often based on politically manipulated forms of franchise and representation. It is a *limited* form of democracy. By contrast, direct democracy is a radical attempt to achieve a more complete democracy by direct citizen participation in decision making. It is therefore skeptical of all forms of representation and bureaucratization of politics.

There are also significant differences in the underlying philosophies of these three modalities of democracy. Notions of direct democracy are often predicated upon democracy as *consensus formation*, while representative democracy considers democratic politics essentially as *compromise formation* in a pluralistic polity. Theories of corporate democracy, by

116 TECHNOLOGIES OF POWER

contrast, emphasize *will formation* as the essence of the democratic process. Will formation is presumed to go beyond nose-counting and electoral politics in order to capture the loftier spirit, the *geist*, of a nation or any other culturally cohesive group. Democratic and antidemocratic historical formations, such as populism, liberalism, socialism, or fascism, have employed these ideas in a variety of ideological configurations. In the United States, for instance, the republican and democratic traditions (not to be confused with the two Republican and Democratic parties) date back to the early debates on democracy between the Hamiltonians and Jeffersonians. While the Declaration of Independence represents a ringing statement on the rights of popular revolt against an unjust government and direct rule by the people, the Constitution embodies those principles of representation and checks and balances designed to rule out "mob rule." To put it less tendentiously, this means to preclude direct interventions in decision making by the public. The tension between these two populist and pluralist principles of government have erupted in American history time and again. The debate on teledemocracy is the latest round in that historic debate—between those who see it primarily as a vehicle for the institution of direct rule (Becker & Scarce, 1987) and those who consider it primarily as a complementary channel of feedback to reinforce representative democracy (Arterton, 1987).

In considering the role of communication in the fulfillment of these alternative visions, it is far more appropriate to begin with the institutional arrangements than with communication technologies themselves. Although the literature on information technologies is replete with the assumptions of their inherent biases for or against democracy, there is no convincing evidence to support these views. To avoid technological determinism, therefore, a typology of teledemocracy projects should focus on the goals and values of the organizers and the institutional arrangements of the projects. Table 5.4 provides such a scheme for classifying the teledemocracy experiments. The matrix pairs the institutional democratic structures of direct, representative, and corporate democracy vis-á-vis the teledemocratic processes of "gate-keeping, agenda-setting, mobilizing and resolving." These processes represent the more general, well-recognized media political functions in society. But in teledemocratic projects, the ultimate goal is the "resolving" of a public policy problem or issue. The gate keeping of information, the agenda setting of issues to be discussed, and the mobilizing of the target audience are, therefore, related to the processes of public decision making.

Examples of each of the above types of teledemocratic projects will further elucidate their possibilities and limitations:[3]

---

[3]Thirteen of the following projects have been extensively discussed and analyzed by Arterton (1987).

Table 5.4.   A Typology of Teledemocratic Projects

Teledemocratic Communication Process:	Gate Keeping/ Agenda Setting/ Mobilizing/ Resolving
Democratic Political Institutions:	
Direct Democracy: Consensus Formation	Electronic Plebiscites and Town Meetings
Representative Democracy: Compromise Formation	Cablecasting or Broadcasting of Public Meetings, Legislative Teleconferencing
Corporate Democracy: Will Formation	Grass Roots Participatory Community Media (rural press, urban media centers, teletopias, telecottages)

Electronic plebiscites. Although this form of direct democracy has not yet been fully tried, electronic plebiscites are technologically feasible. Televoting experiments such as those described above may be considered as partial plebiscites. The Qube system in Ohio, however, has demonstrated the technological feasibility of the more general plebiscites. (The institutional limitations of the Qube system are fully discussed in Chapter 6.) Electronic plebiscites require the kind of political will and institutional arrangements which are currently conspicuous by their absence. To reach the entire population and to avoid abuse of the voting privilege, appropriate electronic facilities (such as videotex) would have to be made universally available to the public. To lead to an informed consensus on issues, intense political dialogue must precede the actual vote.

Electronic town meetings. In the United States, a number of successful electronic town meeting experiments have been conducted. The best known of these include the Honolulu Electronic Town Meeting and Upper Arlington Town Meeting over Qube. The electronic town meetings in Honolulu, starting with the Constitutional Convention of 1978, have taken place over a series of public issues. They combine television shows on the pros and cons of a particular issue with two forms of voting, including a printed ballot from the newspapers and a telephone ballot after the broadcast (Dator, 1983). The Upper Arlington Town Meeting over Qube used the system's capability of instant electronic "voting" to discuss and vote on issues of traffic and zoning problems in that region.

Cablecasting or broadcasting of public meetings. With the abundance of channels, electronic airing of public meetings has become ever more feasible. In the telecommunication advanced countries (United States, Japan, Britain, France, and West Germany), the concept of "Wired Cities" has come to symbolize this era of abundance. As Dutton, Blumler, and Kraemer (1987, p. 459) report,

> since the 1970s, the United States has wired nearly half the nation's households with cable. Japan, France, Britain, and West Germany have yet to wire over 5% of their households. Since the 1970s, however, all five countries have experimented with 'advanced wired city projects,' while no nation has made a major commitment to their widescale diffusion.

In the United States, C-SPAN (Cable Satellite Public Affairs Network) presents the best known use of new technologies to provide access to the deliberations of the U.S. House of Representatives. This service is carried over 2,000 cable systems and is received by some 20 million households. At times of national crisis, some of the commercial networks also join in the airing of dramatic public hearings with high ratings such as those of the Iran-Contra Affair Congressional Hearings in 1987. Many city councils in the United States are also using the cable access channels to air their meetings or special hearings. When and if such programs are also combined with citizen feedback and participation in the questioning of their representatives, greater participatory democracy can be achieved.

Legislative teleconferencing. Alaska's Legislative Teleconferencing Network is the best known example of this method of enhancing representative democracy through mediated communication between the electorate and their representatives. The network consists of audio teleconferencing, electronic mail, and retrievable computer database on pending legislation and committee meetings. The system has proved successful in overcoming Alaska's problem of making government accessible to its remote population (Smith, 1984). But as costs of audio and video teleconferencing fall, this method of active citizen participation in the legislative process can become a powerful tool. At the present time, however—due to prohibitive costs—these facilities are primarily used by organized and corporate groups of lobbyists to peddle influence with the legislators. Less ambitious but no less interesting experiments in this category are the attempts by a variety of politicians and legislatures to establish interactive communication with their constituencies. Congressman Edward Markey (D-Mass) is among the former, while North Carolina's Agency for Public Telecommunications provides an example of the latter. From December 1983 to February 1984, subscribers to The Source Telecomputing Network could participate in an "electure" led by Congressman Markey. By presenting his papers at a computer conference, Markey entered into discussions with his constituency on the American nuclear arms policy. North Carolina's OPEN/net is, by contrast, a continuing project of the state to provide channels of feedback for the citizens at large on current legislative and executive decisions. A combination of cable, telephone, and satellite technologies are used to air a weekly interactive, three-hour show on public issues.

Grass roots community participation. Projects in this category aim at mobilizing participation at the grass roots on a specific issue or a set of issues. These projects are, therefore, typically multimedia channeled with a generous dose of face-to-face community meetings. In addition to the projects discussed in the section on "telecommunity," the following four projects at the neighborhood, urban, state, and national levels provide good examples. At the neighborhood level, the MINERVA Electronic Town Meeting was designed by a well-known sociologist (Amitai Etzioni) as an effort to broaden participation in the regular meetings of an apartment complex. Panelists discussed various aspects of an issue over a cable access channel serving that community, while they could walk over to a studio room to videotape their responses to the presentations. At the end of this mediated discussion, a questionnaire was passed around in which community members could express their views on the issues. At the urban level, Des Moines Health Vote '82 provides one of the most successful examples. Sponsored by the Public Agenda Forum, Health Vote '82 involved a substantial proportion of the Des Moines community in a vote on a decision on the alternatives in health care delivery systems. Citizens returned ballots printed in the Des Moines Register. At the state level, Alternatives for Washington presents a concerted effort by Governor Daniel Evans of Washington to gauge statewide public opinion on the future of the state. From 1974 to 1976, a group of citizens nominated by political leaders and interest groups, were brought together to discuss future directions in detail. The alternative choices developed by this group of "experts" was later submitted to the public in the form of mailed-back newspaper ballots. Public discussion of the issues also was reinforced by the organization of numerous community meetings, questionnaires, and telephone polls. At the national level, the National Issues Forum of Domestic Policy Association provides one of the few examples. A joint project of the Kettering Foundation and the Public Agenda Foundation, the project stages each fall a nationwide series of community meetings to discuss three selected policy issues. Following the local meetings, the DPA holds a national meeting in which representatives from the local meeting can discuss the issues with the "decision makers" through a satellite videoconference.

CONCLUSION

In recent decades, the promise of teledemocracy has fired the imagination of many earnest democrats. Yet, the performance of teledemocracy as reviewed in this chapter falls far short of the progress we have made in the scientific development of interactive information technologies. This suggests that information technologies alone have no inherent biases for or against democracy. Yet the rhetorics of most writings on information technologies tend to privilege them with a will of their own—information technologies have been presumed to isolate or integrate individuals, legitimate or undermine political systems, or act as mobility multipliers or participation dampeners.

These anthropomorphic views of technology have led to both excessively pessimistic and excessively optimistic views of the impact of communication technologies on the three dimensions of political democracy—freedom, equality, and community. The traditional media are supposed to serve the cause of political freedom by acting as watchdog over the government and by airing public opinion. The new interactive media are supposed to demassify mass communication and provide increasing channels for citizen talkbacks, political mobilization, and direct participation. On the other hand, the media (particularly commercial media) are supposed to have narrowed the parameters of public discourse and of public choice by their primary focus on sex, violence, and entertainment. The new interactive media have mostly created an illusion of participation in a declining "public sphere."

As for the contribution of the media to social equality and equity, the verdict has been again polarized around two diametrically opposite views. On the optimistic side, the new abundance of channels is presumed to have broadened consumer convenience and choices in such new services as telebanking, teleshopping, and tele-education. On the pessimistic side, the new technologies are held to have further isolated the individuals from their social contexts while providing them with new "push-button fantasies" (Mosco, 1982).

The same dualism exists with respect to the contributions of the media to a democratic sense of fraternity and community. There are those who have argued that the worldwide penetration of the electronic media into every home has created a new "global village" of human solidarity. Such media events as the assassination of President Kennedy, the landing of humans on the moon, the Sadat-Begin peace making in Jerusalem, or the religious celebrations held by the Pope in Poland or elsewhere have reinforced this solidarity at a global or national level. On the other hand, there are those who would point to the power of television in creating a transient, episodic, and disintegrated view of reality that has rendered its viewers insensitive to the violence, famine, and suffering ceaselessly witnessed on the screen.

What is the verdict? Kenneth Lauden (1977), a thoughtful observer who wrote one of the earliest studies on *Communications Technologies and Democratic Participation*, has come to repent his early optimism to suggest the decisive influence of institutions (in the United States, primarily market forces) over technologies. The "cable fable" of the 1970s which promised a technological wonderland has led, in the 1980s, to more of the same cultural and political fare offered by broadcasting. According to Lauden, cable is now no more independent, accountable, diverse, interactive, and conducive to political participation, economic choice, and information abundance than is broadcasting. The economic reality is that cable is increasingly controlled by the same players as broadcasting with the same fundamental objective of profit maximization from the same cultural and political products—entertainment and entertaining news and information.

Yet, the promise of teledemocracy still remains—as a hope enacted by the scattered experiments and projects discussed in this chapter. Alternative institutional arrangements can bring about real political change while putting the new technologies at the service of greater public discourse and democratic participation. This chapter has argued that when the time comes, teledemocracy would be able to serve the threefold cause of strengthening representative democracy, fortifying corporate democracy, and charting new ways and methods for direct democracy.

6

The Perils of an Orwellian World

It was even conceivable that they watched everybody all the time. But at any rate they could plug in your wire whenever they wanted to. You had to live—did live, from habit that became instinct—in the assumption that every sound you made was overheard, and, except in darkness, every movement scrutinized.

(Orwell, 1948)

Two-way cable is *fun*. Playing the system, subscribers are only vaguely aware that the preferences they state, the products they select, the personal opinions they express can all be stored in the computer's memory and tallied, analyzed, and cross-referenced with the demographic and financial information that is known about them.

(Wicklein, 1981, p. 27)

Nineteen Eighty-Four has come and gone. Clearly, the Orwellian nightmare has not turned into a reality. But, in the meantime, a quiet revolution in information technologies during the past two decades has provided the technological infrastructure necessary for the establishment of a global, totalitarian system of near-complete domination and control. An information-perfect society in which the individual may have, literally, no place to hide *is* clearly in the making. Unless we learn to tame the new technologies by instituting laws, rules, and norms appropriate to the occasion, the threat of total mind and behavior control hangs over our heads even in the most democratic of societies. The Orwellian nightmare may come to pass, as T. S. Eliot prophesized, "not with a bang but with a whimper."[1]

This chapter focuses on the darker side of the new information technologies, particularly videotex, computer data processing, and a new phenomenon of "mediacracy" in politics and religion. It attempts to demonstrate how a number of undramatic developments in the information and communication industries are beginning to concentrate new information powers in the hands of those who control the technologies. The examples provided here have something in common: they show

---

[1]The context is the ending of T. S. Eliot's poem, "The Hollow Men"; "This is the way the world ends, this is the way the world ends, this is the way the world ends, not with a bang but with a whimper."

how some *banal* applications of information technologies to solve the problems of entertainment, business management, political campaigning, and religious proselytizing can lead to dramatic consequences in distributions of political and economic power. These examples all come out of the United States where the technologies are advanced, and political and commercial incentives, relatively unfettered. But there is no reason to believe that other countries are any less immune. On the contrary, in the hands of a less democratic society and government, the same technologies will probably be used with less restraint and more impunity. These caveats should guard us against the utopian temptation to view the new interactive modes as the harbinger of a new age of teledemocracy.

VIDEOTEX: THE QUBE IN OHIO

Qube was the trade name (signifying nothing) for a commercial, interactive, cablecasting system inaugurated in Columbus, Ohio in the early 1970s (Wicklein, 1981, pp. 15–33; Teicher, 1984, pp. 45–50; Bretz, 1983, pp. 110–116). Its owner, Warner Communications Inc., also launched Qube II and III into other cities in the United States, including Houston, Cincinnati, Dallas, Pittsburgh, St. Louis, and New York. While Qube I and II were primarily used for entertainment purposes, Qube III, introduced in 1980, also provided the capability for "teleshopping," a service ranging from grocery shopping and electronic fund transfers to purchases of stocks and bonds. While Qube I was highly experimental and unprofitable, it pioneered a technology that promises many practical and profitable applications (Compaine, 1984, p. 155). As a commercial enterprise, Qube I was terminated in 1984 partly because of its early and by-now outmoded technology. Qube has thus gone down the tube for now. However, as a pioneering technology, it will continue to reappear in more advanced forms at other times and places.[2]

The chief characteristic of the Qube system, attracting worldwide attention, was its digital response interactive capability. Subscribers were provided with a small computer terminal and channel selector. Thirty channels were offered to the subscribers for a monthly charge of $10.95. In addition, 10 premium programs were also offered at an extra charge of $1–$3.50 per month. Moreover, the subscribers could also choose from 10 special community channels and 10 channels of regular broadcast television. The interactive part of this system consisted of the five response buttons on the keyboard which made it possible for the viewer to answer multiple choice and true/false or yes/no questions.

As Teicher (1984, p. 46) put it,

---

[2]For a good account of the rise and fall of the Qube, see Carol Davidge, 1987.

at the heart of the Qube system is the most sophisticated computer set-up ever married to a cable television system in the United States. The computer scans the cable system every six seconds, 'hitting' each of the 35,000 home terminals, and asking them three basic questions: Are you functioning well? What channel are you turned to? Which response button are you touching? Each home terminal instantly responds back to the computer with the appropriate data.

This technology is, however, improving rapidly. The black box designed by the Qube engineers is a microprocessor about a foot and a half long, six inches wide and four inches deep. It is filled with miniaturized circuits encased in small silicon chips that can duplicate the operation of a room-sized computer of the 1960s. But, as the chief Qube engineer once asserted, "This is a second generation black box. We are working on a third" (Wicklein, 1981, p. 16). As the technology has improved, the processors have given the system the capability to make decisions about climate conditions in the house, turning the heating plant and the air conditioners on and off in a pattern that both conserves energy and reduces consumer costs.

The Qube system had enabled a variety of uses, including entertainment, education, public opinion polling, teleshopping, and community interaction. As to be expected from a commercial system, entertainment programming predominated. The first 30 channels provided access to the regular commercial and public television stations, a public access channel, and a program guide channel that most ordinary Cable TV subscriptions also supply. The next 10 premium channels provided a variety of entertainment, sports and pornographic programs for the asking at a price that was automatically billed to the subscriber. The Qube system thus pioneered the pay-per-view system in cable narrowcasting.

Educational programs included courses offered to the subscribers by a consortium of four institutions of higher learning—Ohio State University, Capital University, Franklin University, and Columbus Technical Institute. The interactive system made it possible for professors to electronically update the Socratic method by asking their telestudents to use the Response Buttons to answer True or False, or to pick the correct answer from five multiple choices flashed on their screens. Positive reinforcement was immediately given in the manner of a red flashing light if the student responded correctly. The professors also could receive instant feedback on their delivery by asking the students to tell them whether they are going too fast, too slow, or whether the material is relevant and interesting or not.

Polling, for the purposes of advertising and public opinion sampling, has been the most profitable as well as the most potentially hazardous use of the Qube system. First, the system has made the Nielson and

Arbitron ratings obsolete. "Sampling" guesswork is no longer neces-sary. The system allows the sponsors to know which households are tuned in which channel(s) at any given second. Combined with the demographic data on these households, the commercial advertisers can have an accurate analysis of which age, ethnic, or income groups are watching their advertisements. Targeting particular audiences for partic-ular advertising promotions is thus made so much easier.

As for the use of Qube or similar systems for public opinion sam-pling, the possibilities are limitless. NBC news used the system in 1979 to get an instant reaction of subscribers to a speech by U.S. President Jimmy Carter in which he outlined his plans to meet the energy crisis. Of 7,000 respondents, 39 percent thought his plans were "tough enough," 40 percent thought they were not, and 21 percent were not sure. NBC reported the numbers across the country, instantaneously as they were produced by the Qube computer (Wicklein, 1981, p. 26).

However, public opinion is notoriously capable of manipulation by charismatic leaders and demagogues during times of national crisis. This method of decision making can be abused by leaders who wish to by-pass the due process of democratic discussion and consensus building on the critical issues facing a nation. On emotional issues, such as inter-national confrontations and war, a demagogic leader can arouse citizens to support dramatic actions and thereby silence the dissenters by an "overwhelming show of public support" as registered through "direct democracy." Although this is no more a problem in interactive televi-sion than in one-way broadcasting, the idea of "direct polling" provides greater drama and legitimacy. But in Qube—as in other "direct polling" activities—it is very difficult to ascertain who is pushing the electronic buttons—a child, a house pet, or an adult. Following a 1982 speech by President Reagan on military aid to the Contras, the level of support for such aid shot up from 35 percent to 64 percent (Davidge, 1987, p. 93). Instant democracy thus contradicted other polls taken over a period of time during the 1980s that showed serious reservations on the part of the American public about U.S. military involvement in Central Ameri-ca.

As Margaret Ingelstam, a Swedish community media activist, has suggested,

democracy is based on the idea of man (*sic*) as an actively creative being who should be a party to the decisions affecting him. This means that he needs to participate, not only in the formation of opinion and the specific debate which precedes decision-making, but also that he needs to become a participant in a living culture, in the social dialogue, and in the whole of the process in which people's ideas, feelings, and experiences can meet together, be made visible, and be developed. I am convinced the more people are included in this process, this communication, the broader and deeper democracy will become. . . . (as quoted by Wicklein, 1981, p. 44)

The closest Qube seems to have come to this conception of interactive social dialogue was when, in deference to its community obligations, it offered channel facilities at no cost for "town meetings" and government hearings. As Wicklein (1981, p. 25) reports,

> one such meeting was held in Upper Arlington, a prosperous suburb in Qube's franchise area. Using multiple-choice questions, the Upper Arlington Planning Commission asked Qube subscribers to comment on a draft plan for reviewing a lower part of the city. The computer was programmed to narrowcast the hearing to only those subscribers who lived within the suburb. Two previous public hearings on the issue drew a total of about 125 citizens each. The meeting held by two-way [communications], the computer reported, attracted a total of 2000 residents during its two and a half hours.

The Commission asked a series of questions on which the citizens gave their preferences. Results were displayed within seconds after they had pressed the buttons. To make sure of the freedom that comes from anonymity of response, the Qube hosts assured the respondents that the computer had been set in a mode that would not identify them. Asked if they wanted to do the experiment again, 96 percent pressed the Yes button, and within 10 seconds the computer, having worked out that percentage, relayed it to the home screens.

The invasion of privacy is clearly Qube's Achilles' heel. The management of Warner Amex Cable, aware of this problem and its potential hazard to commercial success, has drawn tight security around the system's polling computer. However, Gustave M. Hauser—its president and chairman—has had to concede also that "people who buy the service will simply have to accept that they give up a bit of their privacy for it." Assuming the good faith and good business sense of the company, however, Wicklein (1981, pp. 28–30) has constructed an interesting scenario in which commercial and political advantage might supersede most scruples of public responsibility. It is sobering to read this scenario at length:

SCENARIO: THE DOSSIER BUSINESS
THE TIME: 1994, when two-way, interactive cable has spread to hundreds of cities across the country.
THE PLACE: San Serra, a city of 150,000 in Southern California.
Colbert Paxton, San Serr's mayor, is running for re-election on a law-

and-order campaign. In a comfortable home on a hill overlooking the city, Martha Johnson, Mayor Paxton's opponent, has just pushed a Response Button to order a book, displayed in a department store's information commercial, that advocates abolition of laws restricting sexual activity between consenting adults. She pays for it by punching in the number on her department store charge card. Next, she takes a look at a shopping channel that features personal products for women, and punches in an order for an aerosol spray deodorant.

Martha leaves for night-time political rally and Arnold, her husband, takes over the controls of the two-way set. Punching up a public-affairs channel, he finds the cable company quizzing its subscribers on their attitudes toward homosexuals:

Lesbians should be allowed to teach in the public schools: Yes: Button No. 1; No: Button No. 2.

Without hesitation, Arnold touches No. 2. Then, making sure their two small children are in bed, Arnold settles into a chair and selects a premium film entitled *The Professional Cheerleaders*. Fifteen minutes later, the Message Light on the key pad flashes on, telling Arnold that the cable company or one of its clients has a message for the subscriber. Cursing the interruption, Arnold dials the Message Light number, and is switched by the computer directly to the department store. In a recording, the store's credit manager points out that the Johnsons are in arrears on their credit payments, and says that the book Mrs. Johnson has just ordered cannot be sent until the Johnsons transfer $15.95 directly from their bank account to the store's account. Angry, Arnold punches in the necessary bank funds transfer, using the Johnsons' Personal Identification Number, and goes back to his movies.

At the cable company headquarters, the Information Sales Department, which works around the clock, is compiling data from its confidential clients from information the computer has collected concerning subscribers who have been interacting with their sets. Several clients have indicated interest in the Johnsons' interactions and have ordered computer profiles from the system.

Client 1, Mayor Paxton's campaign manager, is delighted to learn that Arnold, whose wife is a feminist and a supporter of legislation to eliminate legal restrictions concerning sex, has expressed an opinion against one of her campaign stands. He chuckles at the quiet use he can make of the fact that Arnold also watched a porno movie while his feminist wife was out. He knows what time Arnold's wife left the house, because the cable company, at the mayor's request, has installed a motion sensor to monitor the Johnsons' doorway from outside the house, relaying information about the comings and goings to be checked out by a police surveillance car parked unobtrusively down the darkened street.

Client 2, a publisher of skin magazines, also gets notification of the porno film selection, and sends the Johnsons a sales brochure in a plain manila envelop.

Client 3, a local environmental group trying to decide whether to work for Mrs. Johnson, is disappointed to learn that she would, unthinkingly, order an aerosol product that is dangerous to the ozone layer.

Client 4, a national credit-rating company, gets the information that the department store has rejected Mrs. Johnson's purchase on credit, and notes that information in her dossier for the next customer who purchases credit-rating information on her; it also enters a correction as to the Johnsons' bank balance, which the computer obtained when Arnold paid up for his wife

To prevent such an electronic nightmare from ever coming to life in reality, increasing regulation on protection of privacy will be necessary. Similarly, to provide for community and public-minded uses of the new technologies in addition to their profitable commercial uses, some government provisions will have to be put into motion. However, prospects for such regulation are relatively dim—at least in the United States at the present time. Deregulatory policies have come into force at about the same time as two-way, interactive systems came into operation. The Federal Communications Commission has shown little enthusiasm for the regulation of the communications industries. Under Presidents Carter and Reagan, in fact, deregulation has been increasingly the official policy. The legislative as well as judiciary branches of the government have also followed suit. In the two years of hearings by the House Subcommittee on Communications on bills to revise the Communication Act of 1934, almost no discussion was heard concerning privacy. Few national voices were raised, and Congress—for the most part—ignored the issue as it related to cable. In 1979, the U.S. Supreme Court also struck down the FCC rules requiring cable systems to provide access for any community groups that wanted to use one of its channels. "In a case initiated by the Midwest Video Corporation, a cable company in Arkansas, the court said that because cable systems were an adjunct of broadcasting, the FCC could not treat them as common carriers that had to offer service to everyone on a non-discriminatory basis." (Wicklein, 1981, p. 31) Technologically, however, cable is more similar to common carriers than to broadcasting. Whereas airwaves can be and are indeed allocated by frequency among a number of competing broadcasters, cable-like telephone lines is a technological monopoly. Were it not for its close affinity to broadcasting in terms of commercial programming, cable could have been treated as a common carrier, open to all users regardless of size or ideology.

In the meantime, however, market forces seem to have undermined the Qube system. At issue are the community services that Qube has been offering. As an *Economist* (January 28, 1984, p. 27) article reported,

Warner Amex Cable, which won most of the biggest [cable] franchises a few years ago, is now loudest to be let off the hook. This month the company, which is expected to announce losses of more than $70m for 1983, has asked Dallas and Milwaukee for relief, and Pittsburgh and parts of New York City may also be due for cutbacks. What Warner Amex most wants to trim or postpone are the services in which its promises shone brightest: its celebrated Qube system, for two-way television, and community programmes made by local folk. . . . The new chairman of Warner Amex, Mr. Drew Lewis, complained that it had spent $7.4m on community channels which have drawn only 0.6% of the audience. . . . He announced the suspension of Qube, which has a total of only 325,000 subscribers in six cities.

The Qube system was the first in a series of commercial failures of the interactive cable in the United States. The cable fable of the 1970s which promised wired cities and interactive democracy has been overwhelmed by a cable system that simply follows broadcasting in its focus on commercially viable entertainment programs. The initial insistence of the Cable Act of 1972 for two-way capability and channels for educational, governmental, and public access has fallen by the wayside. In fact, industry opposition to these requirements has led to the elimination of such obligations. Acting in 1979 on a challenge to FCC's rules by a cable operator, the United States Supreme Court affirmed a lower court decision that the FCC had exceeded its authority to establish access, channel capacity, and two-way requirements (FCC vs. Midwest Video Corporation et al., 440 U.S. 689, 1979). The deregulation of cable in 1987 has pushed it further away from public service towards commercial profit (Dutton et al., 1987).

DATABASES: YOU ARE IN THE COMPUTER

What Orwell, Wicklein, and others had barely imagined in science fiction and scenario construction is rapidly happening *in fact* through privatization and commercialization of information services. One of the many instances in which the growing commercial, computer databases threaten individual privacy has been carefully documented in a 1985 PBS "Frontline" documentary, entitled "You Are in the Computer." The documentary provides an insight into how the new computerized information services lock into the existing social structures of domination and control.

David Pavillion, a former security guard and policeman turned slum landlord in Syracuse, New York, decides to rent an IBM computer to collect and store information on his wayward tenants. The experiment proves so successful in differentiating between "good" and "bad" tenants that he starts a new company, Tenants Information Center (TIC), to provide the same service to other landlords. He establishes a database of information on some 8,000 tenants and attracts some 500 landlord subscribers. Due to the small size of the market, the novelty of the service, and his own inexperience, his new information business does not sufficiently grow. He undertakes a campaign to increase subscribers by writing to some 4,800 Syracuse landlords, but only three reply favorably.

Pavillion does not, however, give up. He looks around the country for successful examples of what he had tried to do in Syracuse. He finds one such company in Los Angeles: Unlawful Detainer Registry, Inc. (UDI), headed by a more professional information entrepreneur named David Salks. In a visit to UDI, Salks explains to Pavillion how he has grown from a $40,000 to a $2 million business in a few years. First, the size of the rental market in Los Angeles is significantly large: UDI has about 1.75–2 million tenant names on file; it receives a quarter of a million requests for information per year; there are about 50,000 eviction notices in Los Angeles yearly; and UDI charges $9.00 per request for information for about 900 such requests in a day.

Second, UDI does not rely on the "subjective" impressions and reports of tenants alone to establish and update its files. It uses the Unlawful Retainer Registry of the court system, which contains information on all landlord-tenant complaints, including court actions. This is a public document to which UDI's information workers have complete access. The information is transferred from court documents to UDI's databases, supplementing what information the landlords have contributed on "the lifestyles" of particular tenants.

Credit information services are even larger and more successful than the tenant information service operations. One such company in Los Angeles, T. R. W., maintains files on some 120 million people and checks the credit ratings of some 300,000 people a day at the rate of 8 seconds per request. In the United States, some 100 million people carry credit cards with an average of seven cards per person. With 50 percent of all purchases on credit, the size and complexity of this information market staggers the mind. But the computer technology has made it possible for the creditors to know fully about the financial behavior of any individual who purchases on credit. There is a Federal Fair Credit Reporting Act that attempts to protect the rights of access and reply to these files, but the borrowers are notified only after the credit reporting system harms them. And that is often too late.

The victims of the new information-perfect society, are of many different kinds. First, we witness in the documentary the slum dwellers who often pay rents well above the norm for what they get. They are nearly helpless. The information against them is the most damning, because it is probably the most accurate. They often pay late, are sometimes evicted, and exhibit an undesirable lifestyle from the point of view of the landlords. There is an estimate of 35,000 homeless people in Los Angeles, and many more in other cities. An information-perfect society will increase these numbers, but will not resolve the fundamental social and economic problems that lie behind slums and homelessness.

Second, there are the occasional errants—the respectable middle-class tenants—who have occasionally failed to pay the rent on time, played loud music, partied into the dead of the night, or quarreled with the landlord. These tenants will get black marks in their files, and are denied tenancy at the next round; some fight back in costly court battles, but most have to circumvent the system by other means.

Finally, there is the entire population—rich and poor, young and old, men and women—who are threatened by the information files held on them by the U.S. Internal Revenue Service, Federal Bureau of Investigation, Central Intelligence Agency, National Security Agency, National Reconnaissance Office,[3] credit information services, tenancy information services, malpractice information services, and a whole variety of court records such as traffic violations and paternity suits. The recourse available to these victims of information-perfect society lies not so much in individual court battles as in the development of legislation to meet the invasion of the new information technologies on privacy. The new laws would have to provide for at least three conditions in the conduct of an information business: (a) guarantees of accuracy of information, (b) the rights of access to one's own files, and (c) the rights of reply to allegations contained in the files.

BLOCK MODELING: THE COMPUTER AS JUDGE AND JURY

The introduction of computers in society has also provided enormous potentials for the abuse of information power in personnel management. "Block modeling" is, for instance, one such new computer technique by which corporations, organizations, or governments can harness seemingly innocuous data from the personnel files and adapt it in new and unexpected ways, such as targeting individuals for promotion or dismissal. As described by Boormand and Levitt (1983a), this is a programming technique that evaluates how employees fit within an organization on the basis of their relations with other employees. Recent impetus has come from such diverse independent quarters as Bell Laboratories, the American Broadcasting Company, the Wharton School,

---

[3]For a revealing account of the functions and budgets of these agencies, see Mosco, 1982, Chapter 1.

and even the Institute for Social Management in Bulgaria. Each of these organizations has recently spent time and money to develop advanced computer methods capable of "X-raying" a complex population—several hundred middle managers, for example—to detect structured patterns of interaction and communication. And though these technologies certainly have significant benevolent uses, their premise is a recognizable extension of the "'guilt by association' idea, and can therefore be abused."

As in the previous example of the Qube system, block modeling does not require any particularly sensitive information in order for it to become hazardous to the individual. Rather, it exploits the unexpected, even uncanny synergy of large masses of "relational" data buried in organizational files. Examples might include: whom you talk with in your company; whose phone calls you do not return; whom you eat lunch with; whom you have worked with; who owes you favors; to whom do you send carbon copies of memos and letters; even whom you go bowling with or play tennis with! This kind of information is practically useless in isolation, but when coupled with other kinds of geodemographic data it can turn into a powerful analytical tool for the study of social and communication networks. In this approach, society can be divided into distinct "blocks" in accordance with postal zip codes of residence, rank in any given bureaucratic hierarchy, income, age, sex, ethnicity, race, nationality, voting behavior, expressed consumer preferences, or even views on any given subject. Blocks are thus defined as discrete sets of people occupying similar positions in a network of relationships expected to behave similarly with respect to certain items of interest to the organizaiton.

Although the assumptions made concerning block modeling are still open to serious questioning, the technique has progressed since the mid-1970's to become an increasingly favorite method of personnel management in certain organizations. Boormand and Levitt (1983a) report that they were part of a research team at Harvard that published the first papers on block-modeling's social applications:

The response was revealing. Places like mental institutions and rehabilitation centers in Lithuania were quick to request reprints. Perhaps they saw block-modeling as a means to ferret out dissidents. Later, members of the group received inquiries from the Swiss as well as West Germans whose questions (and travel reports sent back home) were especially exhaustive. Interest then seemed to wane until two or three years ago, when a wave of, if often unobtrusive interest started coming from American business sources.

The uses of block modeling are actually and potentially varied, including a complex mix of legitimate and suspect objectives as follows:

1. Trouble shooting—an early warning system to identify the trouble spots in an organization, for example, when internal tensions get out of hand, producing a wave of firings or resignations.
2. Reward—a systematic way of identifying the "good" employees from the "bad" and the "mediocre" for raises, promotions, funding, and so on.
3. Punishment—identifying the potential grass-roots sources of opposition to corporate or government policies and killing them in the bud.

Is it possible to reap the benefits and avoid the undesirable consequences of block modeling? Clearly, the answer to this question depends to a great extent on the kinds of guarantees for the protection of individual rights we can provide through legislation and the establishment of norms and codes of conduct. Boormand and Levitt (1983b) have offered a series of thoughtful observations on this question that deserve a lengthy quotation:

> One should not look to Congress to pass a law. Waiting for legislation is like Waiting for Godot. One should also not expect easy recourse through the traditional civil suit. In fact, the law has yet to define limits to the block modeling enterprise and little legal fault can currently be found with most of the means of gathering the needed information for its use.
>
> Still, protective rules need to be fashioned, even if they must sometimes fit in the nooks and crannies of legal categories—a new clause in a union contract, for example.
>
> In most situations, an employee should at least be notified if he is the subject of something like a block model analysis by his employer. If you are an unsuspecting victim, there is no way to defend yourself. Then, focusing on rules for employee protection, a range of unique problems must be dealt with.
>
> For example, the thrust of early computer-oriented privacy legislation from the 70's was giving people the right to examine information in their own 'files.' The privacy gains were genuine, but from a standpoint of block modeling, they are largely irrelevant. That is because block modeling classifies people on the basis of where they fit in far larger webs of relationships.
>
> Therefore, one has to be concerned with many more 'files' than just one's own—some belonging to people one has no direct connections with. One is thus vulnerable to all the problems of these third parties. . .
>
> Thus, individuals being classified through a block model or similar method need to be given a carefully calibrated set of rights to information

in order to interpret their assigned positions and respond accordingly. This information should at least include some basic knowledge about the data base, including the scope of the population being modeled as well as what specific types of data have been, or will be, included.

Such data gives a crucial basis for understanding one's recourse. For example, if the block model put you in an unfavorable category, and used such data as whom you bowled with or went to parties with, this use of non-job related information could be attacked as gratuitous.

One might contemplate giving an employee access to the full data base stripped of personal identifying information except his own location in it. However, the wide availability of precisely such tools as block modeling makes recovery of identities from even such apparently 'stripped' files a real privacy risk.

Still, one may disclose the structural role of the different blocks without dipping down to a level of individual identities. This last type of information, combined with a specific right to know your individual block location, can be enough to give a respectable road map for defense against the worst implications of guilt by association.

Very importantly, effective ways also need to be developed to permit members of the same block to get together to mount a common defense. In contrast to abuses like 'redlining' or race, sex, or age discrimination, the new technologies frequently pick out less than obvious groups whose members may easily fail to recognize they are being targeted in common.

Currently, technical progress in block modeling is making it possible to conduct an aggressive defense by showing that in some cases there is an equally good block model leading to very different classifications. In other words, there's more than one way to structure the given data—so that one block model might, for example, stress conflicting factions while a second identifies options for negotiation or cooperation.

The last observation is suggestive of the mystique with which computer-generated data is currently regarded. Most laypersons are easily awed and intimidated by whatever verdict a computer-generated data sheet imposes upon them or others. Bank clients are typically reluctant to challenge the accuracy of computer-generated account statements; students generally accept the grades they receive on computer-generated report cards as well-deserved; faculty evaluations generated by computerized modeling are taken into serious consideration by their peers in decisions on promotion and tenure. A demystification program, therefore, seems to be the first necessary step towards any protective program. The public must, first and foremost, learn to challenge the "findings" of the computer-generated data analysis on several grounds, including accuracy of input data (the GIGO principle, i.e., garbage-in-garbage-out!), relevance or appropriateness of input data, (e.g., use of information on leisure time activities together with work-related information), and the methods of correlation analysis. In other words, responsible users of block modeling should be prepared to have their data inspected as well as to disclose the major alternative ways of organizing their data. In the meantime, however, it is important for the layperson to remember that each time they pick up the telephone or send electronic mail in their offices, they may be adding to somebody's computer database. The computer, just like the Big Brother, never forgets!

ELECTRONIC POLITICS: THE COMING OF MEDIACRACY

The cover story of *Time Magazine*, October 25, 1982, was on a significant new phenomenon in American politics, known as Political Action Committees, or PACs for short. In the United States, PACs have assumed an important role in campaign financing, especially in Congressional races. The more than 3,300 PACs, representing the interests of corporations, trade associations, labor unions, and other groups contributed to Congressional candidates in 1982. Almost 25 percent of the House of Representatives raised more than half their 1982 campaign money from PACs (*World Almanac*, 1984, p. 306). Tables 6.1 and 6.2 summarize the amounts and sources of such financing in recent years. The tables suggest a strong correlation between PAC's major sources of contributions and conservative politicians often wedded to strong corporate interests.

There is nothing inherently pernicious about PACs, except for two ever-growing political facts of life in a modern representative democracy—the rising electronic costs of campaigning and the inability of the candidates or their individual supporters to pay for them. Initially, PACs represented a piece of legislation to deal with these problems. But they have led to some unintended consequences. In the wake of the Watergate scandal that had uncovered some illegal campaign contributions to a variety of candidates, U.S. Congress amended the federal election laws in 1974 to limit the role of wealthy contributors and to end secretive payoffs by corporations and unions.

> The new law formalized the role of PACs, which were supposed to provide a well-regulated channel for individuals to get together and support candidates. . . . Instead of solving the problem of campaign financing, PACs became the problem. They proliferated beyond any expectation, pouring far more money into campaigns than ever before. Today the power of PACs threatens to undermine America's system of representative democracy. (*Time*, October 25, 1982, p. 20)

Table 6.1. Top Congressional Fund Raisers

Senate			House		
	Total	Political Action Committees		Total	Political Action Committees
Jesse Helms (R-N.C.)	$16,522,266	$ 840,530	Andrew Stein[1] (D-N.Y.)	$1,780,130	$ 12,700
Jay Rockefeller (D-W.Va.)	12,093,549	533,322	James R. Jones (D-Okla.)	1,419,585	662,861
James B. Hunt[1] (D-N.C.)	10,063,502	833,046	William S. Green (R-N.Y.)	1,143,653	100,597
Philip W. Gramm (R-Tex.)	9,804,902	1,326,875	Robert K. Dornan (R-Cal.)	1,046,909	86,082
Lloyd A. Doggett[1] (D-Tex.)	6,032,864	802,607	Ronald V. Dellums (D-Cal.)	951,097	51,021
Rudolph Boschwitz (R-Minn.)	5,983,410	998,793	Jack M. Fields (R-Tex.)	945,280	345,216
Charles H. Percy[1] (R-Ill.)	5,331,736	1,084,988	Bruce A. Morrison (D-Conn.)	929,192	357,565
Paul Simon (D-Ill.)	4,586,036	897,395	Tommy F. Robinson (D-Ark.)	921,486	20,550
Bill Bradley (D-N.J.)	4,317,423	662,421	Joseph P. Addabbo (D-N.Y.)	898,556	324,521
Raymond Shamie[1] (R-Mass.)	4,196,521	(2)	Robert W. Edgar (D-Pa.)	880,767	282,828
Carl Levin (D-Mich.)	3,517,444	707,653	Stan Parris (R-Va.)	865,985	269,083
Albert Gore (D-Tenn.)	3,166,007	782,948	Robert P. Quinn[1] (R-N.Y.)	861,034	(3)
William L. Armstrong (R-Col.)	3,105,821	800,156	Chester G. Atkins (D-Mass.)	858,658	(3)
Thomas Harkin (D-Ia.)	2,848,763	770,202	Les AuCoin (D-Ore.)	858,055	399,545
John W. Warner (R-Va.)	2,830,558	691,998	Lindy Boggs (D-La.)	796,527	297,584

(1) Lost 1984 election. (2) Less than $82,000. (3) Less than $231,000.
Source: Federal Election Commission; *The World Almanac, 1986*, p. 249.

Table 6.2. Top Political Action Committees

Political-action committees that reported the highest outlays during 1983–1984

National Conservative PAC	$19,332,000	National Committee to Preserve Social Security	$2,400,526
Fund for a Conservative Majority	5,451,498	National Committee for an Effective Congress	2,381,384
National Congressional Club	5,222,378	Campaign for Prosperity	2,186,144
Realtors Political Action Committee	3,874,782	National Education Association	2,177,756
National Rifle Assn. Political Victory Fund	3,774,796	National PAC	2,154,447
Republican Majority Fund	3,531,125	United Auto Workers	2,131,847
American Medical Association	3,513,763	Associated Milk Producers, Inc.	1,997,805
Ruff Political Action Committee	3,499,272	United Food and Commercial Workers	1,933,898
Fund for a Democratic Majority	2,955,393	Machinists Non-Partisan Political League	1,865,697
Citizens for the Republic	2,754,549	National Association of Home Builders	1,846,987

Source: Federal Election Commission; *The World Almanac, 1986,* p. 249.

Before PACs, corporations and unions were generally prohibited from donating to campaigns. The legislative act of 1974 allowed a PAC to give $5,000 to both a candidate's primary and general election campaigns, while an individual contributor was allowed to give only $1,000. The result was an eightfold increase in the level of contributions of PACs, from over $10 million in 1974 to at least $80 million in 1982. The impact of these donations has been both expected and unexpected. First, the donations have distorted the democratic process by indebting the legislators to their sources of campaign financing. "Dependence on PACs has grown so much that PACs, not constituents, are the main focus of a Congressman's attention," says Common Cause President Fred Wertheimer. "When these PACs give money they expect something in return other than good government," asserts Republican senator Robert Dole. Democratic Congressman Thomas Downey of New York is more blunt: "You can't buy a Congressman for $5,000. But you can buy his vote. It's done on a regular basis." This is one reason why Michigan Democrat William Brodhead decided to quit Congress this year. "I got sick of feeling indebted to PACs. There is no reason they give money except in the expectation of votes" (*Time*, October 25, 1982, pp. 20–21).

Second, however, the more far-reaching and serious consequence of PACs has been to raise the cost of campaigns. To gain more and more television exposure, the candidates need greater and greater access to funds. "It is like getting addicted by a pusher. You become accustomed to lavish campaigns," says Democrat Andrew Jacobs of Indiana." In 1974, the average cost of campaigning for the House was $50,000; in 1980 the average was $150,000. In 1982, Congressional races costing $500,000 and beyond were not uncommon. This cost has steadily gone up with no end in sight.

Third, the increasing importance of the media in political campaigns has led to a level of professionalization of politics unprecedented in democratic societies. Grass-roots candidates can no longer depend on their own intuitive judgments for political strategy. They have to hire professional pollsters and media specialists to do the job for them. A new profession, called "political consultancy," has, in fact, emerged to respond to these needs. The book, *The Selling of the President* (McGinnis, 1968), documents the social psychological and media techniques used by political consultants to achieve their campaign objectives in the election of President Richard Nixon in 1968. Another book, *The Programming of the President* (Perry, 1984) provides insights into how computerized analysis of audiences combined with polling techniques provided clues for the Presidential candidate Ronald Reagan, in 1980, on what to say to whom at what occasions so as to gain maximum electoral returns. Without adequate and carefully calculated television exposure, a candidate will remain unknown and unelectable. However, by careful, calculated, and lavish media campaigning, a virtually unknown candidate, hand-picked by PACs, can be elected to office. The new information technologies have thus created a new profession in the electioneering business. It is difficult to believe that office holders elected through such lavish and sophisticated campaigns would be more committed to public interest than to the special interests of their sponsors. As Ronald Perry (1984, p. viii) has put it most poignantly:

> [The] modern techniques for mass manipulation [are] far beyond the fictional scenario envisaged in 1984. In that masterpiece Orwell was issuing a warning about socialism—as practiced by Stalin in the Soviet Union—infecting Britain in the late 1940s. His 1984 was a vision of 1948. Yet now the Russians themselves want to learn from real U.S. electoral methods, 1984-style. Early in 1981, after Ronald Reagan's election, a senior Soviet official based in Washington D.C. arrived unannounced and uninvited at Wirthlin's offices in McClean, near Washington D.C. He wanted to meet the strategist and learn how he had managed to sell the former actor-governor to the American people. . .

Finally, a new method of campaigning, known as "negative advertising," has also come to be a favorite of some PACs in unseating their political opponents. The National Conservative PAC (NCPAC), known as "Nikpac," mounted a series of harsh negative advertising campaigns in 1980 that were apparently responsible for defeating such illustrious, liberal Democratic Senators as George McGovern of South Dakota, Frank Church of Idaho, Birch Bayh of Indiana, and John Culver of Iowa. Table 6.2 places NCPAC financially at the top of the Political Action Committees by a wide margin.

The increasing domination of the media in politics thus threatens to replace democracies with mediacracies. Mediated political realities cut the citizens off from serious discussions of issues and open them up to unprecedented manipulations based on their hidden hopes and fears. This generation more than any other in history has been exposed to the electronic signals which bring a "manufactured" reality into the most intimate environment of the home. But manufacturing reality costs money, and those in the possession of resources are clearly in a stronger position to impose their own definition of reality on others (Nimmo & Combs, 1983).

In the light of the rising costs of campaigning and the influence of PACs, prospects for reform in United States campaign laws look rather dim. As *The Wall street Journal* reports, "a computer-aided tabulation of the latest campaign-finance report shows that 44% of the contributions raised by this year's [1984] winning House candidates came from PACs. The figure is a record and reflects a remarkably sharp increase from the last election when 35% of the winners' receipts came from special interest groups" (*Wall Street Journal,* December 24, 1984, p. 28). What is more, this growth is likely to continue as new groups band together to exert pressure on the lawmakers through collective contributions. This means, as Common Cause president Fred Wertheimer points out, "that the new Congress comes in more in debt and more dependent on PACs than they ever have been. It is going to make it that much harder to achieve consensus on public policy questions" (*Wall Street Journal,* December 24, 1984, p. 28).

ELECTRONIC CHURCH: THE EMERGENCE OF FUNDAMENTALISM

The convergence of two phenomena, one technological and the other social, has led to the emergence of what has come to be known as "electronic church" in the United States. The combination of broadcasting, cable, and satellite technologies has led to what is known as "vertical programming." In contrast to horizontal programming, aimed at the entire population in a locality, vertical programming aims at a special interest group across the nation. Special interest groups in one locality might be too small to justify the costs of programming especially for them. By putting together separate elements of this special audience via one channel of a satellite service that goes to a number of local cable or broadcasting systems, the audience will be considerably enlarged and costs per unit of audience considerably lowered. U.S. national commercial television considers an audience of 30 million necessary for an entertainment service to survive, while a news or documentary program that reaches only 10 million might be tolerated for reasons of prestige. Vertical programming on satellites and cable reduces costs to an extent that an audience of only 100,000 becomes an economically viable proposition (Wicklein, 1981, p. 23).

Among the first to recognize the significance of this emerging techno-economic reality was a group of fundamentalist Protestant evangelists who have become millionaires themselves while building formidable religious and political organizations around their electronic churches. The phenomenon has already been studied by a number of journalists and scholars (Armstrong, 1979; Gerbner, 1985; Muggeridge, 1977). It has also become the subject of *Time Magazine* cover stories several times in the last few years. The Rev. Ben Armstrong, a Presbyterian conservative who has run the National Religious Broadcasters (NRB) during the past two decades, boasts that his colleagues have "done what Ted Turner tried to do and Rupert Murdoch wants to do—create an alternative fourth network" (*Time*, February 17, 1986, p. 62). A 1984 University of Pennsylvania survey estimated that 13.3 million people, or 6.2 percent of the national TV audience, are regular viewers of the various shows. A Nielson survey in 1985, commissioned by the Christian Broadcasting Network (CBN), showed that 21 percent of the nation's TV households tune in to Christian TV for at least six minutes a month. The findings of this survey are summarized in Table 6.3 for the top six "televangelists."

The new fundamentalist movement has also amassed immense fortunes in the past two decades. In 1986, religious broadcasting companies consisted of 200 local TV stations (more than double the figure a year earlier), 1,134 radio stations (up 91 from the previous year), freelance religious programs, and growing cable and satellite hookups that reach 10s of millions of homes (see Figure 6.1). According to a 1977 estimate by *Television/Radio Age*, televangelists spent $500 million to purchase broadcasting time. A decade later, the total hovered around $1–$2 billion. That does not count an extraordinary variety of other projects attached to the electronic church, including affiliated universities, hotels, resorts, retreats, and political organizations.

Brief portraits of the top six televangelists may provide a profile of the leadership of the neofundamentalist movement:

PAT ROBERTSON, head of the Christian Broadcasting Network and the star in CBN's four-times-a-day *The 700 Club*, is the best known of the televangelists. Son of longtime U.S. Senator A. Willis Robertson, he grew up in Lexington, Virginia, fought in Korea, graduated from Yale Law School, failed the New York bar exam, and was partner in a small business. Then at age 26 he experienced a religious conversion to the Neopentecostal, or Charismatic movement, which emphasizes baptism

Table 6.3. Top Televangelists
in the United States, 1985

	Frequency of TV Show	TV Households Reached per Month, in Millions
Pat Robertson	daily	16.3
Jimmy Swaggart	weekly	9.3
Robert Schuller	weekly	7.6
Jim Bakker	daily	5.8
Oral Roberts	weekly	5.8
Jerry Falwell	weekly	5.6

Source: *Time*, February 17, 1986, p. 67.

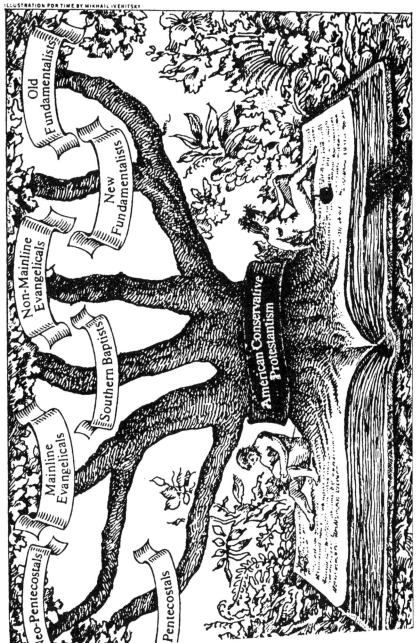

Figure 6.1. The Main Branches of American Conservative Protestantism.

Source: *Time*, September 2, 1985.

in the Holy Spirit to acquire Holy Spirit "gifts," including "speaking in the tongues" (languages unknown to the believer) and faith healing. He started America's first Christian TV station with the purchase of a defunct UHF station at $37,000. CBN's $233 million annual income is now based on active solicitation of contributions from the viewers, including 4 million prayer calls to 4,500 volunteers manning telephone banks in 60 counseling centers. The enormous success of CBN led Robertson to pray about whether to run for U.S. presidency in 1988. Robertson's message includes physical and emotional healing, unity of religion and politics, balancing of the budget, strong defense against Soviet Union and Communism, and policies that are antiwelfare, pro-Israeli, antiabortion, antifeminism, antipornography, and proprayer in the schools. Among the top televangelists, Robertson best understands the need for building bridges to other social groups in society. His CBN includes both advertising and entertainment programming, while his conservative views are not as extreme as others. CBN currently reaches 30 million subscribers, the fifth largest cable operation of any kind. In 1987–88, Robertson made an unsuccessful bid for the Republican nomination for the U.S. presidency.

JIMMY SWAGGART, a Pentecostal preacher and Gospel singer, has his headquarters at his striking 7,000 Family Worship Center outside Baton Rouge, Louisiana. His style is highly dramatic, while his messages assail Communism, Catholicism, and "secular humanism," the last of which he blames for abortion, pornography, AIDs, and a number of other social ills. Through his weekly one-hour broadcasts and sale of some 13 million copies of his albums, he earns $140 million a year. That pays for his TV production costs, daily Bible studies, and his newly-established Jimmy Swaggart Bible College, which drew 18,000 applications for 400 openings. In 1988, Swaggart publicly and tearfully confessed to "sins" of the flesh for which he was temporarily put on probation by the Assembly of God church.

ROBERT SCHULLER, a bland but effective performer, presides over the vast, glittery Crystal Cathederal in Garden Grove, California. At a cost of $18 million, paid for largely by viewer donations, this structure serves as the stage for Schuller's weekly *Hour of Power*. Schuller spends a total of $42 million a year on his TV and non-TV operations. He is the author of several best-selling inspirational books. Affiliated with the mainstream Reformed Church in America, his central message is one of hyperoptimism analogous to that of Norman Vincent Peale, the author of *The Power of Positive Thinking*.

JIM BAKKER, 46, is the Pentecostal proprietor of the PTL (for People That Love or Praise the Lord) Network in Charlotte, North Carolina. The network ranks second to Robertson's CBN in Christian cable (13 million households, 24 hours, all religion). He earns $100 million a year, most of which is spent on his Heritage USA theme park, opened in 1978 near Fort Mill, South Carolina. Following Walt Disney World and Disneyland, this is the third largest attraction in the country with nearly 5 million visitors a year. In 1987, Jim Bakker and his wife Tammy were found "guilty" of sexual misconduct for which they have had to resign from PTL in a continuing battle for the control of the multimillion dollar enterprise.

JERRY FALWELL is president of the 21,000-member Thomas Road Baptist Church in Lynchburg, Virginia, whose Sunday worship reaches 172 television markets. Founder of the Moral Majority, an influential political lobby which was renamed Liberty Federation in 1986, he is the most outspoken of the televangelists. His views on foreign and domestic policies, including his defense of the South African and dictatorial regimes in the Third World, have earned him a prominent place on TV news and talk shows. He also runs Liberty University (7,000 students) in Lynchberg. His income in 1985 was about $100 million but growing, including the proceeds from a new cable hookup he purchased in 1986 (rebaptized the Liberty Broadcasting Network) that reaches 1.5 million homes. During the 1987–88 crisis of PTL, he took custody of the PTL in an attempt to save the religious right from disgrace.

ORAL ROBERTS, of Tulsa, the century's most famous faith healer, has a Sunday service that appears in 192 markets. His enterprises include the 4,600-student Oral Roberts University, the 294-bed City of Faith hospital and research center, and a new $14 million Healing Center which will feature, among other attractions, a three-hour tour of animated films of Bible stories. His income is currently estimated at $120 million. Roberts is gradually transferring his mantle of leadership to his son and heir apparent Richard Roberts, who appears in a daily talk show.

The connection between televangelism and fundamentalism is an intimate one. While televangelism is a relatively new phenomenon, fundamentalism is an old one. About 1,000 of 9,642 U.S. radio stations have a religious format. Regular viewers of TV religious programs number about 13 million. The vast majority of both radio and TV programs are both evangelical and fundamentalist in tone. As the above biographies suggest, they are for the most part run by a conservative and fundamentalist breed of evangelists primarily from southern and southwestern, Baptist, or Pentecostal churches. While the fundamentalist beliefs give a literal interpretation of the Bible, evangelical sermons offer short cuts to salvation in faith healing, positive thinking, and this-worldly success. The lifestyle of the evangelists themselves sets an example of how salvation and success go hand in hand. Robertson lives in a $420,000 mansion, takes rides on his four horses, and travels in a private jet. Bakker drives a Mercedes and owns a $449,000 retreat in Palm Springs. Swaggart lives in a housing compound that is worth $1 million; much of the materials and labor was contributed by the followers.

Mainstream religion is a minor force in religious broadcasting. There seems to be a general bias against the modern, distantiated media of communication. Malcolm Muggridge (1977), a British author and TV personality who has written extensively on religious themes, has argued that television represents a fourth temptation of Christ: a contract from Lucifer, Inc. to go to Rome and anchor a First-Century network variety show. Jesus, "concerned with truth and reality" rather than "fantasy and images" refuses. As a direct result of that choice, across the centuries, poets and philosophers, musicians and mystics celebrate "the brightest and most far-reaching hopes ever to be entertained by the human mind and the most sublime purposes ever to be undertaken by the human will." Others have argued that Jesus engaged in dialogical communication, not in emaciated broadcasting messages to undifferentiated masses.

Nevertheless, the new fundamentalist revival in the United States is presenting a powerful and growing political and social force to be reckoned with. As fundamentalism elsewhere (e.g., in the Islamic world), it represents a reaction against the permissive character of modern, commercial, and consumerist capitalist order. The commercial media system, sustained through advertising and the battle of ratings, tends to reinforce all of the permissive values. It has thus become one of the chief targets of fundamentalist criticisms as well as one of its vehicle for proselytization. However, the views of the religious right are shared by large numbers of people outside the fundamentalist churches. "A majority of Protestants are simply dissatisfied with what they regard as a moral breakdown in American society," asserts Sociologist Phillip Hammond of the University of California at Santa Barbara (*Time*, September 2, 1985, p. 49). Conservative Roman Catholics, Eastern Orthodox Mormons, Orthodox Jews, and even some secular humanists—themselves a target of fundamentalists—deplore such developments as over 16 million abortions performed since 1973, the fourfold increase since 1970 in children raised by unwed mothers, the rise in drug use, the emergence of gay liberation, and the glamorization of promiscuity.

What is paradoxical about the American fundamentalist movement, however, is that it is wedded to the same economic and social forces that breed the permissive values of an affluent, capitalist society. It also uses some of the same this-worldly values and tactics to achieve its astounding success. The Bakker-Swaggart fall from grace has dramatized both of these facts. In this respect, the new religious right is fundamentally no different than the old secular right. Fascist and Nazi movements also employed an ideology of antiliberalism to achieve a new capitalist order in which worldly success, power, and glory were the ultimate objectives. The sources of social support for the rightist movements also seem to be fundamentally the same: the lower middle class and marginalized sectors of the population provide the mass movement, while a group of charismatic and entrepreneurial leaders give it organizational shape and direction. The tonic of salvation, money, and mass organization is proving to be as powerful in the United States as the blending of extreme nationalism, racism, and mass hysteria proved to be in Europe during the interwar period. However, the ultimate political success of the new fundamentalists in the United States is still in need of a major political and economic crisis as big as the depression of 1930s. The forces of the extreme right and the extreme left would have to join battle then in a polarized society.

CONCLUSION

This chapter has reviewed some of the instances in which the new electronic technologies and their increasing abundance might augur ill for democratic ideals and institutions. These examples might be considered as anecdotal, but they cannot be dismissed as fanciful. The convergence of the old and new information technologies are creating ever-growing opportunities for centralized control, citizen surveillance, and corruption of the political and religious institutions. Each example cited here (the Qube, databases, block modeling, electronic politics, and the electronic church) demonstrates an instance of such threats. Precisely because these encroachments on democratic institutions are piecemeal, they often go unnoticed. But, in the long run, their cumulative effects may prove disastrous. In the information age, the price of liberty is— more than ever before—eternal vigilance.

7

Prospects at the Centers

> The problems which are generally associated with office automation make up the final chapter of a story which began with the industrial revolution, that is with the supreme assertion of capitalist production revolution over all preceding types of production and over those that exist today. . . . It [information technology] is in fact an organizational technology and, like the organization of labor, has a dual function: as a productive force and a control tool for capital.
>
> (Franco de Benedetti, Managing Director, Olivetti Corporation)

> In the past, leadership in business organization was identified with the entrepreneur—the individual who united ownership and control of capital with capacity for organizing the other factors of production and, in most contexts with a further capacity for innovations. With the rise of the modern corporation, the emergence of the organization required by modern technology and planning and the divorce of the owner of the capital from control of the enterprise, the entrepreneur no longer exists. . . [It is replaced by] all who bring specialized knowledge, talent or experience to group decision making. This not the management, it is the guiding intelligence—the brain—of the enterprise. There is no name for all who participate in group decision-making or the organization which they form. I propose to call this organization the Technostructure.
>
> (Galbraith, 1967, pp. 81–82)

The last two chapters focused on the promises and perils of the new information technologies; this chapter and the next will focus on their overall performance at the world centers and peripheries.

Due to the relative abundance of information technologies at the world centers of power (North American, Western Europe, and Japan), the debate on communication and democratization has primarily focused on the issues of *political democracy*—that is, information and freedom. At the centers of peripheries (the metropolitan sectors of the newly-industrializing countries such as South Korea, Brazil, Argentina, Mexico, India, Singapore, Hong Kong, Taiwan), the problems of access loom large and the debate on communication and democratization has consequently revolved around the issues of information and equality, namely *social democracy*. By contrast, at the peripheries of peripheries (the rural hinterlands of Africa, Asia, and Latin America), the disintegrating impact of cultural domination of the centers has raised the problem of information and identity to the highest levels of public consciousness and debate. At the peripheries, therefore, *cultural democracy* has become a central focus of the democratization debate. The three dimensions of democratization are, however, inextricably tied together in the struggles for political freedom, social equality, and cultural identity.

DEMOCRACY VS. TECHNOCRACY

The problems of freedom, access, and identity are central to any discussion of communication and democratization in advanced as well as developing countries. But the impact of the new information technologies has renewed the risks of overwhelming liberal democracies with a technocratic system that arrogates to itself the right to determine what citizens need to know and thereby restricting their information freedom and access. In this process, the traditional boundaries of censorship and control have dramatically shifted from the mass media to libraries and online information services. To appreciate the significance of this shift, it would be useful here to review the recent policies pursued by the Reagan Administration in the arena of U. S. federal information policies.

In its eight years in office, the Reagan Administration has pursued a mosaic of information policies that may be considered relatively harmless—that is, if each piece of the mosaic is looked at in isolation. But when put together as a whole along with the Administration's media and communication policies, the picture becomes alarming. Anne Mintz (1987), director of information services at *Forbes* magazine, has singled out seven areas of concern that deserve to be studied extensively and in depth. I will review them only briefly here in a modified order to suggest that the democratic and technocratic forces are now fully engaged in wholly new arenas.

First and perhaps foremost, U. S. federal information policy has been always subject to considerations of national security. But in the 1980s, the phenomenal growth of electronic data bases to some 3,200 worldwide has posed a new problem (*Business Week*, December 1, 1986). The Reagan Administration is taking aim primarily at computer databases because they are presumed to be "gold mines for foreign agents." The Administration nailed down its new policy in a November 5, 1986 memorandum signed by National Security Adviser John M. Poindexter. This memorandum gave federal agencies unprecedented powers to suppress information by resorting to what amounts to a new security classification: "sensitive." This new power gives the federal bureaucrats an open-ended authority to refuse to divulge any information that they consider "sensitive." The old-fashioned policy of dividing information between "classified" and "unclassified" had the virtue of focusing the debate on what should be classified, who should have access to this classified data, and by what standards do we classify information? The new policy blurs the boundaries and opens the door for abusive and arbitrary treatment of information by the technocrats. The exclusion of a vast array of scientific and technological information from public access will surely deprive the investigative U. S. citizens while only blocking the unimaginative foreign spies. The implementation of the new policy has already begun with four government databases run by the National Technical Information Service (NTIS), the Defense Technical Information Center, the Energy Department, and the National Aeronautics & Space Administration (NASA). The application of the same policy to the private sector raises horrendous questions of technological feasibility. Dialogue's counsel Robert A. Simon has posed the question rather aptly: "Will we all need a passport to enter a library?" (*Business Week*, December 1, 1986, p. 39) That may be, in fact, what is in store if the policy is carried to its logical conclusion. *The New York Times* (September 8, 1987) reported the following in a front page story:

> FBI agents have asked librarians in New York City to watch for and report on library users who might be diplomats of hostile powers recruiting intelligence agents or gathering information potentially harmful to the United States' security. Officials of the FBI acknowledged in response to inquiries yesterday . . . that staff members at fewer than 20 libraries, most of them academic rather than public, had been asked to cooperate with agents in a library awareness program that is part of a national counterintelligence effort. This was cleared through the Deputy Assistant Director of the New York FBI office, James Fox. "We're just contacting the ones that would be logical for hostile intelligence people to use."

The security fetishism in the Reagan Administration's information policies is thus just catching up with the security fetishism in its media policies. The following well-documented cases demonstrate the ubiquity of the security syndrome in the Administration's media and information policies: the denial of media access to the Grenada operations, the new requirement for public officials to submit all their writings (including fiction) for clearance before publication even years after the end of their service, the misinformation policies pursued in cases of the Libyan invasion and the Korean Airlines crash, and—most dramatic of all in the Iran-Contra Affair—the denial of access to information to key cabinet secretaries and congressional leaders as well as the public-at-large.

Second, the Reagan Administration's preoccupation with national security is matched equally with its enthusiasm for privatization in all arenas—including information. In fact, the two policies go hand in hand. National security is perceived as the primary means for the protection of private corporate interests at home and abroad. The privatization policy in information has been extended to federal government libraries, NTIS, and Government Printing Office (GPO). The privatization of federal government libraries began with the Office of Management and Budget (OMB) Circular A76 of 1983. The argument presented in this circular was an economic one, that it is more cost-effective to have a consulting firm from outside to run a government department's library. That argument falls apart if we consider the revelations about the defense contractors' ever-increasing bills, including $1000 ash-trays and $2500 toilet seats. The argument also opens the possibility that a U.S. company which is a subsidiary of a foreign company could obtain a contract to run the White House Library. Given the Japanese advances in this field, that is not as fanciful as it seems. But the directive also gives the libraries the same cavalier treatment rendered to food, janitorial, and landscaping services. That leads us to the conclusion that if there is a conflict between the objectives of national security and private profit, the latter may command policy. The Iran-Contra affair may have, in fact, substantiated that proposition. The two other government agencies most affected by the privatization policies are NTIS and GPO, whose services are vital to the dissemination of scientific, technological, and general information to scientists and the public-at-large. According to Nancy Kranich, chair of the American Library Association's Coalition on Government Information, since 1982, one out of every four of the government's 16,000 publications have been eliminated.[1]

Third, the major federal legislation that protects the public's right to know, the Freedom of Information Act, has been systematically subjected to curtailment during the Reagan era. The federal agencies, most notably the Office of Management and Budget, have developed new criteria that make duplicating government documents under the Act increasingly more expensive for scholars and other investigators. The response time to requests for information has progressively increased, but in some instances, access has also been denied on grounds that the information *might* become classified as "sensitive." Access to government documents assumes a vital importance when viewed in the light of recent revelations that the FBI had been keeping a tap over such notable American writers as Faulkner and Hemingway for a very long time. In 1988, the higher education community saw once again how valuable the

---

[1] For further details, see American Library Association, *Less Access to Less Information By and About the U. S. Government*, 1988.

Act is when the Center for Constitutional Rights released over 1,200 pages of FBI documents. These papers, all obtained under the Act, show a pattern of FBI surveillance of faculty and students associated with the Committee in Support of the People of El Salvador, a group critical of U.S. government policy in Central America (*NEA Higher Education Advocate*, March 7, 1988).

Fourth, the OMB proposals to reduce the job grades and educational prerequisites for federally-employed librarians spells out another budget cutting policy with far-reaching consequences for the quality of service the public can expect in the future from its federal information specialists.

Fifth, the FCC proposals for the imposition of a hefty surcharge for telecommunications of data over phone lines will have a chilling effect on any number of information customers. Business customers can pass the cost on to the consumers, but public information services (public libraries, university research institutes) will be cut out of the information markets. Such services as BITNET, an electronic mail service connecting universities in North America to Western Europe, Japan, Israel, and some other parts of the world will probably be the casualty of this policy.

Sixth, taxing information has not yet become a universal policy, but indications point in that direction. Some states—such as New York—consider information a commodity to be taxed. Cultural products (books, magazines, records) are already taxed; so are databases. If the policy of charging telephone services by duration of use rather than type of service becomes universal, all manner of transmission of information over the telephone lines will be taxed.

Seventh, the policy of cutting budgets on the collection of statistics by the federal government has already done irreparable damage. It has even produced political consequences such as the protests by the Asian-American community objecting to the Census Bureau's new policy of collapsing all the different Asian ethnic groups (the Chinese, Japanese, Koreans, Vietnamese) into one. But the reduction of census information on such vital issues as housing, income distribution, economic forecasts, and population movements will in due course affect negotiations over labor union contracts, congressional district borders, and government, economic, and social policies. Can the calculable government cost reductions in information-gathering justify these incalculable social cost increases?

What can be done to control and reverse these antidemocratic information policies? Two of the leading professional associations in this field, the American Library Association and the Association of American Universities, have closely monitored these developments and have made thoughtful policy recommendations. An ALA resolution recommends that "there should be equal and ready access to data collected, compiled, produced, and published in any format by the government of the United States." A reliance on commercial organization, the ALA points out, can lead to the dissemination of only information that can find enough buyers. Privatization also leads to the removal of publications from public depository libraries where they are available to scholars and citizens. The ALA also objects to attempts to prevent dissemination of unclassified scientific research (ALA, 1988).[2]

The Association of American Universities has also published a report on "Government Information Controls," prepared by John Shattuck and Muriel Morisey Spence of Harvard University. The report considers the negative impact of the restrictive information policies so severe that it calls for bold action on the part of a new president in 1989 to correct and reverse those policies. The report particularly focuses on legislation needed in such areas as the Export Administration Act, the Paperwork Reduction Act, and the Freedom of Information Act. It concludes that (*Chronicle of Higher Education,* March 30, 1988, p. A28):

> A new Executive Order on Information Policy should be premised on principles that justify revision of the existing system of controls. The first principle should be a presumption of free and open communication, consistent with the First Amendment, of information generated both inside and outside the federal government. This presumption of openness should be overcome in particular cases involving information generated by the government only when there is a demonstration of substantial public necessity.

But the information policies of the Reagan Administration represent only the tip of the iceberg in a technological revolution that is transforming the nature of capitalist societies. The impact of the current technological revolution on communication and democratization in the advanced capitalist societies may be further analyzed in terms of three major trends which seem to characterize the situation: (a) from scarcity to abundance, (b) from regulation to reregulation, and (c) from public to private discourse. Each of these trends can best be understood in terms of the interplay of technological and socio-economic-political forces at work. All three trends have entailed profound consequences for the classical liberal ideals of freedom of speech, assembly, and public discourse.

---

[2] A weekly newsletter called *Access Reports* also provides up-to-date news on the subject of freedom of information in the U.S., Canada, and Europe.

FROM SCARCITY TO ABUNDANCE

Rapid technological innovation and convergence in recent decades have put telecommunication at the forefront of most industries in the advanced capitalist countries. As *The Economist* (November 23, 1985, Survey 5) has observed, "Twenty years ago telecommunications was one of the world's most boring industries. Economics and technology have turned it into one of the most exciting. It has become the key to the biggest industrial change of the next few decades: the developed world's shift to an information economy. The plunging of an industry long dominated by cautious utilities into innovation-driven chaos has" irritated some people and exhilarated others.

From the consumers' point of view, a trend from relative scarcity to increasing abundance of channels of information and communication may be considered the single most important consequence of this technological revolution. The new abundance has come via three roads: (a) increasing channel capacity in each of the traditional media of communication, (b) increasing convergence of the traditional media into a single transmission network of voice, data, and images (the integrated services digital network—ISDN), and (c) increasing versatility and low cost of communication hardware and software.

Increasing channel capacity has been achieved through new technological innovations as well as more efficient uses of the three most scarce natural resources in communication, that is, paper-producing materials, the electromagnetic spectrum, and the geostationary orbit. The introduction of broadband coaxial cable, fiber optics, computers, satellites, and microchips has each contributed immensely to the growing channel capacity for the transmission, storage, and retrieval of information. But more efficient techniques in the production of paper, increasing use of those bands on the electromagnetic spectrum that were traditionally left unutilized, and more effective uses of the geostationary orbit all have led to a broadening and deepening of channel capacity.

The revolution is far from over. The introduction of fiber optics and laser technologies, for instance, is expanding capacities beyond all measure. Light is a better messenger than electricity. It is immune to electromagnetic interferences; it also dispenses with the high voltages and powers which generate heat and cause electrical systems to fail. Light also has a higher bandwidth than electricity. By spanning more frequencies, it squeezes more information into less space; it costs less too. Light travels through cheap silica (glass), not costly copper. Due to all of these reasons, the world's telecommunication systems are fast changing to optical-fiber cables. The Atlantic and Pacific oceans were crossed by optical-fiber cables in 1988. Meanwhile, terrestial networks are expanding fast. British Telecom expects half of its long-distance telephone routes to be optical by 1990. Despite its legacy of more than 800m miles of installed copper wires, in 1988, AT&T acquired optical-fiber routes that stretch over about 10,000 miles. Other smaller telecommunication companies are also following suit. But the application of optical fibers is also extending to Local Area Networks (LAN). "Their high bandwidth is a blessing for information-hungry computers and video terminals. Their immunity to interference is attractive in factories with heavy machinery; their immunity to eavesdropping useful in offices. . . . If optical circuits can be integrated on chips as efficiently as electrical circuits already are, optical fibers will become cheap enough to use in the smallest of LANs" (*The Economist*, March 22, 1986, p. 85). This means computers that run on light instead of electricity. It will have far-reaching implications not only for increased information handling but also for the development of more "intelligent" computers that differentiate between "yes" and "no" and the gradations in between, as light can go on and off as well as vary in intensity. Researchers have already made experimental chips from lithium niobate, gallium arsenide, and indium phosphide. On them, light travels along grooves, called optical waveguides, etched on the chip's surface.

On the storage and retrieval side, laser technology is also contributing immensely to increasing capacities. Laser discs and digital audio and video recorders have already reached the markets. But the compact-disc read-only memory (CD-ROM) promises to go well beyond the existing floppy discs. One compact disc can store as much as a thousand of the standard magnetic floppies used by microcomputers. "A laser encodes digital information on the disc in the form of pits, and a second laser reads the information by converting the pattern of pits into a digital message. Since lasers can burn and read 100m pits a square inch, the disc's storage capacity is stunning" (*The Economist*, March 22, 1986, p. 87). An entire Encyclopaedia Britannica can be stored on a disc with room to spare for computer programs or other needed information. Instead of using them to store music or 300,000 pages of text, publishers could fill them with 5,000 photographs, a stereo soundtrack, or even some anima-tion (although the digital discs cannot yet handle full-motion videos). A company in New York has already produced 39 laser discs that contain a video encyclopedia of the twentieth century with a price tag of $10,000. This encyclopedia will bring home to teachers and students alike all the dramatic moments of modern history from 1893 onwards: the Monkey Trial featuring Clarence Darrow against William Jennings Bryant, the signing of the Peace Treaty at Versailles, George Bernard Shaw introduc-ing Albert Einstein, scenes from World War II and its aftermath, the March on Washington, the assassinations of President Kennedy, Martin

Luther King, and Senator Robert Kennedy, the landing on the moon, the combustion of the spaceship Columbia, and much more. This educational use of the new media is not, however, a dominant trend. The new capacity is of dubious social value unless it can be employed to raise the levels of material and cultural life. Under the commercial system, most of the new capacity is engaged in handling business and military information or narrowcasting more of the same old media fare to differentiated audiences with special preferences and the ability to pay. Deregulation policies have been flaunted as a mechanism to foster pluralism in media programming, but their net effect, so far, seems to have been differentiated packages of the same fundamental media fare appealing to the lowest common denominator and highest audience ratings. As a consequence, levels of sex, violence, and titillating entertainment have dramatically increased in television programming to meet the challenges of the new competitive environment.

The new abundance also has to be measured against equality of access. In its first report on computer use in the United States, for instance, the Bureau of the Census has confirmed the suspicions about a widening gap between information-rich and information-poor. According to this report based on a survey conducted in 1984, some 15 million American adults had computers at home, but only 53 percent used them. Predictably, "the figures also suggest the creation of a computer elite based on race, sex, and income. Only about 3.4% of children in households with annual incomes of less $10,000 had a computer at home, compared with 37% of children in families with incomes of $50,000. Of those who had them, boys were more likely to use a computer than girls (80% to 66%) and, among adults, 63% of men used computers at home compared with only 43% of women. As for race, 17% of all white children used computers at home, compared with 6% and less than 5% of black and Hispanic children, respectively" (*The Economist*, April 23, 1988).

FROM DEREGULATION TO REREGULATION

During the past two decades, rapid technological innovation in telecommunication has led to a convergence of the print, telephone, broadcasting, cable, computers, and satellites media. Industries which were at one time separate are now indistinguishable in the emergence of such new information services as teletext and videotex. Figures 7.1, 7.2, 7.3, 7.4, and 7.5 show the effects of this convergence of technologies, industries, and professions. The emerging map of the world telecommunication industry (including publishing, broadcasting, computer hardware

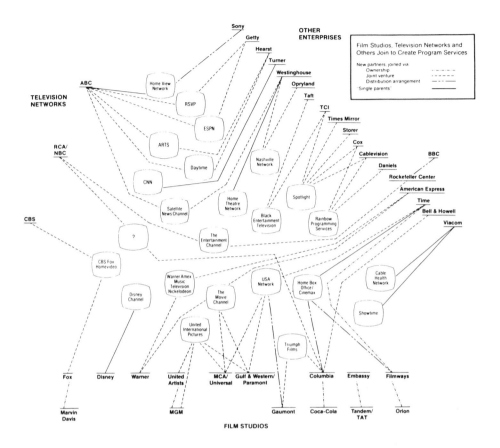

Figure 7.1.   New Partnerships for Home Entertainment

Source: Pool, 1983, p. 48.

and software, satellite, telephone, and data processing) has ushered in a new era of intense competition for the old and emerging markets. This, in turn, has changed the rules of the game in rather dramatic and unpredictable ways.

Government and industry responses to the new realities have assumed a variety of different forms and labels. In the United States, the new set of policies have come to be known as "deregulation." In Britain and Japan, they have been labeled "privatization." In France, they are called "decentralization." The different labels reflect the different economic and political environments of each country. But insofar as the world telecommunication industry should be increasingly viewed as a single market with differentiated products and services, it refers to a

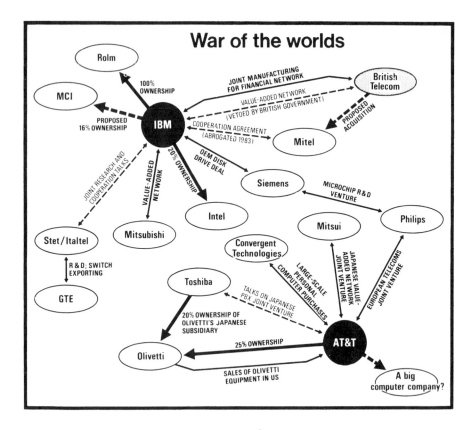

Figure 7.2.   The Battle of the Giants: IBM, AT&T, and the Convergence of Telecommunication and Computer Industries

Source: The Economist, June 29, 1985, p. 69

single process of restructuration and reregulation of the industry towards convergence of technologies, industries, services, and professions. As the current wave of technological innovations subside, we may also anticipate a new market structure dominated by a few giant transnational conglomerates (such as IBM and AT&T) interlocked with the major national companies through a variety of financial and corporate arrangements. (For a view of the emerging patterns, see Figure 7.2.)

Whatever the lables, two distinct trends are unmistakable: privatization and liberalization. Privatization means the sale of public telecom monopolies (such as the British Telecom or Nippon Telegraph and Telephone) to private stockholders, their diversification into computer and electronic publishing industries, and an increasing commodification of

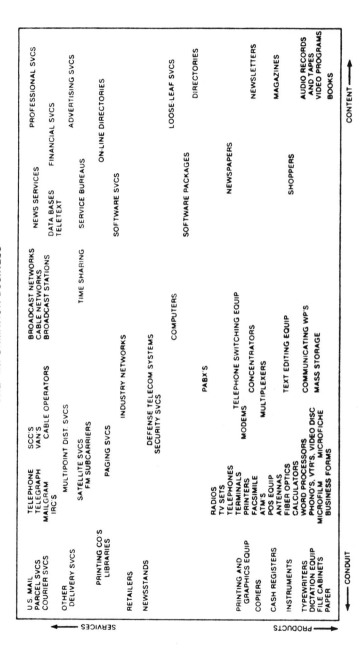

Figure 7.3. The Information Business

Source: McLaughlin & Birinyi, 1980, p. 3.

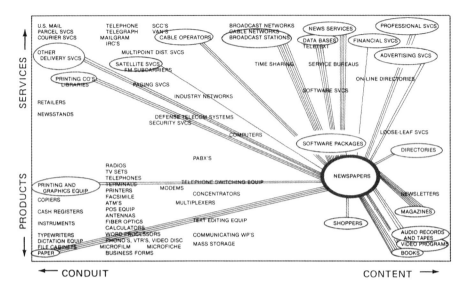

← CONDUIT   CONTENT →

Figure 7.4. Diversification by newspaper companies.
Each line indicates entry into a particular field by one of a group of seven publishers. These newspaper companies display a variety of diversification strategies. Broadcasters, publishers, and other media companies are repositioning themselves to deal with new ways of collecting, packaging, and distributing information.
Source: Report of the Program on Information Resources Policy, Harvard University, 1980, p. 11.

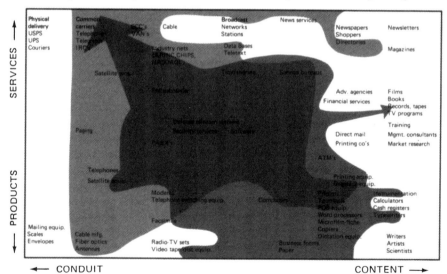

← CONDUIT   CONTENT →

Figure 7.5. Mapping possible future competition between two major information firms.
(AT&T plus ACS, and IBM [domestic and foreign, plus technological capabilities] plus SBS and Discovision.)
Program research provides affiliates with analytic tools. This chart is from *Mapping the Information Business* by John McLaughlin with Anne E. Birinyi.
Source: Report of The Program on Information Resources Policy, Harvard University, 1980, p. 9.

160

information. Liberalization has meant deregulation to allow greater competition in industries which traditionally had distinct boundaries. As the market forces play themselves out and the small are absorbed into the big, new oligopolies will emerge to take the place of public or private monopolies of the past. As *The Economist* (November 23, 1985, 34 Survey) has noted:

> There is a place in telecommunications for thousands of entrepreneurial suppliers of products and services: they have revolutionized the industry by introducing competition to it over the past 20 years. But telecommunications is an expensive game—around $400 billion is sunk in the world's telecoms assets—with some very big players. There are several that might one day play it on a global scale: among them the Bell holding companies, the big Japanese companies that do business in both computers and telecoms—NEC especially—perhaps Siemens, conceivably NTT or BT, even the future owners of great private networks like GM or the American Televisions networks. But today there are two—AT&T and IBM.

What does all this mean for democratic freedoms? The response cannot be an easy one. In the long run, increased capacity, diversification of sources and types of information, and greater interactivity all point to increasing possibilities for the fulfillment of the democratic ideals of direct citizen participation in the management of private and social affairs. But without public control and management, the new capacity will be more likely utilized for commercial advantage or political mind management. Deregulatory policies seem thus far to have had that set of consequences. They have generally led to increased automation, lowered employment, increased privatization of information, rising costs of information and telephone services, lessened government control of broadcasting and cable, and increased diversification of information and entertainment at higher costs. But deregulation has involved few efforts to harness the power of the new technologies towards democratization of access or participation. Only in countries where government policy has committed itself to public service, as in Canada and France, have the new technologies extended "the right to communicate" beyond its traditional boundaries.

In the United States, deregulation came in January 1984 with the breakup of the giant AT&T into 22 operating companies grouped under seven regional holding companies. The new AT&T inherited the Bell system's long-distance network, manufacturing arm (Western Electric), and most of the R&D establishment. "Deregulation" should perhaps be considered a misnomer for this scheme. In fact, long distance continues to be regulated by FCC, while local services are subject to regulation by the states and FCC. The complex settlement reached between AT&T and the Justice Department's antitrust division sealed an arrangement that both technological convergence and economic necessity had made nearly impossible to avoid. Some argue that "the company saw the writing of a guilty verdict on the wall and forestalled it with the best deal it could make; others that the settlement was a sweetheart deal between the Justice Department and AT&T that let the telecom giant unload the local, low-profit part of its business, keep its profitable long-distance service, and go into businesses like computers that had been off-limits before. The result in any event bore an only-in-America stamp: the world's biggest corporation was dismembered, and a national telecommunications policy with major social and economic consequences was set, by a solitary unelected judge" (*The Economist*, November 23, 1986, 10 Survey).

The combination of deregulation and divestiture has created an American telecom market of enormous complexity and mixed blessings. Long distance rates have gone down (mainly to the benefit of large business corporations), while local rates have considerably increased (chiefly to the detriment of local consumer households). More complex telephone bills and greater diversity of services are now the order of the day. The office equipment market has been completely opened up to competition. The network facilities (such as line or satellite capacity) and services (like voice transmission) that run on them are subject to a patchwork of regulatory practices. The value-added networks (VANs) were not included in the divestiture scheme. But the AT&T and the operating companies are not allowed to enter the electronic publishing business (in protection of the newspaper publishers) or data processing. As computer and telecom technologies become ever less distinguishable, pressure for mergers of the two businesses will increase. The net effect of all this is, however, an increasing commodification of information and telecommunication services that threatens to price the lower income groups out of the market.

Japan's deregulatory policies have a Western appearance but a uniquely Japanese reality. They resemble the British policies of "privatization" more than the American policies of "deregulation." They aim at transforming Japan into a fully automated, information-intensive economy by the turn of the century. On April 1, 1985, Nippon Telegraph and Telephone (NTT), was changed from a public monopoly into Japan's biggest private corporation. Up to two-thirds of the shares have been gradually sold off (only to Japanese buyers). The same technological and economic pressures leading to the breakup of AT&T also caused the privatization of NTT. Competition came from the same two basic sources: alternative long-distance services and VANs. But the Japanese policies are part of a concerted effort towards an Integrated Services Digital Network, which the Japanese call their Information Network System (INS). The system will be built by the expenditures of some $80 billion—$120 billion by the year 2000, which will probably generate another $250 billion in private spending for products such as PBXs and computers to be attached (20 Survey). Moreover, "Japan is expected to end up in the early 1990s with a more competitive long-distance market than either Britain, where only one alternative carrier has been authorized, or America, where anybody can enter but there is a good chance that only two or three will survive as nationwide competitors. The Japanese VANs market has been thrown wide open to competition" (*The Economist*, November 23, 1986, 18 Survey).

In Britain, privatization of the British Telecom has layed the cornerstone of policy. When the British government sold off 50.2 percent of BT in 1984, it received £3.9 billion ($5.6 billion). Those who bought BT shares enjoyed the pleasure of watching them double in value in a year. BT was thus left virtually intact, but as a private company it now has moved into a more competitive market environment for service and equipment, PBXs and VANs. Teletext and videotex services in Britain present, however, a mix of private and public systems. There are currently three teletext channels in use throughout Britain, including CEEFAX run by the BBC and ORACLE run by IBA. PRESTEL, a videotex service run by the British Telecom on a commercial basis, provides business customers (87 percent of the total) with computer-based information services.

West Germany seems to have no deregulation policies—manifest or latent. The Bundepost, a public monopoly, has near absolute control over German telecommunications. Conventional services are nowhere better or cheaper than in Germany, but equipment and services invented after 1965 fare badly (*The Economist*, November 23, 1986, 28 Survey).

France, like Japan, has followed a concerted policy of moving towards a "societe telematique." France's Telecom public monopoly, the Direction Generale des Telecommunication (DGT), "earned a great deal of credit during the 1970s by swiftly transforming one of Western Europe's most archaic telephone systems into the most modern. France now has Europe's highest proportion of digital switching and transmission. France has also made one of the world's few successful videotex experiments. The DGT has given away or cheaply sold to home and business users hundreds of thousands of small terminals called Minitels that can connect over the telephone lines to remote information services and databases. . . . The French have already become the world's biggest videotex users" (*The Economist*, November 23, 1986, p. 26). TELETEL, as the French videotex service is called, includes a variety of services from electronic yellow pages to shopping, banking, and even teleprayer. A combined teletext/videotex service, known as ANTIOPE, has also been run by the French PTT since 1977. The system has been aggressively marketed outside of France, particularly under the name of INTELTEXT in the United States (Mosco, 1982, p. 79). Deregulation, privatization, and liberalization policies are, however, deeply political issues in France, the details of which are to be fought out between a socialist President Francois Mitterand and a Conservative Prime Minister Jacques Chirac. But the writing is clearly on the wall. Both socialists and conservatives seem to agree on a policy of denationalization (*The Economist*, April 19, 1986, pp. 14–16).

Canada has followed the French pattern with a substantial government commitment to the growth of national videotex services that might compete successfully with the American information venders. TELIDON, as the service is called, is run by the Canadian Department of Communications. As Mosco (1982, p. 82) notes, the Canadian program is unique in the extent of public involvement and social application in these field trials. The Department of Communications guarantees the representation of public and educational authorities on its videotex bodies. The Department has funded more than the standard market feasibility studies. It has supported studies of public access and social impact. Moreover, schools are more closely involved in Canadian field trials than in either Britain or France. As Mosco (1982, p. 83) notes further:

> Canada has always been an information colony, first of the British and now the United States. This colonial status has spread a spirit of nationalistic resistance through not only the Canadian working class, where such resistance is not surprising, but to the Canadian bourgeoisie as well. This nationalistic desire to create some measure of cultural sovereignty in the face of wave after wave of U. S. media/telecommunications penetration helps us to understand why Canada is more open to some degree of public interest involvement in the development of videotex. The interest in cultural sovereignty is reinforced by the resistance of French Quebec to *both* U. S. hegemony and that of English-speaking Canada. In this climate of resistance, the federal government must rely on grass-roots mobilization to achieve market success with videotex. This is particularly important because with market success may come an instrument to further unify

Canada's loose federation. Communication is thus particularly critical as a form of nationalistic resistance *and* as a means to achieve a great degree of national cultural unity.

The foregoing comparative analysis suggests that deregulation and denationalization policies have generally had a set of contradictory consequences for democratization: (a) They have come in the wake of rapid technological innovation and are aimed at encouraging it further; (b) they have led often to the divestiture or privatization of private telecom (e.g., AT&T), or public telecom (e.g., BT) monopolies; (c) in the short run, they have also led to an increasingly more competitive market environment, some lowering of consumer prices for such products as telephones and computers and such services as long distance telephone, but some price increases such as local telephone and VAN services; (d) in the medium and long run, consolidation of smaller companies into the bigger transnational conglomerates will probably mean higher information prices all around; (e) as for access, participation and public service facilities, the present policies have generally strengthened the market forces at the expense of public service. Only in countries such as Canada and France, where for cultural or political reasons, nationalist policies have required greater public access, the new technologies have become available to nonbusiness consumers on a large scale.

In the longer run, increased automation and robotization is undoubtedly the most dramatic and far-reaching consequence of the new technologies (*The Economist,* April 5, 1986, pp. 32 and 97–99). The factory of the future will resemble Henry Ford's assembly-lines of human toil only in its central objective: higher and higher productivity and profits. However, the era of *mass* production of homogenized products will be increasingly eclipsed by a new era of *batched* production of differentiated products to meet the changing tastes and demands of differentiated consumer markets. In the words of *The Economist,* "Henry Ford's soul-destroying, wealth-creating assembly lines are out of date. Most of the things factories make now—be they cars, cameras or candlesticks—come in small batches designed to gratify fleeting whims. The successful manufacturing in the twenty-first century will be those whose factories change their products fastest" (*The Economist,* April 5, 1986, p. 97). This is analogous to what has happened to mass communication. Differentiated consumers and products are overtaking mass consumers and mass products just as differentiated audiences and programs have been overtaking mass audiences and programs. But just as in the new differentiated communication marketplace, the new differentiated products market will cater to those who have the ability to pay.

FROM PUBLIC TO PRIVATE DISCOURSE

Classical liberal theory considered democracy essentially a form of government by public discussion and consent. Public discourse lies, therefore, at the heart of modern democratic theory and practice. If representative government is to have any meaning at all, equal access to the means of production (from factories to farms), of representation (from local councils to national legislatures), and of public discourse (from meeting places to printing, broadcasting, and the new telematic facilities) must be maintained. While automation of production is limiting access in the economic sphere, bureaucratization of representation (through political machines and expensive campaigns) is narrowing access in the political sphere. In the cultural sphere, privatization of communication and information industries is undermining the public sphere, while creating a cleavage between mass and privileged audiences.

The decline of the public sphere in Western democracies in recent decades has considerably undermined the liberal democratic theories and practices. This decline is not necessarily of recent origin. The rise of mass movements in the 19th and 20th centuries, an ensuing "tyranny of the majority," the emergence of mass societies and mass communication as homogenizing forces, the self-appointment of "power elites" as the representatives of the public, and the cult of experts in the form of "opinion leadership" have each contributed to a progressive decline of the public spheres of discussion. But the emerging media structures and policies threaten to widen the existing gulfs between elite and mass even further. As Nicholas Garnham (1986, p. 28) has argued:

> This change is characterized by a reinforcement of the market and the progressive destruction of public service as the preferred mode for the allocation of cultural resources; by a focus upon the TV set as the locus for an increasingly privatised, domestic mode of consumption; by the creation of a two-tier market divided between the information-rich, provided with high-cost specialized information and cultural services, and the information-poor, provided with increasingly homogenized entertainment services on a mass scale; by a shift from largely national to largely international markets in the spheres of information and culture.

Whereas the national press, public broadcasting systems, and voluntary associations such as the political parties and trade unions assumed the existence of an intelligent and critical public, the emerging media system in Western democracies is increasingly catering to two distinctly different kinds of tastes and preferences: "the mass audiences" whose preferences for cheap entertainment is presumed to outweigh their desire to know, and the segmented audiences whose ability to pay for their own differentiated cultural and informational preferences can underwrite the growth of an ever-growing market of differentiated products and services, from personal computers and videocassettes, to the Playboy cable services.

These latter developments have been dubbed in the literature as the dawn of an "information society" (see Chapter 3). But "information society" as proposed by its theorists and proponents means primarily privatization and commodification of information and *not* public information service and equal access. The effects of this process are transforming the public sphere into a trichotomous mass/elite/segmented structure. These effects can be witnessed in the increasing preponderance of a number of interrelated phenomena: decline of public broadcasting, public telecommunication, and public information services, rise of privatized entertainment, rise of mediacracy in politics, decline of public universities and libraries, depreciation of public affairs into media events, news management, and disinformation campaigns.

I will briefly discuss each of these phenomena under the rubrics of three interlocking processes of commodification of information, including those of information senders, receivers, and contents. First, the commodification of information senders is best seen in the shift of emphasis from public to commercial broadcasting systems in the Western countries and a concomitant process of commodification of public figures (politicians, academics, astronauts, musicians, etc.) into "stars" to be discovered, commercialized, packaged, and sold to the consumer public. In the meantime, the traditional democratic channels of public discourse have considerably declined to give way to the preponderance of media personalities in politics, academics, arts, or culture. These channels traditionally resided in such voluntary associations as the political parties, trade unions, professional organizations, and grass-root movements. The new "mediacracy" has turned the traditional forums into podiums for media exposure and impact rather than for policy debate and deliberations. The two American political party conventions in 1984, for instance, exemplified the central importance of media pomp and ceremony as opposed to policy deliberations. During his tenure of office, President Reagan has demonstrated more than any previous chief executive how to stay popular by "communicating" through one-way broadcasting without holding frequent press conferences in which he might have to respond to critical questions. His techniques have been extremely successful in projecting an image of a strong but congenial president without having had to engage in serious public discourse on important policy issues. He has entertained the public without having engaged them intellectually. The turning of politics into entertainment by the new commercial media has thus given a new meaning to the old definition of politics as bread and circus.

The commercial media is particularly prone to three D temptations— to *dramatize, dichotomize,* and *distort* the public issues. To capture larger audiences and ratings, the three U.S. networks as well as Cable News Network (CNN) have increasingly treated news for its entertainment value focusing mostly on the three Cs—crimes, coups, and catastrophies. To further dramatize political events, they have dichotomized national and international conflicts into a series of stories of cowboys against Indians, baddies against goodies and, of course, the United States against the forces of evil in the world (Communism, Islam, and drug traffickers). The total impact of this particular style of treating the great issues of our times has been a process of trivialization and distortion of the problems facing the nation and the world. Bombarded by a constant stream of episodic catastrophies, audiences have become desensitized to the shock and violence of much of current affairs. Devoid of context and stripped of meaning, the news has thus become "a tale told by an idiot signifying nothing."

But politics is not the only casualty of commodification of news. The principles of the "star system" developed by Hollywood for the promotion of its film productions has now been extended to virtually every field of human endeavor, from music (Michael Jackson), to science (Carl Sagan), to newscasts (Dan Rather), to sports (Dale Murphy) to best-selling authors (Clavell and Michner), in order to promote particular brands. The stars themselves (e.g., Marilyn Monroe) are often victimized by a commercial system which is more keenly interested in profits than in their originality and humanity. But without a coterie of corporate managers, advertisers, and public relations figures, the star would not be a profitable commodity. The depreciation of the stars' talents through commercialization is a price most of them have been all too willing to pay for the "social success" they achieve.

Second, by contrast to the commercialization of public figures, the commodification of audiences has had an even longer history. Dallas Smythe (1977) was among the first communication scholars to recognize the central importance of the audience as a commodity under the commercial media systems. Smythe pointed out that the commercial media do not sell advertising time, as it is conventionally thought. Rather, they sell audiences to the commercial advertisers. The implications of this new theoretical perspective for a new understanding of the functions of work, leisure, and audiences under capitalism is significant. As Smythe (1977, p. 3) points out:

> The material reality under monopoly capitalism is that all non-sleeping time of most of the population is work time. This work time is devoted to the production of commodities-in-general—both where people get paid for their work and as members of audiences—and in the production and reproduction of labor power—the pay for which is subsumed in their income. Of the off-the-job work time, the largest single block is time of the audiences which is sold to advertisers. It is not sold by the workers but by the mass media of communications. . . But although the mass media play the leading role on the production side of the consciousness industry the people in the audiences pay directly much more for the privilege of being in those audiences than do the mass media.

But with the birth of the new information services, particularly those of teletext and videotex, the commodification of audiences has taken a new dramatic turn. Qube of Ohio (see Chapter 6) has already invented a new category of commercial, called *informercial*, that will have devastating implications for the traditional distinctions between programs and commercials, news and editorials, documentaries and promotionals. "Columbus Alive," a Qube interview program, was actually one long, disguised commercial. Interviews with authors of books were, for instance, paid for by book publishers to promote their wares. But the programs were at no time identified as such (Wicklein, 1981, p. 22).

Third, the commodization of information content should perhaps be considered the most far-reaching consequence of the current information revolution in the world. Ivan Illich (1983) has drawn an insightful analogy between what happened to the public domain land under the Enclosure Movement in England and what is happening now to the public domain information. The Enclosure Movement, a long and gradual process taking place in England between the 13th and 17th centuries, led to the incorporation of public domain lands by the big landlords into their estates. It signified the transition from a preindustrial to an industrial system of land tenure and use. It effectively transformed much of the existing agricultural land into the commercial production of sheep and wool for England's burgeoning textile industry. It may be argued that similar processes are occurring in the information markets of the advanced industrial countries. Much of the public domain information, from library holdings to government documents, scientific publications and yellow pages, has been gradually incorporated into commercial data bases and value-added networks that operate in the commercial information markets. Once this process works itself out, the low-income groups will be virtually priced out of the information marketplace.

Together, the commercialization of information senders, receivers, and contents should be considered in light of a longer historical process of what Jurgen Habermas (1979, p. 200) has called "the decline of the public sphere":

The political public sphere of the social welfare state is characterized by a peculiar weakening of its critical functions. At one time the process of making proceedings public—publizitat—was intended to subject persons of affairs to public reason, and to make political decisions subject to appeal before the court of public opinion. But often enough today the process of making public simply serves the arcane policies of special interests: in the form of "publicity" it wins public prestige for people of affairs, thus making them worthy of acclamation in a climate of nonpublic opinion.

In recent years, this decline has been further probed (among others) by Richard Sennet's *The Decline of the Public,* Theodore Lowi's *The End of Liberalism,* Stuart Ewen's *Captains of Consciousness* and *Channels of Desire,* John Wicklein's *Electronic Nightmare,* Vincent Mosco's *Pushbutton Fantasies,* and Nicholas Garnham's journal, *Culture, Media and Society.* The commercial media (including the public opinion survey agencies such as allup and Harris) have managed to reduce public issues to publicity by personalizing, trivializing, and dichotomizing the public debate. To maximize on the entertainment value of public events, the media have personalized the news around colorful and bizarre media personalities; by doing so they have trivialized the views or policies for which these public figures stand; by catering to the public figures who present sharp images they have dichotomized conflicts and views; by dichotomizing social issues they have oversimplified them; by oversimplication they have paved the way for at best muddled rather than enlightened public discourse. In all of this, the media have abdicated their traditional critical functions vis-á-vis the centers of power in business or government.

This may seem an overgeneralized indictment of the modern media of mass communication. What about the role of the media in the Vietnam and Watergate crises? In both those instances, the media played a central role in bringing about the end of U. S. policies and presidencies that went against the political interests and moral sensibilities of the American people. But in both instances, the media were responding to a social movement critical of the existing policies and practices of the U. S. government. That demonstrates that the media continue to play a Janus role—looking in two diametrically opposite directions towards their own interests as they are tied with governments and business and towards their audiences with whom they have to seek credibility and popularity. In instances (such as the Falklands War between Argentina and Britain or the invasion of Grenada or the air attack against Libya by the United States), when no social movements opposed these policies, the media's role has been largely uncritical and even laudatory. Only a traditionally autonomous public media, such as the BBC in Britain, still attempts to perform its critical functions. But as the coverage of the Falklands War and the Irish Republican Army's activities have demonstrated in recent years, even the BBC is not immune to government silencing and curtailment.

The role of the media in the Vietnam and Watergate crises is rather illustrative of how these tensions and conflicts work themselves out where a social movement of resistance exists. The war in Vietnam represented a variety of different center-periphery conflicts: an imperialist war of centers against peripheries (the French, Japanese, and Americans against the Vietnamese struggle for independence), a civil war of the periphery's centers against their own peripheries (a variety of French and U.S.-dominated, urban-centered regimes fighting the Viet Cong, rural-based guerrilla forces), and finally on a larger scheme, a struggle among the world centers of power (the West) against the peripheries and semiperipheries (Second and Third Worlds). As the war intensified and U. S. direct involvement increased during 1960s, certain sectors of the center's peripheries (including the youth eligible for draft, their families, and the blacks and women struggling for their own civil liberties) began to oppose the war. The media was thus continually torn between the policies and directives of a belligerent U. S. government at command of a powerful war and propaganda machine and an increasingly resentful and militant audience protesting the war. A state-controlled media would have completely followed the directives of the government without much regard to the sentiments of its audiences. But the commercial media played a critical role in its criticisms and exposure of the government policies and positions without, however, challenging the fundamental precepts on which much of those policies were based. The American media have thus failed to bring about a change of public opinion with respect to the U. S. policies towards the Third World. The U. S. has continued to pursue the same set of policies in Central America, Libya, and South Africa which brought about the tragedies in Korea, Vietnam, Iran, and Lebanon. An uncritical media has thus bred an uncritical public and public policy.

The case of the Watergate crisis demonstrates the same set of partial successes and failures in a domestic situation. Loyalty to the office of the presidency and what it stands for symbolically has traditionally deterred the American media from exposing those of the Presidents' weaknesses that might prove embarrassing to the office or the country-at-large. (Witness the media's voluntary silence on President Franklin Roosevelt's partial paralysis or President Kennedy's love affairs.) The excesses of President Nixon's presidency in media harassment and wire tapping put this principle to a severe test. In many ways, Nixon and his "Orange County" White House staff also represented a group of outsiders to the U. S. corridors of power long dominated by the Eastern Establishment. It was not that Nixon was the first to tape-record his White House conversations; Eisenhower and Kennedy had done that before him. What set the Nixon team apart from the others was the blatancy and brazenness of their operation and the fact that they were caught at it. The Holy War that vice president Spiro Agnew declared on the "impudent snobs" of the media establishment was thus turned against the Nixon Administration. Watergate became the *cause celebre* of a media that had been too long accused of following the Presidency rather sheepishly. In collaboration with an outraged public and Congress, the media succeeded in a historic feat of exposing and forcing an "outlaw" president to resign. But a decade later, the lessons seemed to have been forgotten. In a convention of the American Newspaper Publishers Association, Nixon received a standing ovation for proposing that the U. S. bombing of Libya in April 1986 should be followed by a blockade of the Gulf of Sidra. Nixon's proposal for acting against international law was matched by his suggestion that the only lesson he had learned from Watergate was that "other presidents should just destroy all the tapes."

The contempt for the public and its right to know reached new heights in the Iran-Contra Affair. The significance of this scandal lies not so much in its much publicized arms-for-hostages deals but in the fact it represented a successful effort to create a government within a government running a covert operation in which none of the duly elected or appointed responsible officials (notably secretaries of defense and state and congressional leaders) were allowed to have a say (Draper, 1987; Wills, 1988). Unfortunately for the U.S. media's watchdog functions, the news of this outrage also broke out first in an obscure Shi'ite newspaper in Lebanon and not in the American press.

CONCLUSION

I have argued in this chapter that the performance of the new information technologies with respect to democratic institutions and processes should be understood in terms of their linkages with the "technostructures" of power and participation. This perspective cautions us against any universal generalizations about the effects of a diverse variety of information technologies and requires us to look empirically and critically at the social and political contexts of their use.

At the centers of power in the advanced capitalist societies, I have argued that rapid technological innovation seems to have combined with a period of restructuring of the telecommunication markets to produce three distinct trends: from scarcity to abundance of channels, from regulation to reregulation of telecommunication industries, and from public to private discourse in national and international affairs. I have also suggested that the present competitive environment, caused principally by rapid technological innovation and an ensuing breakup of traditional boundaries in the communication and information industries, will be followed by a period of reconsolidation and reemergence of traditional oligopolistic market structures. Democratic social movements can and have employed, to a certain extent, the increased channel capacity and the new competitive environment to broaden their base. But as the examples of the movements against the war in Vietnam and the Watergate scandal demonstrate, the critical role of the media is contingent upon the existence of broad-based democratic movements. Otherwise, the decline of the public sphere under the present commercially-dominated media systems spells a continuing decline of the critical functions of the media in public affairs. The ultimate threat in this process will be an imperceptible but effective evolution of democratic institutions into technostructures that are insensitive to and intolerant of public needs and interests.

8

Prospects at the Peripheries

> For the West the notion of progress replaced the notion of tragedy. With a sense of tragedy the history of the world could be understood as a conflict of equal values: Creon's spirit of order as against Antigone's spirit of freedom. Whatever the outcome, the experience was a lucid one. But once you believe that you are ordered to progress, failure becomes not tragedy but a crime. Those who oppose you are no longer equals but figures of evil. If there is one thing that is happening around the world, it is the determination of peoples not simply to accept the two versions of inevitable progress—that of Western capitalism or Soviet socialism—but to find ways of combining the power of technology with the energy of their own traditions.
> (Carlos Fuentes, as quoted by Gibbons, 1985, p. 122)

> Brazil has taken off, leaving the Brazilians behind.
> (Comment attributed to a recent Brazilian President)

The performance of information technologies at the peripheries of world power, in the urban ghettoes and rural hinterlands of Africa, Asia, and Latin America, is radically different from that at the centers. It is characterized by a dualism of economic, political, and cultural conditions generally absent in the advanced capitalist or communist worlds. In Brazil, which typifies some of the newly-industrializing countries (the so-called NICs), the top one percent of the population appropriates more of the national income than the bottom 50 percent[1]. This kind of dualism has to be understood in terms of the asymmetries brought about by the developmental process characteristic of most of the Third World societies.

In this chapter, I will first provide a conceptual framework for the understanding of these asymmetries before going on to present case studies of the competing strategies of communication and development, including the high accumulation, high mobilization, and high integration strategies. (For a glimpse of world media asymmetries, see Figure 8.1.)

DEVELOPMENT VS. DEVELOPMENTALISM

The postwar decades have been characterized by the worldwide spread of an ideology of economic growth which we call "developmentalism."

---

[1] See *The Economist*, November 15–21, 1986, pp. 55–64.

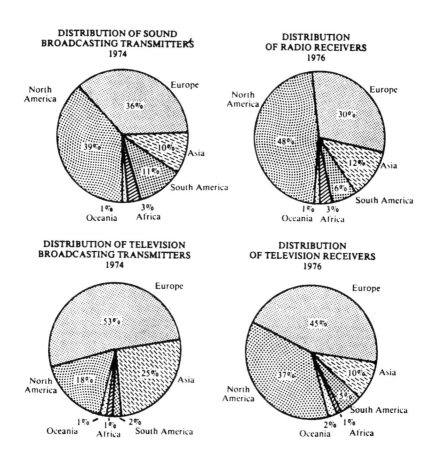

DISTRIBUTION OF SOUND
BROADCASTING TRANSMITTERS
1974

North America
Europe 36%
39%
10% Asia
11%
South America
1% Oceania
3% Africa

DISTRIBUTION
OF RADIO RECEIVERS
1976

North America
Europe 30%
48%
12% Asia
6%
South America
1% Oceania
3% Africa

DISTRIBUTION OF TELEVISION
BROADCASTING TRANSMITTERS
1974

Europe 53%
North America 18%
25% Asia
1% Oceania
1% Africa
2% South America

DISTRIBUTION
OF TELEVISION RECEIVERS
1976

Europe 45%
North America 37%
10% Asia
5%
South America
2% Oceania
1% Africa

Source: Statistics on Radio and Television, 1960–76, Unesco Office of Statistics, Paris, 1978.

INSTALLATION OF COMPUTERS IN THE WORLD
(monetary basis)

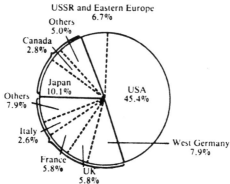

USSR and Eastern Europe 6.7%
Others 5.0%
Canada 2.8%
Japan 10.1%
Others 7.9%
USA 45.4%
Italy 2.6%
West Germany 7.9%
France 5.8%
UK 5.8%

Note: IDC Survey as of the end of
1976 (total amount: $82.189 billion)

Source: Report on Present State of Communications in Japan, The Look Japan, Ltd. 1978

Figure 8.1. World Media Disparities
Source: MacBride et al., 1980, pp. 127, 130

This ideology is fundamentally rooted in the 18th century "Idea of Progress" that sees material development in and of itself as good and inevitable. The liberal and Marxist versions of this ideology have viewed cultural development as a derivative of material progress. Material backwardness (in science, technology, levels of production and consumption) is viewed *ipso facto* as cultural backwardness. Both views tend to see the process of development essentially in terms of accumulation of capital and the mass production of consumer goods. Development policies derived from these ideological premises, whether under capitalism or communism, have thus been characterized by a kind of "growth mania."

The vision of an "industrial system," rich in material production of goods and services, lurks behind these theories and ideologies of development. In this view, sociocultural progress is seen as derivative of the economic sector, to be also measured by the production and distribution of commodities. The literature of development is thus replete with an array of economic, social, and cultural indicators that measure "the progress" of nations along some preconceived targets of competition—from per capita income to radio and television sets per 1,000 of population.[2] In this sense, therefore, economic indicators express the commodity fetishism that is characteristic of some of the advanced and highly secularized industrial societies. In 1983, however, *The Economist* provided a fascinating set of development indicators which demonstrated how per capita income does not necessarily give a good indicator of the quality of life as judged by the staff of that journal. (See Table series 8.1 but watch out for the biases of the *The Economist* staff!)

The concept of development indicators owes much of its popularity to normative theories of social change. The indicators always objectify a desired model of development. However, they tend to reveal as much as conceal the normative premises upon which much of their legitimacy rests. To select one set of development indicators as opposed to another suggests preferences, conscious or unconscious, for certain social goals as opposed to others. Indicators thus stand as intermediate variables between development theory and development policy. While it is the function of development theory to clarify the theoretically possible choices, development policy makes choices and pursues them in practice.

Development theory itself, however, has gone through considerable transformation in the last three United Nations Development Decades. Extremes of pessimism (as in Nurkse's vicious circles-of-poverty theories) have given way to extremes of optimism (as in Rostow's stage

---

[2] See the publications of the United Nations agencies, particularly The World Bank's *World Development Report* and UNESCO's statistical yearbooks.

Table 8.1. **Nirvana by Numbers**

	Political	Cultural	Social	Health	Economic	Climate	Grand Total
France	204	140	167	173	171	179	1034
West Germany	196	147	157	162	195	179	1028
Australia	192	156	160	175	175	154	1002
Japan	188	132	168	184	186	160	1002
Italy	190	129	169	173	154	188	989
Switzerland	182	153	113	179	168	186	980
Sweden	181	150	153	179	164	142	978
United States	181	160	147	149	181	150	974
Britain	187	160	156	161	160	152	965
Canada	180	147	147	175	175	110	950
Spain	177	134	153	183	143	154	944
Israel	176	113	154	180	141	162	911
Mexico	176	114	149	110	146	173	882
Bahamas	175	142	142	147	135	134	880
Hungary	172	132	145	139	147	165	879
Russia	168	135	166	152	143	127	856
China	161	81	139	150	131	184	828
Sri Lanka	151	94	130	143	134	126	802
Singapore	148	108	127	159	166	101	792
Brazil	143	93	146	114	139	159	782
Kenya	133	83	135	105	112	159	762
India	131	73	109	94	108	164	729
Saudi Arabia	131	77	115	112	158	113	721

The Great Divide		
Gdp Per Capita, 1981, US $		Overall Rank from Staff Questionnaire
Switzerland	17,430 •	• 1 France
Sweden	14,870 •	• 2 W Germany
W Germany	13,450 •	• 3 Australia
USA	12,820 •	• 4 Japan
Saudi Arabia	12,600 •	• 5 Italy
France	12,190 •	• 6 Switzerland
Canada	11,400 •	• 7 Sweden
Australia	11,080 •	• 8 USA
Japan	10,080 •	• 9 Britain
Britain	9,110 •	• 10 Canada
Italy	6,960 •	• 11 Spain
Russia	5,860 •	• 12 Israel
Spain	5,640 •	• 13 Mexico
Singapore	5,240 •	• 14 Bahamas
Israel	5,160 •	• 15 Hungary
Bahamas	3,620 •	• 16 Russia
Mexico	2,250 •	• 17 China

(*continued*)

Table 8.1. (*Continued*)

Gdp Per Capita, 1981, US $		Overall Rank from Staff Questionnaire
Brazil	2,220 •	• 18 Sri Lanka
Hungary	2,100 •	• 19 Singapore
Kenya	420 •	• 20 Brazil
Sri Lanka	300 •	• 21 Kenya
China	300 •	• 22 India
India	260 •	• 23 Saudia Arabia

Source: *The Economist*, December 24, 1983, pp. 53–59.

theory of takeoff into self-sustained growth), to be in turn challenged from the left by the world system and dependency theories (Baran, 1958; Frank, 1969; Wallerstein, 1974; Blomstrom & Hettne, 1984). As a result, the importance of cultural and structural factors have come to be better known and appreciated. While liberal theories have focused primarily on the internal dynamics of modernization, Marxism has emphasized the international linkages of dependency in the processes of "development of underdevelopment" (Frank, 1969). The more recent literature attempts to combine both perspectives, while emphasizing historical specificity. In the meantime, development indicators have broadened in scope to include economic as well as social and cultural (communication) factors. The concept of qualitative as opposed to quantitative indicators has also been introduced into the literature in order to suggest the importance of historical and structural variables (Tehranian, 1985).

The concept of development is so value-laden that any examination of its derivative concepts, such as development or communication indicators, must guard against any facile notions of progress. However, much of the literature of communication development is replete with the linear, one-dimensional, and commodified notions of progress. UNESCO's set of suggested minimal standards for the mass media provides a glaring example of such a theoretical bias (UNESCO, 1961, p. 16). In the call for a new World Communication and Information Order, however, UNESCO's emphasis changed from quantitative to qualitative changes. But in the earlier policies, UNESCO had urged that every country should provide at least the following media facilities per 1,000 people: 100 copies of daily newspaper, 50 radio sets, 20 cinema seats, and 20 television receivers. Now that many of the less developed countries have nearly achieved or surpassed these standards (albeit unevenly), it is increasingly apparent that more media facilities do not necessarily and automatically mean higher standards of economic or cultural development, better communication, or greater democracy.

If anything, in the context of the LDCs where media programs are often dominated by Western imports and government propaganda, the contrary may be argued. In many instances, where the big media (the national press, broadcasting, satellites, mainframe computers) are often in control of the government, and the small media (cassettes, transistor radios, copying machines, mimeographing, personal computers, and traditional networks of communication) are in the possession of grass-roots organizations, dualistic systems of communication have also emerged alongside the dualistic economic, political, and cultural structures. In revolutionary social situations (as in Iran, the Philippines, Central America, and South Africa), one media system has been pitted against another (Tehranian, 1979, 1981). Communication indicators that are thus insensitive to the small media cannot capture, let alone monitor, communication and social change. The growth in the indicators of the big media primarily measure the availability of capital, the government's commitment to the expansion of the communication infrastructure often in pursuit of centralization and penetration (as in the Shah's Iran and Suharto's Indonesia), and possibly the existence of high income and effective demand for communication consumer products (as in the Persian Gulf states). The dual processes of transnationalization and tribalization have been considerably hastened by the global processes of mass communication and homogenization of culture. As Illich (1978, pp. 17–18) puts it poignantly:

> Fifty years ago, most of the words heard by an American were personally spoken to him as an individual, or to somebody nearby. Only occasionally did words reach him as the undifferentiated member of a crowd—in the classroom or church, at a rally or a circus. Words were mostly like handwritten, sealed letters, and not like the junk that now pollutes our mail. Today, words that are directed to one person's attention have become rare. Engineered staples of images, ideas, feelings and opinions, packaged and delivered through the media, assault our sensibilities with round-the-clock regularity. Two points now become evident. One, what is occurring with language fits the pattern of an increasingly wide range of need-satisfaction relationships. Two, this replacement of convivial means by manipulative industrial ware is truly universal, and is relentlessly making the New York teacher, the Chinese commune member, the Bantu schoolboy, and the Brazilian sergeant alike.

In the Third World, where these processes have taken place piece-meal and unevenly, the social system is torn between a "modernizing elite" and a "traditional mass." Frequently, the two sectors of population live in separate quarters as well as in separate realities and centuries. What goes under the rubric of "development" often includes the processes of growth in physical output, its lopsided distribution among the traditional and modern sectors of the economy and society, and increasing dualism and alienation. In the meantime, a number of concurrent developmental processes are undermining the general sense of community solidarity and well-being. These processes include increasing levels of division and alienation of labor in the economic sphere, bureaucratization and professionalization of power and authority in the political sphere, functionalization and atomization of human relations in the social sphere, and secularization and homogenization in the cultural sphere.

As *bits* and *watts* (the indicators of information and energy units) increase in mass production and consumption, life is impoverished under a system of modernized poverty. Whereas poverty in traditional societies is made tolerable by relative equality, ethics of self-denial, and mutual obligation, and strong bonds of community, modernized poverty is characterized by the ethics of relentless acquisition, conspicuous consumption, and unabashed self-gratification. Modernized poverty thus breeds atomistic mobility, status anxiety, social envy, rising expectations, frustrations, and regression. The negative *internalities* of dualistic modernity (such as time-consuming acceleration, sick-making health care, stupefying education, countercommunicative mass communication, and information-void news) thus outpace the positive *externalities* of growth and development.

Given the global power of developmentalism as an ideology, can the concepts of "communication" and "development" have any meaning at all? Under the prevailing ideology, development has come to be identified all too frequently with economic growth and its measurements of increases in material output in time. Communication has come to be identified all too synonymously with mass communication and its ideological apparatus of persuasion and manipulation. Any task of theoretical reconstruction has to begin, therefore, with a reexamination of the normative and historical contents of the two concepts.

The processes of social communication and development are thus complex processes that appear radically different from the perspectives of the top and bottom of the social structure. Table 8.2 attempts to capture some of these contradictory perspectives on developmental goals and the ensuing noise and dissonance in public discourse.

There is sufficient reality to this table to propose that social and economic development involves contradictory processes and perspectives. Table 8.3 attempts to reduce these processes to three fundamentally contradictory processes, viewed from top-down, bottom-up, and democratic perspectives. These processes cut across national boundaries, simultaneously taking place at the global as well as national contexts while creating centers and peripheries of development both within and among nations.

If we consider the processes of accumulation, mobilization, and dif-

Table 8.2.   Contradictory Perspectives on Developmental Goals

Development Goals as Viewed from the Top	Development Goals as Viewed from the Bottom
National security and power	Individual choice and freedom
Social mobilization	Social mobility
National unity and identity	Subnational unity and identity
Economic growth	Income distribution and social justice
Political socialization	Political participation
Property and business rights	Public and consumer rights
Educational/professional competence	Educational/professional opportunities
Information control	Information access
Communication surveillance	Communication privacy
Majority rule	Minority rights
Central authority and control	Regional and local autonomy
Cultural and artistic direction (sometimes censorship)	Cultural and artistic creativity (sometimes subversion)

ferentiation as *generators* of development, and the processes of concentration, repression, and domination as the *deterrents,* we may argue that the three historical *crises* of development can be viewed as the crises of *distribution* to fulfill the promises of equality, *participation* to meet the hopes of freedom, and *integration* to achieve a sense of community that is often undermined by the dislocations and conflicts during the developmental process. The processes of legitimation, socialization, and signification generally correspond to the cultural and communication aspects of the developmental process. Figure 8.2 attempts to demonstrate the same set of relationships in terms of a multiple feedback loop model. The underlying arguments of this model may be summarized as follows:

1.   Capital accumulation, whether undertaken through private or state enterprises, often leads to economic concentrations of power, which in turn has a negative impact on the equality of income distribu-

Table 8.3.   Contradictory Processes and Perspectives in Development

Dimensions:	Generators: Center Views	Deterrents: Periphery Views	Crises: DevCom Democratic Views
Economic	Accumulation	Concentration	Distribution/Legitimation: To Maximize Equality
Political	Mobilization	Repression	Participation/Socialization: To Maximize Freedom
Sociocultural	Differentiation	Domination	Integration/Signification: To Maximize Community

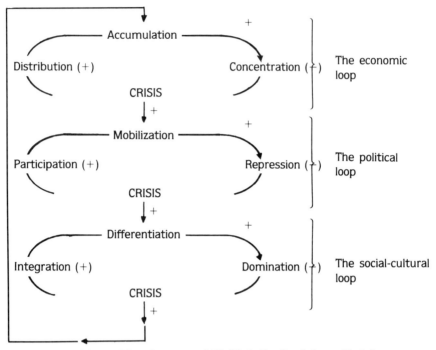

Figure 8.2. Crises of Development: A Multiple Feedback Loop Model
Source: Adapted from Tehranian, 1977, p. 33

tion. Most empirical studies of economic growth bear this out (Kuznets, 1971).

2. Political mobilization takes place primarily through increasing levels of physical, social, and psychic mobility characteristics of the processes of industrialization and urbanization. Physical mobility mainly involves the movement from rural to urban areas. Social mobility includes both horizontal (movement from traditional to modern professions) and vertical mobility (movement up and down the social and economic hierarchy). Psychic mobility involves the increasing demand for cognitive flexibility and adaptation in the modern world, requiring greater learning capacity, multiple identities, and the ability to empathize with others. But political mobilization also entails militancy on the part of the disenfranchised groups and classes in society. This, in turn, often produces increasing levels of political repression by the regime in power unless channels and institutions of political participation (e.g., political parties, labor unions, voluntary associations) also develop along the way.

3. Sociocultural differentiation occurs as a result of increasing levels of division of labor, professionalization, and social stratification along caste or ethnicity, class, and status lines. But this also means that some leading elites (the entrepreneurs, the military, the party leaders, and the sociocultural groups associated with them) begin to exercise new forms of social and cultural domination. In the meantime, the traditional ties of community have broken down and replaced by the less organic and more tenuous ties in the new urban and commercial settings. The social and psychological dislocations of this process produce a national integration crisis focused on the competing interests, authorities, and identities that reflect the economic, political, and cultural struggles in the developmental process.

4. It is thus argued here that only through the processes of fair income distribution, political participation, and national integration can society regain the solidarity it often loses through the dislocating and alienating processes of development. In this model of development, as represented by Table 8.3 and Figure 8.1, positive and negative feedback loops operate in multiple directions to produce a series of developmental crises centered on conflicts of values (interests, authorities, and identities). If the threefold crises between economic concentration and distribution, political repression and participation, and sociocultural domination and integration are not satisfactorily resolved, a development deadlock inevitably unfolds. This often leads to political instability, economic stagnation, and sociocultural decay.

Under historical conditions in which the rates of accumulation have been generally faster than the rates of mobilization (as often was the case in the Western historical experience), the social and political contradictions of development have been largely absorbed and integrated within the emerging economic, political, and cultural institutions of modern industrial society. But wherever the rates of mobilization have outpaced the rates of accumulation and integration, the ensuing imbalances have produced revolutionary upheavals.

The quickening of the processes of worldwide accumulation, achieved through the extraordinary power and reach of the transnational corporations and the modern bureaucratic state, has coincided with the even faster tempo of mobilization achieved through the communications revolution (mobility, literacy, and media exposure). This combination has created serious imbalances in the Third World, between market demands and supplies, political and cultural claims, and opportunities. In the face of the temptations of a new age of high mass consumption promised by the international media "channels of desire" (Ewen & Ewen, 1982), a number of distinctly different strategies have presented themselves to the developing countries.

Table 8.4 attempts to provide a typology of these strategies and policies, focusing on "internal development policies" and "external communication policies" while at the same time providing examples of countries that might illuminate the underlying concepts. Table 4.1 has already shown a range of policies from exogenous/growth to endogenous/integrated development strategies, and from manipulative to participatory communication strategies. This table also identifies the emerging strategies of high accumulation with capitalism, high repression with totalitarianism, high mobilization with communism, and high integration with communitarianism. Table 8.5 provides examples of what the development strategies of high accumulation, high mobilization, or high integration might mean in terms of development and communication policies.

Figure 8.3 provides a synopsis of what is to follow in the next three sections. The figure suggests a tradeoff between capital and political mobilization while high integration is shown to provide an equilibrium position between the two competing strategies. The historical cycles from periods of high accumulation to high mobilization represent what has been discussed in terms of the cycles of American history (pp. 83–84) and Chinese politics (pp. 192–193). The usefulness of these tables, figures, and their organizing concepts will become more apparent as we begin to discuss the three alternative development strategies in the experiences of a number of nations.

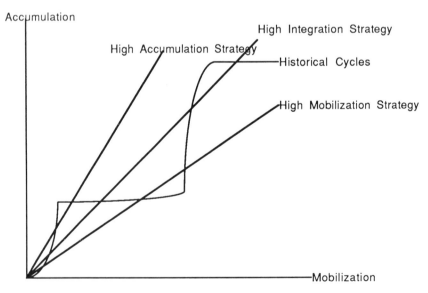

Figure 8.3.   Development Strategies and Historical Cycles

Table 8.4.   Alternative Communication and Development Strategies: A Matrix of Policies

INTERNAL DEVELOPMENT POLICIES:	High Accumulation	High Mobilization	High Integration	High Repression
EXTERNAL COMMUNICATION POLICIES:				
Assimilation:	Iran (Shah) India (Gandhi II & III) Philippines (Marcos) Egypt (Sadat) Turkey (Ataturk)	Philippines (Aquino)	India (Gandhi I)	S. Africa Iraq (Hussain)
Dissociation	USSR (Stalin) PRC (56–66)	USSR (1917–27) PRC (49–56, 66–76) Vietnam	Burma Albania Japan (Tokugawa)	Iran (Ayatollah)
Selective Participation	Saudi Arabia PRC (76–89) NICs Japan (Meiji) Egypt (Mubarak) Pakistan (Zia)	Algeria Indonesia Malaysia Egypt (Nasser) Pakistan (Bhutto I & II) Iran (Bazargan)	Tanzania	Spain (Franco) PRC (89– present)

KEY:
INDIA: Gandhi I refers to Mahatma Gandhi; Gandhi II refers to Madam Gandhi; Gandhi III refers to Sanjay Gandhi.
PRC (PEOPLE'S REPUBLIC OF CHINA): 49–56 refers to the early revolutionary period; 56–66 refers to the Great Leap Forward; 66–76 refers to the Great Proletarian Cultural Revolution; 76–present refers to the Modernization Period.
NICs (NEWLY INDUSTRIALIZING COUNTRIES) refers to S. Korea, Singapore, Taiwan, and Hong Kong.
PAKISTAN: Bhutto I & II refers to Zulfaghar Ali Bhutto and his daughter, Benazir Bhutto.
USSR: 1917–27 refers to the periods of War Communism and New Economic Policy before the rise of Stalin and Stalinism.

Table 8.5.   Alternative Communication & Development Strategies: The Main Policies

	Development	Communication
High Accumulation	Heavy Industry	Telecom Infrastructure
High Mobilization	Material Incentives (consumer goods)	Ideological Exhortation (nationalism, communism)
High Integration	Intrinsic Needs	Dialogical Communication

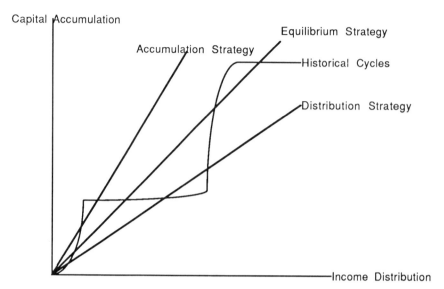

Figure 8.4.   Tradeoffs between Accumulation and Distribution

HIGH-ACCUMULATION STRATEGIES

High-accumulation strategies are founded on the proposition that all economic growth is derived from savings and capital investment. This belief has been the cornerstone of the classical and neoclassical theories of economic growth, from Adam Smith to John Meynard Keynes and Paul Samuelson. A corollary of this belief is the proposition that income distribution has to be for a time, somewhat lopsided in favor of the high-income groups, who tend to save and invest a higher proportion of their income. Another corollary of this belief is that as per capita income rises, a more equal distribution becomes increasingly possible through wage increases and extensions of welfare benefits. From a liberal perspective, this so-called "trickle-down theory" of income distribution justifies the constraints imposed on wage increases and consumption that periods of "take-off into self-sustaining growth" require (Rostow, 1960).

Figure 8.3 attempts to depict this tradeoff between capital accumulation and income distribution. A perfect equilibrium line at 45 degrees is considered a virtual impossibility, while the historical cycles of booms and busts are depicted by a sharply fluctuating curve. As Table 8.5 suggests, high accumulation strategies also are characterized by heavy investments in infrastructure and heavy industries, such as roads, railroads, telecommunications, steel, and petrochemicals. Although high accumulation strategies are most typical of the capitalist road to development, from time to time, communist countries also have adopted this strategy. Stalin's crash industrialization program during the 1930s and Mao's Great Big Leap Forward in the 1950s provide such examples for the Soviet Union and the Peoples' Republic of China.

As for international communication policies, three alternative strategies of *dissociation, assimilation* and *selective participation* present themselves as alternative strategies (see Table 8.4). Dissociation strategy is a road often taken by countries that have experienced major social revolutions. It is a typical and perhaps necessary reaction against a prolonged period of colonialism or foreign domination preceding such revolutions. The strategy is prompted by a dual threat facing new revolutionary regimes, including (a) the ever-present threat of counterrevolutionary forces attempting a comeback in collusion with those imperial powers who have lost out by the revolution, and (b) the ever-pressing need for revolutionary regimes to consolidate their ideological and political power base in an often prolonged period of internal strife and reconstruction. The strategy is thus based on a period of strict dissociation from the international capitalist system. This rupture often cannot be complete or permanent; its intensity and duration depend on the size, resource endowments, and the will of the leadership of the country in question. Whereas revolutionary Soviet Union and China tried and succeeded in dissociation policies each for more than a decade, the revolutionary regimes in the smaller Third World countries have faced enormous difficulties in pursuing such policies (witness Tanzania and Iran).

Following the ascendency of Stalin in 1927, the Soviet Union provides a classic example of the pursuit of a strategy of dissociation. In the debates over whether the Soviet Union should continue to export its revolution to the rest of the world, the dissociation policies were proposed under the slogan of "Socialism in One Country." The international revolutionary hopes had already subsided by 1927, Stalin had achieved a firm control of leadership after a bitter internal struggle, and the Soviet Union was embarking on its road to agricultural collectivization and heavy industrialization during the next 13 years. The underlying policy imperative during this period of self-imposed isolation was to achieve the status of an industrial economy that could withstand the economic, political, and military threats from the West. Nevertheless, the lure of trade with the West and the threat of a rising Nazi movement in Germany dragged the world's only socialist regime into many commercial deals with UK and U.S. as well as into a pact with Hitler. Culturally, however, the country substantially sealed its borders in order to concentrate on an intense ideological struggle for a high accumulation strategy of growth—high savings and investments, low wages and low consumption. Revolutionary China, Cuba, and Vietnam provide other examples of the pursuit of the same strategy with the exception that each of these countries has been able to receive, at least for a time, economic and political support from the communist bloc. The assimilation strategy coupled with a high accumulation strategy is most typical of periphery capitalist countries with large populations and capital resources (either domestic or borrowed), such as monarchical Iran and Brazil. During the 1960s and 1970s, Iran became the recipient of ever-growing oil revenues that reached some $25 billion per annum. The combination of these windfall "savings" in the form of hard foreign exchange earnings and a policy of rapid industrialization and Westernization, led the country into a period of reckless spending on all fronts—transportation and telecommunication infrastructures, heavy and import substitution industries, and imports of consumer goods of all kinds. These policies were combined with an utter disregard for sound economic investment criteria, inattention to the Islamic cultural sensibilities of the population, and heavy-handed treatment of the opposition.

In Brazil, essentially the same set of policies were followed by a military regime that took over the country after 1964. However, at least two significant differences between the two countries has thus far prevented a revolutionary situation from developing in Brazil. First, Brazil's economic growth during this period has been based on capital borrowings to the tune of over $100 billion of foreign debt; this has, in turn, provided some measure of economic discipline imposed from the outside. Secondly, Brazil has already made a transition from a military to a civilian regime in the mid-1980s. This promises to provide some measure of political participation as a safety valve against the excesses of a high accumulation strategy of economic growth. The contrast between Iran and Brazil can be best appreciated in their telecommunication sector. While both countries became media-intensive consumers of imported Western cultural products, Brazil has managed to develop its own domestic productions in print, broadcasting, and computer industries. Brazil's peripheral capitalism may thus have a reasonable chance of survival, while Iran's crony capitalism (controlled mainly by the royal family) was perhaps doomed to failure from the start.

The selective participation strategy is typically followed by both peripheral capitalist as well as communist countries. The Peoples' Republic of China (PRC) during the Modernization Period (1976–present) and some of the Eastern European countries (such as Yugoslavia, Hungary, Poland, and Romania) provide examples for the latter. Saudi Arabia and Singapore, two countries which lie worlds apart geographically and culturally, provide examples of the former. Following a devastating period of the Great Proletariat Cultural Revolution, China dramatically shifted its policies of self-isolation and dissociation to one of selective participation in the international capitalist regime. This has, in turn, prompted a communication policy of ideological diversity, materialist incentives, advertising, and rising Western cultural imports. Following the Hungarian Revolution of 1956, Soviet Union's firm control of the Eastern European communist countries has proved too difficult to maintain. In the wake of Yugoslavia's experiments with market socialism and active opening to the West, Romania, Hungary, Czechoslovakia, and Poland have gradually moved in the same direction. In this respect, the Hungarian experiments seem to have been the most successful of all in Eastern Europe.

Saudi Arabia and Singapore provide two dramatically different examples of the pursuit of the same policies of selective participation and high accumulation. Saudi Arabia enjoys the benefits of a huge oil income (about $40 billion per annum) and small population (overestimated at 11 million) with one of the world's highest per capita incomes (approximately $12,000). However, unlike some other oil exporting countries (Venezuela and Iran, for example), Saudi Arabia has followed a closed-door cultural policy while pursuing an open-door economic policy. High rates of economic growth are thus coupled with strict, fundamentalist Islamic controls on Western cultural imports, from alcohol to media products. This has led to a covert rather than overt dualistic society, in which the privileged upper strata of society (including the proverbial 2,000 Saudi princes) carry on Western living styles in private while, in public, life is outwardly Islamic. However, in reaction to the Islamic revolution in Iran, the fundamentalist controls have become even more strict. This has gained the Saudi regime a degree of stability that would have been otherwise impossible under the conditions of "free flow of information." Nevertheless, "The Death of a Princess" could get through the censors to be shown in Riyadh the very next day after its premier in London. This fictionalized documentary was a BBC-WGBH television production that embarrassed the Saudi royalty by telling the story of the summary execution of a Saudi Princess who had eloped with a commoner. The video cassette recorders and other small media that make such escape from official censors possible are undermining government efforts to control the flow of cultural products (including pornography) from the outside world (Boyd, 1982).

Singapore, by contrast, is a Confucian and newly-industrializing country (NIC). With few other resources except its geography and the high levels of education and ingenuity of its citizens, Singapore has followed a strategy of high accumulation and selective participation since its independence from Malaysia in 1965.[3] But after two decades of impressive growth rates of about 9 percent per annum, the city-state of

---

[3] For a survey, see *The Economist*, November 22, 1986.

Singapore experienced its first recession by showing 1.8 percent of nega-tive growth in 1985. An export-driven strategy of growth has thus proved itself as much vulnerable to the vagaries of the international market as the import substitution strategies that have faltered in the face of high indebtedness and collapse of the world prices for raw materials (including oil). Singapore, however, achieved its success during its first two decades by high degrees of diligence, discipline, and social control. As Prime Minister Lee Kuan Yew has put it (*The Economist*, Survey, November 22, 1986, p. 3):

> I say without the slightest remorse that we wouldn't be here, would not have made the economic progress, if we had not intervened on very personal matters—who your neighbor is, how you live, the noise you make, how you spit—or where you spit—or what language you use. . . . It was fundamental social and cultural changes that brought us here.
>
> We are not homogenous, never will be. . . . One language is a social glue that helps to keep a society together, but it is not stronger than religious or ethnic pulls. . . . Never deceive ourselves that we can become like Hong Kong, Taiwan or Korea—tight, cohesive, with one social response.

Singapore's high accumulation strategy has been based on a combina-tion of export orientation and low wages. Both factors are facing serious difficulties. Other Asian competitors—Korea, Taiwan, Hong Kong—are competing for the same markets in a recessionary world economy with lower wages. As *The Economist* (November 22, 1986, p. 7) reports, "Sin-gapore's unit labor cost in 1980 was 34 American cents for a dollar of output—lower than any newly industrializing country in East Asia apart from South Korea. By last year the Singaporean figure had risen to 48 cents, only two cents below America's. Meanwhile, the South Korean Figure had risen to just 30 cents, and the Hong Kong figure had fallen from 41 to 32 cents." This discrepancy may best be understood by the ethnic composition of Singapore's population. Singapore's population is divided into unequal lots of Chinese, Malays, Indians, and Euroasians; they speak different languages[4] to ensure mutual misunderstanding—with Malay as the lingua franca. Since independence, government pol-icies have insured that the young have a common bond of English and Mandarin, the labor unions are brought to heel, and the multiethnic population behave according to a doctrine of inequality based on educa-tion and merit. To quote the inimitable Prime Minister Lee again:

> We are born unequal and we've got to make the best of the lot. And whether it is fruit trees, whether it is race horses, whatever it is, this is the

---

[4] Mandarin, Malay, English, and Tamil were the official ones, but there were assorted Chinese and Indian dialects, too.

way nature works. . . Don't we want to use some sense and say to our-selves, 'The more we have of people who can run this economy better, the better it is for everybody'? Because one outstanding man who discovers how to do a microchip, or whatever, can transform our lives and provide jobs and raise standards of living.

The doctrine has led to a eugenics program in which the government rewards the higher educated couples who breed more of themselves. In the context of a multiethnic population with differential income and education levels, this policy is clearly skidding on the thin ice of racial politics. According to the government statistics, Malays and Indians are procreating with enough enthusiasm to more (the Malays) or less (the Indians) replace themselves; the Chinese are falling far short of the replacement rate—last year by 31.5 percent. In fact, last year's births by racial group divided into 69.1 percent Chinese, 19.1 percent Malays, and 7.7 percent Indians. Since the present racial composition is 76.4 percent Chinese, 14.9 percent Malay, and 6.4 percent Indian, it will not take long for the ethnic balance of Singapore to shift. The government policy of favoring education and merit as a criteria for breeding more or less may thus be viewed as a thinly disguised policy of favoring the Chinese and disfavoring the minorities (i.e., the Malays and Indians who show lower education and economic achievements).

Singapore also illustrates the difficulties facing many multiethnic, multilingual Third World countries. In an effort towards national and international integration, a bilingual communication policy has been adopted in Singapore—English to foster modern and internationalist values, and Mandarin Chinese to insure a single, dominant Chinese cultural identity. As *The Economist* (November 22, 1986, pp. 10, 15) reports:

> 'With language comes values', as one American-educated Chinese economist puts it. In the colonial days of Singapore, Chinese education nurtured either traditional Confucian values, including a blind loyalty to the ruler, or Mao-inspired communism. English education inculcated be-liefs in law and democracy. Language was fundamental to Mr. Lee's idea of independence. If English became the common language, three benefits would follow: Singapore would gain access to English-dominated interna-tional trade; the power of the communists would be diminished; and a certain levelling of the economic balance would occur between the Chi-nese majority and the Malay and Indian minorities.

High accumulation strategies have thus succeeded in a number of historical situations to achieve high rates of growth without disrupting the social balance; in most other circumstances in the Third World, the same strategies have produced insurmountable social and economic contradictions leading to political instability and revolt. Soviet Union and China provide examples of the former where dissociation policies were pursued, while Iran and the Philippines present examples of the latter where assimilation into the international capitalist regime was the dominant policy. If combined with conservative, selective participation cultural policies (as in Saudi Arabia and Singapore), high accumulation strategies may achieve some measure of success. But it is important to note that the NICs (South Korea, Taiwan, Hong Kong, Singapore, and Brazil), where high accumulation strategies have produced remarkable growth rates during the past two decades, are facing serious challenges in overcoming a world recessionary period and domestic political problems.

HIGH-MOBILIZATION STRATEGIES

High-mobilization strategies are typical of the early periods of revolutionary movements and regimes, but they can also be consciously adopted later as in the Chinese Great Proletarian Cultural Revolution (1965–68). Mobilization does not, however, automatically lead to political participation. Orderly participation in the processes of decision making requires an institutionalization of direct or representative democracy. That is why periods of mobilization are castigated by conservatives as "mob rule" and extolled by radicals as "moments of enthusiasm."[5] A historical hiatus thus always stands between political mobilization and participation during which the regimes in power resist and repress the democratic forces.

Figure 8.4 proposes a tradeoff between mobilization and participation on an assumption, born out of recurrent historical experience, that high degrees of political mobilization need to be either severely repressed or somehow institutionalized into revolutionary or reformist channels of political participation. As Huntington (1968) has argued, a rapid rate of mobilization unaccompanied by a commensurately high rate of institutionalization of political participation often leads to political decay, that is, disorder and violence. We may argue, therefore, that political development consists of processes of institutionalization of political participation. The 45 degree line of perfect equilibrium between political mobilization and participation is thus very difficult to achieve; the curve fluctuating between periods of mobilization and participation represents the historical realities more closely.

To correlate high-mobilization strategies with the three alternative communication strategies of dissociation, assimilation, and selective participation in the international capitalist regime, we may consider the cases of China, the Philippines, and Algeria. The Chinese communist

---

[5] See Leonard Binder's book on Egypt, *In a Moment of Enthusiasm* (1978).

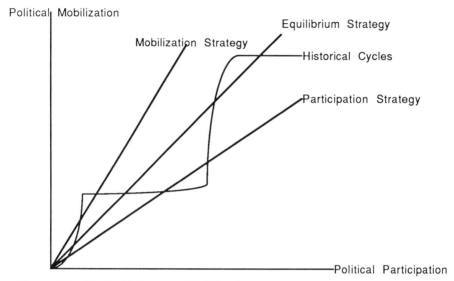

Figure 8.5.   Tradeoffs between Mobilization and Participation

regime seems to have gone through four distinct development strategies during the following four periods: (a) From 1949 to 1958, revolutionary high mobilization was virtually in effect in order to consolidate the power of the new communist regime. This period was also characterized by close affiliation with the Soviet Union and a rejection of the West; (b) From 1958 to 1960, a strategy of "Great Leap Forward" inaugurated a high-accumulation strategy in order to achieve China's ambitions for industrialization. Relations with the Soviet Union deteriorated in 1960 by the open rupture of the Sino-Soviet ideological disputes and the withdrawal of Russian technicians and economic assistance; (c) From 1965–1968, the Great Proletarian Cultural Revolution was set into motion by Mao as a measure of renewing revolutionary enthusiasm and purging the bureaucratic elements from the party and the government. This high-mobilization strategy brought millions of young peasants from the countryside into the cities and disrupted the course of China's modernization in industry and agriculture; (d) Following the death of Mao and Premier Chou En-lai in 1976, a power struggle between the radicals (the so-called Gang of Four) and moderates led to the ascendency of the latter group led by Deng Xiaoping. This continuing stage, known as "The Modernization Period," is characterized by high-accumulation development strategies domestically and selective participation in the international capitalist world. China's experience in recent decades have thus demonstrated the cyclical nature of the developmental process, driven by contradictory forces that call for capital accumulation and political mobilization from the centers of power while the peripheries of power demand income distribution and political participation. The transition from Deng to a new generation of Chinese leaders has been so far peacefully achieved, but the inequalities generated by modernization may result in political upheavals. These prophetic words were written over a year before the tragedy at the Tiananmen Square in June 1989. The new phase in Chinese politics has ushered a new high-mobilization cycle led by the Chinese students facing state repression.

The Philippines presents yet another example of the same set of forces at work. Following some 400 years of Spanish colonial rule, nearly 50 years of U. S. colonial domination, and Japanese wartime occupation, the Philippines gained its independence on July 4, 1946. The Philippines's American-style democratic institutions have not, however, worked in practice. From 1965 to 1986, under President Ferdinand Marcos, the Philippines followed a strategy of high accumulation (and indebtedness), high mobilization, and high repression (particularly after the martial law of 1972) that led finally to a mass revolt. The new government, under President Corazan Aquino, is attempting to redress the balance by pursuing a strategy of accumulation and democratic participation. In the meantime, the open-door policies of economic and cultural assimilation have continued to keep the Philippines within the U. S. sphere of influence. The communist and Muslim resurgency movements that feed on economic and political grievances also continue to undermine the political stability of the Aquino government. While maintaining a precarious balance between the left and the right, the Aquino government is thus faced with the twin threats of a revolutionary movement and a military coup. If and when either of these two possibilities materialize, the Filipino communication and development strategy will probably have to shift radically towards high accumulation and repression, while a policy of assimilation (in the case of a military regime) or dissociation (in the case of a revolutionary regime) would become dominant. Western and particularly U. S. cultural and media influence have been a continuing source of inspiration for some and corruption for others. The Filipino struggles for democracy have clearly been inspired by the American example, but the corruption of the Filipino elite is also to a large measure due to their alienation from their own people and close economic and commercial ties with the United States.

Algeria provides yet another example of a high-mobilization strategy combined with selective participation in the world capitalist regime. Emerging out of some seven years of a guerrilla war against French colonial rule, Algeria gained its independence in 1962. Blessed by moderate levels of oil income and a population of no more than 21 million, Algeria has pursued a development policy of nonalignment (selective participation), a single socialist party regime (controlled levels of political mobilization and participation), and moderate success at economic growth and income distribution. Algeria has thus managed to maintain friendly relations with the Soviet Union while actively engaging in the international capitalist markets by the exchange of its oil exports for Western capital and consumer goods. Algeria's cultural and communication policies, however, have maintained a high level of nationalist and Muslim consciousness, thus stemming the tide of Western cultural and media imports.

The high-mobilization development strategies have combined with the three international communication strategies of dissociation, assimilation, and selective participation to produce a variety of developmental patterns in the Third World. The internal developmental pressures have also combined with the external constraints/possibilities to provide many opportunities as well as obstacles on the way of the LDCs. As the examples of Singapore, China, the Philippines, and Algeria demonstrate, the role of a clear-headed leadership with democratic sources of support has been critical in achieving success against the considerable obstacles that the developmental road presents. But it is also clear from the foregoing analysis that the high accumulation and high mobilization strategies to development have produced some great social and political contradictions, from socioeconomic dualism (as in the Philippines) to serious socioeconomic disruptions (as in the Chinese Cultural Revolution). Both paths thus present severe social and economic dislocations that are difficult to overcome.

HIGH-INTEGRATION STRATEGIES

The high-integration strategies of communication and development come closest to the ideals of communitarian democracy. Except for a few contemporary social movements, however, we can cite few successful national efforts towards the realization of a communitarian style of development. In the light of their past colonial experiences and present aspirations for national identity and unity, many Third World countries have espoused the communitarian ideals in their postindependence years. But countries that have opened their economies and societies to world capitalist penetration have generally experienced patterns of economic growth accompanied by increasing socioeconomic dualism, including class, status, and ethnic antagonisms.

Many of these contradictions are fundamentally due to the nature of development itself. Figure 8.5 attempts to demonstrate that, in the developmental process, another tradeoff exists between levels of so-

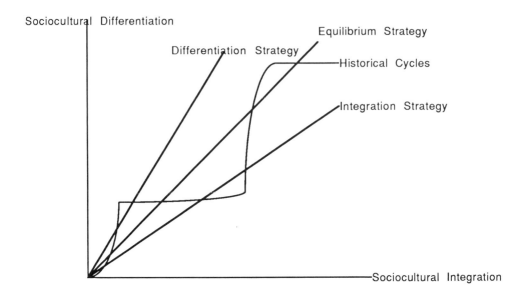

Figure 8.6.   Tradeoffs between Social Differentiation and Integration

cioeconomic differentiation and integration. As in the case of the previous tradeoffs, perfect equilibrium along the 45 degree line is nearly
impossible to achieve. But the degree of fluctuation between rates of
differentiation and integration can be somewhat modified by appropriate developmental policies. A high-integration strategy of development
does not ignore the fact that socioeconomic development involves increasing levels of specialization, division of labor, and stratification of
society along new class and status lines. But it would emphasize endog-
enous technologies, self-reliance, basic needs, decentralization, and political participation in order to moderate the income, class, status, and
ethnic differentials generated by the developmental process.

To illustrate this point, I will use the examples of some of the high-
integration development strategies that have combined with dissociation, assimilation, and selective participation strategies of international
communication.

There are few examples of complete dissociation from the international system. Albania and Burma provide the only two countries in
recent memory that have attempted such a strategy with consequences
fairly unknown to the outside world. India and Tanzania also espoused
such a philosophy in their immediate postindependence years, but both
countries have been increasingly sucked into the international system.
More recently, the leaders of the Islamic revolution in Iran have strongly
advocated a strategy of complete dissociation and independence from
both the capitalist and communist blocs, but even more dramatically
than the other countries, Iran has been increasingly drawn into interna-

tional conflicts (the Iran-Iraq war) and trade relations (oil for arms) that have undermined its ambitions for socioeconomic development. Smaller communities fortified by strong religious convictions, such as the Amish in Pennsylvania and the Robinson Family on the island of Niihau of the State of Hawaii, represent the more successful efforts in this direction. But even these communities stand constantly in danger of dissolution in the face of the encroachments from the "more advanced and civilized" world.

Dissociation strategies have thus been espoused by many Third World leaders in their revolutionary heydays, but the realities of the world situation have often dictated increasing assimilation. Mahatma Gandhi's philosophy of development represents perhaps the most notable example of a dissociation philosophy that was aborted by the postindependence historical realities of India. Gandhi advocated a rejection of Western-style industrialization in favor of a return to the social solidarity and self-sufficiency of the Indian village communities. But India's development patterns in the postindependence years typify much of the schizophrenia in Third World societies, torn as they are between the temptations of modern materialism and a traditionalist nostalgia for community and fraternity. In much of the Third World, this has led to developmental patterns that significantly differ from the official ideological pronouncements of national goals. India provides the most dramatic example in this respect. Indian leaders continue to pay lip service to their Gandhian heritage, but in the meantime, the country has achieved the status of the world's seventh largest industrial power. This is no mean achievement for a country that had almost no industry at the dawn of its independence. This achievement should be, however, weighed against the fact that more than half of India's population of 767 million continue to live in conditions of abject poverty.

The introduction of satellites and television into India demonstrate how meeting the demands of an urban elite and the needs of the rural poor might collide. Satellites and television came to India through a well-known, international experiment—the SITE experiment. SITE is the acronym for the Satellite Instructional Television Experiment (SITE), a project that took place during 1974–76, when the Indian government in collaboration with NASA, provided access to ATS-6 for educational experiments in the subcontinent (Filep & Haq, 1977). Community television sets were placed in 2339 villages to receive educational transmissions. Programs were videotaped in four languages and the subjects included government (15%), culture (28%), agriculture (29%), social (9%), national awareness (9%), religion (5%), and other (6%). The project attempted to provide educational television as well as training on the technical aspects of satellite technology. More specifically, the project aimed at (a) contributing to family planning, agricultural productivity, and national integration, and (b) supporting general school and adult education, teacher training, occupational skills, and improvement in health and hygiene. Evaluations of the experiment showed, however, that few of these objectives were reached to any appreciable extent. The hardware aspects of the projects were deemed to be successful but the software did not offer the appropriate development-support (Gore, 1983).

Nonetheless, the project has had a number of spinoff effects, including the introduction of an Indian satellite system and a significant effort towards participatory television—the Kheda Communication Project. The credo of this project reflects a melange of ideals, including a developmentalist emphasis on economic growth but also a Freirian concern with awakening and self-realization:

> Development—economic, social, cultural or ideological—implies a break from the status quo, from inertia; it implies movement, change. Change requires a certain attitude, motivation, information and, of course, appropriate physical and social infrastructures. It also requires an objective understanding of one's predicament—the family and social constraints one works within. This necessitates the development of rational outlook, a scientific attitude towards life.
>
> Development implies social change, education, awareness and of course economic development. However, economic development cannot take place in isolation; it requires changes in the social system and in the attitude of the individual; it implies breaking away from bondage and oppression; and most importantly—it necessitates an "awakening" of the individual and his self-confidence.
>
> In trying to accelerate development, communication can play a very major role. Television, in particular, can be a powerful tool in creating a "climate" for development. Our attempt at Kheda will be to use TV—and also to supplement it by other means—for development in the broadest meaning of the term. Concretely, the attempt will be to:
>
> i)   Focus on the oppression and bondages in the present social and economic system in such a way as to heighten understanding.
>
> ii)   Mobilize the community and the individual himself to break away from these bondages.
>
> iii)   Promote self-reliance among the individuals and the community:
> • involving a reduction in apathy, in dependence on God or others;
> • implying improvising an optimal use of local resources;
> • necessitating a cooperative spirit and a willingness to take risks.
>
> iv)   Educate the community, particularly the deprived about their duties and rights, including minimum wages, etc.
>
> v)   Provide utility programmes in areas like agriculture, animal husbandry, health, family planning, crafts and skills, functional literacy so as to improve the social and economic condition of the masses.
>
> vi)   Broaden the horizon of the viewers by showing them persons, places and events outside their immediate environment.

vii) Improve horizontal communication between the village communities and vertical communication between the masses and decision
makers.
viii) Inculcate a scientific temper among the younger generation by
improving the educational level of children, particularly in the areas of
science and mathematics.
The prime target audience will invariably be the lower classes/castes
who are the most oppressed and who need the catalytic input that will
help them to help themselves. Accordingly, program content, presenta-
tion, etc. will be designed keeping the audience in mind.

A collection of articles entitled "Another TV" (Pal et al., 1978) provides
a comprehensive analysis of the Kheda experiment. Although Kheda is a
relatively developed district in India, the majority of the television audience proved to be of lower classes and castes—small and marginal
farmers, landless laborers, artisans, Rajputs, Harijans, and so on. There
were about 40 percent children, and of the adults 65 percent men and 35
percent women. There were an average of about 120 people watching TV
programs per set. This implies that the programs were watched by about
12,000 people every day. Audio-visually, Kheda Television reached
about 5000 children, 5000 men, and 3000 women of the small and remote
villages. The programs consisted of both news and public affairs (produced mainly by Doordarshan, the national TV network) as well as
developmental fare produced by the Space Applications Center (agriculture 6%, animal husbandry 5%, health 7%, children 7%, general
information 43%, socioeconomic 11%, miscellaneous 11%, and entertainment 5%). The socioeconomic programs included themes such as un-
touchability, prohibition, superstition, minimum wages, exploitation,
cooperation amongst the oppressed, women's problems, and so on.
The Kheda experiment seems to have successfully tackled one of the
most intransigent problems of RTV programs conceived by the urban-
biased producers for rural audiences (Joshi, 1978, pp. 39–40):

In spite of being in close touch with the rural audience, we have found
that establishing authenticity and credibility can be a problem. One possible solution is to go to the people themselves as was done by one of our
producers. He wanted to make a series of programmes on the theme of
exploitation—caste exploitation, sexual exploitation, economic exploitation, bonded labour, etc. . . . He went to the village and gave the Harijans
[i.e., the untouchables] the plot, they were allowed to choose their parts,
improvise dialogues and situations. These Harijans, from a village which
is extremely backward, have no electricity and from where very few people had even seen movies, came up with brilliant performances. The force
and ingenuity of their performance, the nuances they brought in were
really excellent. The programmes had no problems about authenticity and

credibility because their "acting" was almost reliving their own experiences. . .

Another strategy that we are adopting in this connection is to invite scripts through daily announcements over TV, from the villagers. . . . We also produce many programmes in the field wherein villagers talk about their problems, difficulties and their views on various issues. There is a greater tendency toward making participatory programmes. This produces a sense of identification with the medium.

I should make special mention of a programme based on a real incident—an incident which created waves of shock and horror in the whole State. A child—the only son in the family—was kidnapped and killed as a sacrifice in the belief that such a sacrifice would beget a child. This programme consisted of interviews with the child's parents; the sadhu who advised this sacrifice, the two accused—the kidnapper and the childless man. Feedback on the programme showed that there was pin drop silence and complete comprehension.

The programmes created a sense of anger and revulsion, but it also came out that there was ignorance about the biological facts of how a child is conceived. While they considered child sacrifice to be shocking, they also thought that sacrifices of animals, etc., could help in begetting a child. We therefore decided to make a few programmes against this superstitious belief. Thus, we try to make it a continuous process of finding out what the people know, what should be clarified.

The laudable aims and achievements of SITE and its offshoots should be, however, considered against what has taken place subsequently in terms of the development of television as a medium of mass communication. Indian television is following the basic patterns of development of this medium in other developing countries. It caters to the consumer needs and tastes of a burgeoning urban elite that represents a small minority of the population. Although India is still far behind some other countries in TV set ownership (see Table 8.6), the production of TV sets has already become a booming business. Government policies have helped to create an industry with 120 manufacturers. Former Indian Prime Minister Indira Gandhi started the boom when she concluded that government-controlled television could be helpful. As *The Economist*, December 13, 1986, reports:

> Transmitters were installed to cover 90% of the country in time for the 1984 elections. Then commercial sponsorship of programmes was allowed—and television became watchable. Middle-class Indian families now sit glued to nightly soap-operas. The government threw industrial licenses at aspiring manufacturers of televisions. But, in line with its preference for small scale industry, most were for 10,000 sets a year.
> . . . Of India's 150m families, 145m do not yet have a set. Televisions

Table 8.6.   Television Set Ownership

	TV Sets Per 1,000 People 1984	GDP Per Head ($) 1985
Malaysia	90*	2000
Thailand	67*	750
Iran	48	3750*
Indonesia	35*	500
Pakistan	15†	300
China	10	220
Sri Lanka	3*	380
India	3	250
Bangladesh	2	140
Burma	1	160

Source: *IEAS, Europe Yearbook 1986.*
*1983   †1985
Source: *The Economist,* December 13, 1986,
p. 79.

can be imported only as personal baggage and bear a 150% duty. Most of the market for sets is among the middle class: civil servants, doctors and traders. Everybody who can nearly afford it has to buy a television for his daughter's wedding. Along with a scooter, it is required dowry.

The problem for the television manufacturers is that poor Indians are not getting better-off fast enough. . . [Emphasis added].

The Indonesian experiment with satellites has been somewhat different in scope and strategy (Abramson, 1979; Alfian/Chu, 1981). It has come about as a result of a high-accumulation strategy of development inaugurated after the tragic failure of Sukarno's high-mobilization strategies ending with the military coup of 1965. The New Order Government, led by General Suharto and the military, enlisted the support of an elite of technocrats in its efforts to reconstruct the Indonesian economy. A series of Five-Year Development Plans, known as the REPELITA, was launched in 1969 that aim at increasing agricultural productivity (particularly rice production) and lowering population growth. However, the ensuing economic growth, characterized by Indonesia's increasing involvement in the global economy, has led to some unintended consequences—"serious problems of corruption, a high consumption of imported luxury goods, and widening gap between the haves and the have-nots, and increasing social and political tensions" (Alfian/Chu, 1981, p. 8).

Indonesia's national communication policies have therefore been a reflection of the country's geopolitical realities as well as its developmental objectives and strategies. Indonesia's 13,677 islands constitute the largest archipelago in the world with a total land area of about 735,000 square miles stretching across a territory of some 3,200 miles from east to west and 1,100 miles from north to south. Reaching a population of some 140 million peoples of diverse cultural, religious, and ethnic background spread throughout these scattered islands is a challenge. The objective of Indonesia's developmental policies for the last three decades of independence from the Dutch has therefore been twofold: to promote a sense of national identity and to raise the standards of living. Both objectives clearly require popular support and participation, but the three universal developmental goals (growth, solidarity, and participation) are not necessarily compatible. Indonesia has thus fluctuated, like other developing countries, between high-mobilization strategies (typical of the anticolonial struggles and the Sukarno periods), high-accumulation strategies (typical of the Suharto period), and high-integration strategies (typical of Sukarno's Guided Democracy and Pancasila principles attempting to forge national unity as well as the New Order Government's communication policies).

Satellites were thus conceived as a solution to Indonesia's horrendous development communications problems. On August 17, 1976, an Indonesian domestic communications satellite, known as PALAPA I, was inaugurated. PALAPA I has 12 transponders, each capable of transmitting one color television channel or 400 circuit telephones with two-way communication or 800 circuit telephones with one-way communication. The satellite is connected with 40 ground stations, one for each of the 27 provinces and 13 for industrial areas. Television signals can reach some 81 percent of Indonesia's mostly rural population. For the first time in history, the country is thus in possession of a communication system that can reach most of its population instantaneously (Alfian & Chu, 1981, p. 2). However, it had also become clear to the Indonesian communication policy makers that unbridled television programing can have disastrous social and political consequences. The lessons of Iran seem to have made an impression on the Indonesian policy makers. Subsequent to that revolution, by direct orders from General Suharto, advertising was completely banned from television. It is reported that when Suharto had asked his director of broadcasting "how much is earned from advertising," he received an underestimated figure reflecting the director's fear of losing government budgetary allocations. Suharto concluded therefore that advertising revenues are not worth the social discontent they might arouse. Another indication comes from the fact that the author's article on the role of communication in the Iranian revolution

(Tehranian, 1979) appeared in translation in *Prisma*, the Indonesian Journal of Social Sciences, almost immediately after its publication. The
lessons of the Iranian revolution clearly pointed to the need for a more
conservative television programming in the context of the developing
countries, where the flaunting of Western programs and standards of
living (agreeable to the high-income urban dwellers) alienates and radi-
calizes the urban and rural poor.

The policy goals of Indonesian television were thus set as the promotion of national unity and integration, national development, and political stability. Advertising and Western-style entertainment programs
were banned, while the following five guidelines for television programming have set the rules (Alfian & Chu, 1981, pp. 30–32):

> First, Indonesian television should stimulate the process of "nation and
> character building," which includes, among other things, strengthening
> national objectives and enhancing spiritual development. Second, televi-
> sion should play the role of preserver and protector of the national culture,
> meaning it should stimulate the development of various aspects of Indo-
> nesian culture. Third, television should support and promote the various
> developmental activities that are going on throughout the archipelago.
> Fourth, it should also carry on its educational function, including the
> promotion of public appreciation of cultural shows and other wholesome
> entertainment programs. Finally, television should be guided by what the
> general public wants to satisfy their needs and promote their welfare.

Given this basically top-down approach to communication policy, the
Indonesian efforts towards participatory projects is limited to the areas
of family planning, agricultural extension, and public health promotion
where interaction with the audiences is an essential requirement for
success. In fact, by avoiding ideological issues in its news and public
affairs programming, the mass media attempt to channel social mobilization into progovernment sentiments and projects.

A development strategy that can combine selective participation in
the global system with a policy of high integration at the domestic level
is a far more difficult enterprise to undertake. It demands a high level of
awareness of the international context as well as a full commitment to
integrated and participatory development at home. Dialogic and interactive communication rather than vertical communication via the noninteractive, one-way systems would characterize such a strategy. I have
called this approach to communication and development "communitarian," because it begins *not* with the technological imperatives *but*
from community needs and aspirations.

To reach and activate participation among the remote rural populations in the Third World societies, new approaches are needed. Participatory modes of communication range all the way from the traditional media (tribal dances, peasant festivals, religious passion plays, etc.) to modern literacy or family planning campaigns and multifunctional participatory community media (the rural press, RTV or VCR clubs, etc.). Sylvia Moore (1983) reports a number of often untapped potentials for the use of traditional media that are worthy of note. One great advantage of traditional media is that they are multifunctional, encompassing ancient rituals and living cultures. However, they are largely untapped—ostensibly because traditions are considered by most development workers to be a deterrent to progress. The urban-biased media systems and the top-down message flows thus defy the traditional media and folk cultures as sources for participatory communication. In Southern Colombia, Moore reports (1983, pp. 20–23), the social panorama of some 900,000 inhabitants includes Indians, mestizos, black communities, and rich and poor urban dwellers. "Klestrynge" is the annual ceremony of the Sibundoy Indians. It expresses the Indian view of the world in which the individual, the group, the ancestors, and the land are indivisible. "Klestrynge" is a cultural process in which everyone in the community has a voice. This process of social participation brings about social awareness; it reinforces the existing political and economic system and generates change by consensus. However, it is rarely considered a communication vehicle in plans for social change.

Another example is the Santa Cruz settlement project in Bolivia (Moore, 1983, p. 23). The project, sponsored by a National Agency for Settlements, aimed at resettling highland Indians in Santa Cruz, a lowland area suitable for agricultural development. The World Food Program (WFP) of UN/FAO found that the infrastructure to be provided by the government was less than adequate. Consequently, the Indians who were transferred from the highlands found that their living conditions had deteriorated. Moreover, the Indians found no social structures to which they could belong in the new community. In fact, they became outcasts even though for the first six months they were given communal living facilities. Many consequently returned to the highlands because poverty was preferable to isolation. Absence of interactive communication was found to be the key factor in the failure of this kind of top-down project. Government officials, for example, were often in conflict with local project organizers. To remedy the problem, WFP tried to ensure that there were sufficient local staff who could relate both to the national elite and the local Indian population. "WFP found that this intermediary role was best carried out by agronomic social promoters. These technicians speak the languages (Quenchua, Aymara), understand environmental problems as well as modern techniques which can be utilized by the new population. Because their messages were based on practice, they established permanent contact with the people and were accepted by the local community, whereas social promoters were not."

Participatory traditional media, however, suffer from one major drawback. They incorporate the traditional social structures of power and sources of knowledge and authority. The modern participatory community media, by contrast, tend to undermine much of that authority by bringing into play modern ideas, techniques, and change agents. Both forms of participatory communication, however, depend vitally on the intent for which they are used. If consciousness raising through full community participation is the objective, either method could have mobilizing and emancipatory effects. Conversely, the idea of participation itself can be used to reinforce existing social and political structures.

Freire recognized this when he critiqued his own earlier concepts of "conscientization." His earlier formulations implied that the discovery of reality itself would transform reality without actually considering the dialectics between individual consciousness and the dominant social structures. However, Freire (1976a) came to the conclusion that rational-cognitive activity was not enough, for revolution "heeded a commitment and partisanship rooted in everyday political struggle." After his experiences in Guinea Bissau, he concluded that "there is no liberation without a revolutionary transformation of the class society, for in the class society, humanization is impossible. Liberation becomes concrete only when society is changed, not when its structures are simply modernized." In Guinea Bissau, Freire recommended a fusion between the work of the educator and student with those of other workers, so that the content of learning is based on practice, educational materials are created on site, and action is the point of departure for reflection.

This conception of participation has led to another form of participatory media work represented by the techniques of action research. This technique brings the scientific pretentions of neutrality and objectivity of established academia into serious questioning. Orlando Fals-Borda, for instance, has argued: "There cannot be a 'popular' science or a 'bourgeois' or a 'proletarian' science . . . rather, at certain historical junctures various constellations of knowledge, data, facts and factors become articulated according to the interests of the classes which enter into struggle over social, political or economic power" (Moore, 1983, p. 27). Fals-Borda runs the Foundation for the Analysis of Colombian Reality, engaged in participatory action research with popular movements and organizations. Some UN programs and agencies also recommend this method as the most effective technique of combining action and reflection. UNRISD, The United Nations Research Institute for Social Development, for instance, has set "popular participation" and "livelihood" as the two main themes for it's work in the coming years.

Another project in Peru, known as Tierra Fecunda (Fertile Land), comes closest perhaps to the consciousness raising functions of community media by providing channels through which the concerns, problems, and alternatives available to the rural people may be expressed. The project has some affinity with Paolo Freire's ideas. However, it employs radio alongside traditional channels of communication for its conscientization goals. In Peru, the most important means of mass communication is the radio. The project began in 1980 for strengthening rural radio programs; it was sponsored by the Peruvian Center for Social Studies (CEPES). The program began with the publication of a monthly bulletin aimed at rural population. However, distribution of the papers and the educational leaflets proved difficult. For this reason, in the second half of 1980, the publication was supplemented with a daily radio program in the morning that reaches the remotest villagers. The main objective of "Fertile Land" has been to enlist the participation of the rural population in the preparation and evaluation of the programs. A system of feedback was set up combining different mechanisms:

1. A network of more than 500 rural correspondents to provide regular information on the problems facing their regions.
2. Invitation to listeners to write or visit the radio station to give their point of view.
3. Direct reporting from the rural areas on the conditions and feelings of the rural population.
4. Coordinated input from other rural and agricultural agencies on the conditions and needs of the rural poor.

CONCLUSION

This chapter has considered the performance and prospects of information technologies in the peripheries and semiperipheries of the world. We have viewed the impact of these technologies in the context of a variety of different development strategies, including the high-accumulation, high-mobilization, and high-integration strategies. These development strategies have historically combined with different communication strategies towards the former colonial powers and the global capitalist world. In a matrix of three by three, nine basic strategies of development communication were identified that characterize the experiences of a variety of different countries in the Third World. The struggles for political independence, economic development, social democracy, and cultural identity have been clearly conducted in response to the center-periphery tensions both within and among nations.

As argued in Chapter One, the forces of transnationalization and homogenization of culture has been countered in the Third World by the drives towards democratization of politics and indigenization of culture. Traditional as well as modern media of communication have played a central part in these struggles. Whereas the big media (the national press, broadcasting, and the emerging mainframe computerized databases and communication) have largely served the purposes of the centers, the small media have opened up new channels for democratic participation at the peripheries. With the increasing introduction of transistor radios and cassettes, portable VCR equipment, and personal computers connected via modems into data and communication networks, the community media experiments by scattered groups of enthusiasts and idealists can turn into social movements. By the end of this decade, we may witness the synergy effects of the new technologies spreading to many parts of the world. However, for this to happen, strong linkages between the emerging technologies and democratic ideologies and institutions would have to come about. In the developing world, this also means linkages with the traditional patterns of culture and communication. Otherwise, one may consider the traditional Adowa funeral dance of the Ashanti tribes in Ghana far more participatory than the new electronic media introduced from above and conveying a stream of one-way, alien messages and metaphors.

9

Prospects for Communitarian Democracy

> We represent a total concept, as opposed to the one-dimensional, still-more-production brand of politics. Our politics are guided by long-term visions for the future and are founded on four basic principles: ecology, social responsibility, grassroots democracy, and non-violence.
>
> (From The Federal Program of the Green Party of West Germany, as quoted by Capra & Spretnak, 1984, p. 30)

> The 1950s, the period in which Sarvodaya Shramandana Movement was conceived and initiated, can be viewed as the heyday of blind imitation of western values, developmental goals, technologies and institutional forms by the elites of Sri Lanka who took over the administration of the country from the colonial powers. . . The few national leaders who stood for indigenous life-styles, spiritual and moral values, simplicity, culture, right livelihood, character building, and meditation as a learning process were ridiculed as chauvinists or religious fanatics. . . . From its inception, Sarvodaya has been motivated and inspired by this Buddhist solution to the problem of human suffering—dukkha. Sarvodaya perceived the need for a method of learning that would inculcate the value of sharing among human beings as a means of achieving freedom and happiness during one's present life, short and fragile as it is. Even though Sarvodaya's goal is to make this sharing universal, it recognizes that sharing begins at the grass-roots level, at the level where a human being is conceived in the mother's womb.
>
> (A. T. Ariyaratne, 1986, pp. 109–110)

This concluding chapter will begin with a brief examination of the theoretical origins of communitarian democracy as an ideal. It will then recapitulate our central thesis on the dual effects of the new information technologies and the contradictory prospects they hold for communitarian democracy. The chapter will go on to provide an analysis for those prospects at the centers and peripheries of the globe by focusing on two significant communitarian movements, that is, the Green Movement in West Germany and the Sarvodaya Movement in Sri Lanka. Finally, we will conclude by focusing attention more specifically on the necessary ingredients of communitarian media systems.

THE COMMUNITARIAN IDEALS

The ideals of communitarian democracy have deep historic roots, but the rise of communitarian democratic movements may be traced back in modern history only to the rise of industrial society. The onslaught of industrialization, wherever it has occurred and in whatever form, has dislocated the traditional community structures and values and has given rise to longings for a recapture of "the lost innocence," "the natural harmony," and "the noble savage" of the preindustrial society. This is the "romantic" side of a whole host of antimodernist movements in modern history. It is what might be considered as "the Rousseau Effect" of the early processes of industrialization when the social costs often far outweigh the social benefits (Tehranian, 1980a).

As a pioneering philosopher of communitarian democracy, Jean Jacques Rousseau began with the assumptions of innate human goodness and possibilities for freedom. In the ringing, opening passage of his classic work, *The Social Contract,* he boldly declared, "man was born free, but he is everywhere in chains" (1968, p. 49). As a first theorist of communitarianism, Rousseau put together both a devastating critique of the emerging industrial society in Europe as well as a plan for its reconstruction along more democratic and communitarian principles. His views and theories found their way into all subsequent revolutionary movements in Europe and North America. The utopian socialists in France and England, the Transcendentalists and Jeffersonians in the United States, and the Narodniks in Russia have each expressed their disillusionment with the institutions of modern industrial society by prescribing a return to nature, decentralized communities, and often communal modes of ownership and control of the means of social production and public communication. Rousseau's vision of an ideal community, born out of a social contract of free and equal citizens to enter a civil society, became the focal point of revolutionary theories and enthusiasms of the eighteenth and nineteenth centuries. But Rousseau's proposed vision was to retain the innate goodness, freedom, and equality of human conditions while substituting enlightened reason for the brute force and instinctual selfishness of the state of nature:

> The passing from the state of nature to the civil society produces a remarkable change in man; it puts justice as a rule of conduct in the place of instinct, and gives his actions the moral quality they previously lacked. It is only then, when the voice of duty has taken the place of physical impulse, and right that of desire, that man, who has hitherto thought only of himself, finds himself compelled to act on other principles, and to consult his reason rather than study his inclinations. And although in civil society man surrenders some of the advantages that belong to the state of nature, he gains in return far greater ones; his faculties are so exercised

and developed, his mind is so enlarged, his sentiments so ennobled, and his whole spirit so elevated that, if the abuse of his new condition did not in many cases lower him to something worse than what he had left, he should constantly bless the happy hour that lifted him for ever from the state of nature and from a narrow, stupid animal made a creature of intelligence and a man. (Rousseau, 1968, pp. 64–65)

Rousseau thus may be viewed as a revolutionary conservative. He is as devoted to recapturing the original state of human freedom as he is committed to the Reign of Reason. His way out of this dilemma is his theory of "the general will" (volonte generale) as opposed to "the will of all" (volonte de tous). The will of all is a kind of headcounting that necessitates delegation of authority and representative government. But Rousseau is fundamentally against any delegation of individual legislative responsibility. "If the general will is to be clearly expressed," writes Rousseau, "it is imperative that there should be no sectional associations in the state, and that every citizen should make up his own mind for himself" (1968, p. 73). And, earlier, he argues that "sovereignty, being nothing other than the exercise of the general will . . . cannot be represented by anyone but itself—power may be delegated, but the will cannot be" (1968, p. 69). As a realist, however, Rousseau recognizes that such exercise of the general will cannot be practically carried out in big states; his preference is thus for smallness. Rousseau's political thought thus encapsulates the three fundamental principles of contemporary communitarian movements: natural community, direct democracy, and small size.

If Rousseau in Europe and Thoreau in the United States are to be considered as the first theorists of communitarian democracy, de Tocqueville should be perhaps considered as its first serious critic. De Tocqueville's view of history, as exemplified by his study of democracy in America, considered "liberty" and "equality" as the two driving forces of modern history that inexorably push all modern societies towards democracy. But contrary to most theorists of democracy, de Tocqueville perceived an inherent conflict between the twin drives towards liberty and equality of conditions. He argued that modern democracies suffer from a peculiar pathology: In their search for security, most people would gleefully sacrifice liberty at the altar of equality. He called this phenomenon "the tyranny of the majority"—a tyranny more devastating than the traditional, monarchical tyrannies. This tyranny is sanctioned not by the will of a ruling tyrant or an oligarchy but by the vast majority of a conformist public. It thus penetrates and controls the remotest sectors of the population and the minutest forms of conduct. The historical phenomenon de Tocqueville had so well recognized and diagnosed has come to be known to us as modern totalitarianism.

But de Tocqueville failed to recognize a third and equally powerful force in modern history—the drive to community. Nevertheless, much of his critique of modern democracies should be considered a critique of how the desperate need for security and community can destroy the traditional civil liberties. Undermined by the dislocating and disequalizing effects of capitalist growth, modern societies have often been driven to mass movements based either on communist or communitarian (or populist) philosophies—promising either radical equality or pristine community. To the extent that capitalism has been able to fulfill the promises of equality and community through the welfare state or the communal bonds of religion, nationalism, or voluntary associations, capitalism has been able to withstand the communist or communal challenges. However, capitalism is normatively and structurally biased in favor of freedom and property. It cannot as successfully fulfill the democratic promises of equality and community. By contrast, communism is normatively and structurally biased in favor of equality and (party) elite domination. It cannot as successfully fulfill the democratic promises of liberty and community. Both systems tend to be highly centralized, elitist, and ultimately hierarchical.

In the less developed countries, however, where the experiences of colonialism and neocolonialism have often led to economic devastation as well as cultural depersonalization, the longing to recapture the lost natural community and indigenous institutions has been even more powerful. The search for community has thus overshadowed the principles of direct democracy and small size. Third world national liberation movements have been characterized by a mixture of modern (such as nationalism and Marxism) as well as indigenous, religious ideologies (such as Islam or Buddhism). The more powerful movements, such as the Gandhian movement in India or the Islamic revolutionary movement in Iran, have also relied heavily on the communitarian perspectives of the traditional ideologies to penetrate the mind and the soul of the masses. Thus, communitarian movements have sometimes led to the rise of theocracies, as in the case of the Calvinists in Geneva, the Puritans in New England, the Mormons in Utah, the Amish in Pennsylvania, and the Shi'a clerics in Iran. These movements have sometimes been based on direct democracy (as in the New England Town Meetings), but with the growth of the size of the community, they have increasingly become characterized by central, authoritarian control.

Like liberal and communist democracies, communitarian democracy also has its progressive as well as reactionary tendencies. Its ideals, as the ideals of any other social movement, can be corrupted into their very opposite. The potentials for totalitarian formations are no less powerful in communitarian movements as they are under capitalism or communism. Nevertheless, the critiques of industrial society presented by some of the current communitarian democratic movements present some of the most penetrating and progressive perspectives and possibilities politically alive today. Communitarian negation of the other two dominant world systems, capitalism and communism, could be considered on the whole as a positive democratic force on the world scene today.

TECHNOLOGIES OF DEMOCRATIC POSSIBILITY

We have argued throughout this volume, that technologies in general and information technologies in particular are neither good nor evil— nor neutral! Technologies are powerful tools inextricably tied to the structures of power and domination in society. Their impact on society is mediated through social structures and social relations. In the particular case of information technologies, the dual-effects hypothesis comes perhaps closest to the mark in that it recognizes both the centralizing and dispersive effects of the modern media on the structures of power. The burden of social and political analysis is thus to begin with those structures before moving on to an analysis of the impact of the technologies on society and polity. This analysis has to be historically situated and culturally specific to be relevant; valid generalizations on the effects of the media can arise only after considerable and careful comparative studies and analyses.

I have called this theoretical position "technostructuralism" and "symbolic structuralism" in order to emphasize the interdependency of technologies and social structures and of the ideal and material in social formations. Others have called it the critical or structuralist approach.[1] In order to be better understood, this approach should be contrasted to what Jennifer Slack (1987) has called the "mechanistic" and "expressive" perspectives on the relations between technology and society. The *mechanistic* view is rooted in a long tradition of Cartesian analysis of causality in Western thought. In this perspective, technology is considered as "the cause" whose effects can be studied in a series of linear causations in the economic, political, cultural, or personal spheres of life. In this perspective, technology tends to be viewed as central, autonomous, and ultimately decisive in social formations. The technological determinism of this perspective remains implicit in most of the literature on media technology and society, but in the works of such mediacentric authors as Marshall McLuhan it assumes a rather explicit statement.

By contrast, the *expressive* views consider technology as a total social

---

[1] For a thoughtful review of the different theoretical approaches to the impact of communication technologies, see Slack (1987).

system that encompasses all forms of thought and behavior. Lewis Mumford (1962) and Jacques Ellul (1983), for example, tend to view the social impact of technology in sweeping, all-encompassing terms such as "mechanical civilization" or "technological system." In this perspective, all causality is internal to the whole. The technological *weltanschauung* thus permeates all manifestations of social life. Both views, the mechanistic as well as the expressive, tend to be technologically determinist perspectives. There are, however, two basic differences between them with respect to their views of causality and normative preferences. While the mechanistic view has a linear view of causality, the expressive perspective offers a holistic and multilinear model. While the mechanistic view tends to be technophilic, the expressive school is technophobic.

The technostructuralist and critical perspectives begin with a normative perspective that sees technology per se as neither good nor evil but rather as another manifestation of the social structure, including its coherence as well as its contradictions. In the technostructuralist view, technologies are both causes and effects. Whereas in the mechanistic view the origins of technology are not problematized, and in the expressive view Technology (spelled with capital T) is perceived as a dominating and all-encompassing *weltanschauung* of the modern world, in the technostructuralist view, technologies (note the plural) provide commodities among many other commodities. As extensions of our senses (to use McLuhan's apt phrase) and as leverages of power, however, technologies replicate as well as augment the existing power relations. For this reason, in the critical school, the origins, development, and applications of technologies are systematically problematized. Instead of assuming a psychological and atomistic approach to the uses and gratifications of technologies, the technostructuralist perspective adopts a sociological perspective in order to view the role of technologies in their socioeconomic-political contexts.

Despite this seeming subordination of technologies to social formations, it should still be possible to speak of the counterintuitive effects of technologies. The technostructuralist view, perhaps in contrast to a purely structuralist view, considers contradictory effects of technologies as possible. That is fundamentally because it views the social structure not as a uniform monolith but as contradiction-prone and constantly changing. Anthony Giddens (1984) has employed the notion of "structuration" to suggest that social structures themselves should be considered in terms of the processes of social change. That is why information technologies that often have their origins in military uses end up having far-reaching civilian uses and sometime antisystemic effects. The technology of radio broadcasting, for example, originated in naval communications and soon came to be employed as a powerful medium of mass communication for commercial advertising and subsequently as a social revolutionary tool for reaching the illiterate masses. In other words, once a given technology reaches the marketplace, its applications are deeply intertwined with the contradictions of the social structures of which it is a part. From a technostructuralist view, it is neither the technology nor the social structure that is central. It is rather the nature of the dialectical relations between the two in historically specific situations that should become the focus of analysis.

There is ample evidence to suggest that modern information technologies have already made considerable impact on both democratic as well as totalitarian formations. The origins of modern liberal democracy can be traced back in part to the impact of the print technologies on democratization of knowledge and the dispersion of information and power. But the modern print and electronic media can be argued to have also been in part responsible for the rise of all forms of modern bureaucratic domination, from the state apparatus to the modern transnational corporation. Large state and business bureaucracies have centralized power and information to unprecedented degrees. The modern census bureaus and their statistics (note that the etymology of the word "statistics" relates to the state) have created for the state modern information gathering, storage, and retrieval systems about the citizens and their minutest identities and activities. In the same fashion, the market pricing system (including the stock exchange markets) has created an information gathering, storage, and retrieval system for the modern corporation without which it cannot operate. Information technologies, from print to the online date bases, have only augmented the speed, accuracy and efficiency of such new tools of power.

With the introduction of the new interactive media, however, the dual-effects hypothesis takes on new and ominous dimensions. Possibilities for democratization as well as for totalitarianization of power increase by leaps and bounds—an increase in quantities nearly amounting to a change in qualities of mind and behavior control. The democratic promises of the new technologies are vast and still largely unexplored. If democracy is considered government by dialogue, the new technologies have turned the theoretical possibility of direct democracy and democratic will formation into a real opportunity. The new technologies have contributed to the communitarian democratic potentials in the following three specific ways:

First, the new technologies are rapidly transforming an era of scarcity into an era of abundance in channels of communication. The increase in channels may be considered under increases in two types of resources— natural and man-made. The three most important natural resources for technologically-mediated communication consist of woodpulp, the electromagnetic spectrum, and the geostationary orbit. The production of trees, woodpulp, and paper has dramatically increased in the last century or so by increases in the efficiency and scale of paper production. Although the same cannot be said of the electromagnetic spectrum and geostationary orbit, which are both relatively fixed natural resources, the electronic channels of communication derived from both have dramatically increased by technological improvements—by employing more radio frequencies and achieving a higher level of efficiency in the use of the geostationary orbit. But the most dramatic increases in channels of communication have taken place primarily as a result of the invention of new man-made resources, including broadband cable, satellites, computers, fiber optics, robotics, photonics, and a variety of increasingly more miniaturized, speedy, and efficient (i.e., less distorted and costly) channels of communication. The new channels of communication have thus become more accessible and more universal. It is necessary, however, to remind ourselves that despite the dramatic increases in channel capacity, media distribution still remains lopsided. About 90 percent of the media in world communication are in the hands of approximately 10 percent of the world population living in Western Europe, North America, and Japan.

Second, the new information technologies have ushered in a new era of telecommunication characterized by a transition from broadcasting to narrowcasting. Some media critics have viewed this development with alarm. Richard M. Neustadt, President Jimmy Carter's policy adviser, has argued that today's nationwide news broadcasting, for all its superficiality, provides "a homogenous information base for the most diverse society in the West." But this homogeneity is now under threat from narrowcasting: (Neustadt as quoted by Qvortrup 1984, pp. 108–109)

Some channels will provide only news about their particular themes, and many—such as the movie and sports networks—will offer no news at all. Narrowcasting may fragment Americans' perception of events, and the vast menu of entertainment channels may draw some people away from the news altogether. An electorate awash in video information may end up less informed. One result is that when the president goes on television in 1990, he may be carried on six networks, but he will not be on two dozen others. For the first time since F.D.R.'s fireside chats, the mass audience that presidents have automatically commanded will begin to erode. . .

BizNet will use satellite to broadcast six hours per day of business news, interviews, and—of course—lobbying messages, directly to receivers placed at corporate headquarters around the country. The Chamber has spent $5 million on studios and will spend several millions more each year to run the operation. . . . The new technology will touch off a new scramble for money to buy teleconferencing studios, satellite transmitters, and fancy computers, and only the well-heeled interest groups will have the money to use all the new machines. Few liberal groups can match BizNet's millions.

Under the commercial media systems, the closing of the public sphere has thus become a reality no less tangible than the heavy hand of the government censors. But the potentials for democratic uses of the new technologies are begging for attention. These potentials may be considered under narrowcasting's three distinct democratic features: pluralism, access, and interactivity. In place of broadcasting's homogenizing effects, narrowcasting differentiates and pluralizes the audiences. Direct television coverage of the U. S. congress on C-SPAN and local coverage of City Councils would have been impossible without increases in cable channel capacity and the accommodation of pluralistic audiences, but the Playboy and MTV channels also provide differentiated products to a differentiated audience. Cable's "public access channels" provide opportunities for local, ethnic, cultural, and political groups to produce their own programs and to organize campaigns. Finally, audio, video, and computer teleconferencing add interactivity to our telecommunication systems that have been for long characterized by one-way channels of mass and undifferentiated public communication.

Third, and perhaps most significantly, the new information technologies are making horizontal as distinct from vertical communication increasingly possible. Mass communication by its very nature and technology tends to be heavily centralized, bureaucratized, and manipulative. It therefore lends itself magnificently to the purposes and designs of the modern bureaucratic state and corporation. It expands and penetrates the channels of public communication to the remotest regions and populations. But this additional capacity is one-way. It carries messages from the centers to the peripheries without much feedback. It is vertical communication to the utmost. Horizontal communication requires technological networks that connect a complex web of nodes to each other without the interference of the centers. With the convergence of telephony, broadband cable, and computers, such a technological communication system has become a partial reality. However, as we have seen in the Qube system in Ohio, the new technological networks can be employed in electoral polling and citizen participation to advance primarily commercial advantage. They also hold the potential to snoop on the citizens. Their democratic uses are, at present, largely conspicuous by their absence.

In the face of the immense possibilities of the new information technologies for democratic participation, their conspicuous lack of use calls for an explanation. Traditional telecommunication structures are either state or commercial or "publicly" controlled. Even if democratizing experiments with the new information technologies are allowed to be conducted, they are often conducted under the severest of budgetary and political restrictions. Technological possibilities divorced from social movements thus play at best a neutral or, at worst, an antidemocratic role. To turn these technological possibilities into democratic social realities, it would take democratic social movements and enthusiasms. However, technologies have to be understood and mastered before they can be exploited for the purposes of progressive social movements. The following two examples of communitarian democratic movements in Europe and Asia demonstrate some of the problems that, in this respect, are faced by the democratic movements.

THE GREEN MOVEMENT IN WEST GERMANY

The Green Party in West Germany provides one of the best known and most successful efforts in communitarian politics in Western democracies. For this reason, it also provides a model for the understanding of the strengths and weaknesses of the communitarian democratic movements elsewhere. Moreover, the movement presents a model for the role of communication technologies in the struggle for democracy.

Who are the Greens?[2] Known as *Die Grunen*, the Greens may be considered as an antiparty party in German politics. The Green Party was officially established in 1979. The Green movement, however, has a longer history. It has grown out of the postwar ecological and nuclear crises in which liberal and Marxist politics have failed to reduce the mounting threats to human survival. These movements, spread throughout the Western world, gained some momentum during the 1960s. In the United States, they came to be known as the "counterculture" movement or the Flower Revolution, combining the anti-Vietnam War, black civil rights, and student and feminist movements. In Western Europe, where the ecological and nuclear threats have been more keenly felt, they turned into massive student revolts that culminated in the events of 1968 in France and Germany. The student revolts of 1968 throughout the United States and Western Europe served as the symbolic peaks of that movement. Subsequently, the establishment par-

---

[2] For a general introduction to the Greens, see Porritt (1985). For introductions to the Green movement in Germany, see Capra & Spretnak (1984) and Langguth (1986), providing two sympathetic and critical perspectives.

ties in Western democracies adopted some of the postures and positions of the peace, ecology, and civil rights movements. In the meantime, the generation of students that grew up as activists during the 1960s had graduated.

The reemergence of the Greens in the late 1970s and early 1980s as a party of peace and ecology may thus be interpreted as the political contribution of the flower children of the 1960s. Peter Berger (1973) has called this phenomenon "the Soft Revolution." A postwar generation of middle- and upper-middle-class children in the advanced industrial countries, raised up in relative comfort and inculcated in high democratic ideals, have found the impersonal and anonymous machineries of the modern bureaucratic state and corporation intolerable. Their demand for humane politics is thus a desperate cry for a stop to the kind of policies that have brought about postwar "peace and prosperity" at the cost of ecological disasters, nuclear threats, social injustice at home, and imperialist wars in the Third World (Korea, Vietnam, Algeria, the Middle East, Africa, and Central America). These wars have already claimed some 17 million lives in an era of postwar "peace." Insofar as the issues of social justice have generally taken a back seat to the issues of ecology and peace, Green politics reveals its middle-class origins and biases. But in some circumstances, such as those in the United States, the alliance between the blacks and a nascent Green movement have also produced Martin Luther King's nonviolent civil rights movement and Jesse Jackson's Rainbow Coalition. Both of these efforts represent coalition politics, in which the communitarian concerns of the whites for peace and ecology have converged with the blacks' more urgent agenda of civil rights, social justice, and gainful employment.

The Greens in Germany have achieved a degree of electoral success and visibility that has eluded communitarian movements elsewhere. The founding convention of the Green Party of West Germany was held in March 1979. In the parliamentary elections of the same year, the Greens won a stunning 3.2 percent of the votes—short of the minimum 5 percent necessary for parliamentary representation. The first Constitutional Convention was held in 1980. But in the national elections of the same year, the Greens lost some ground by obtaining only 1.5 percent of the vote. This may be partly due to the fact that communists had decided by this time to join the Greens. In the mind of the electorate, this created a confusion about the true political identity of the Greens. The tension between the Marxist Greens and the Ecological Greens is a continuing one. But in the parliamentary elections of 1983, the Greens managed to obtain 5.6 percent of the vote, which admitted them to the Bundestag. In the elections of the European Parliament, the Greens received over 2 million votes or 8.2 percent of the total votes cast, and as a result they sent seven members to that body. In 1987, the Greens gained further ground by obtaining 8.3 percent of the national vote. In this election, the Greens picked up about one million votes more than they did four years ago, mostly perhaps at the expense of the Social Democrats (see Figure 9.1.). Langguth (1986, p. 113), a critical observer of the Greens, estimates that the Party has a voter potential of approximately 9 percent where it would stabilize. Most Greens do not envision themselves as a majority party; some consider themselves as a small "teaching party" of about 8 to 10 percent (Capra, 1984, p. 161).

The rapid emergence of the Greens as a political party has had its splintering effects. In addition to the tensions between Marxists and ecologists, the Greens also are divided between a "realistic" wing which favors some sort of link with the Social Democratic Party and the "fundamentalists" who do not. This division is expected to become deeper as the party grows bigger and more well-established. An older anecdote about the Greens was that they are like tomatoes: green at the outset but red as they mature! The newer anecdote goes like this: two Greens, two opinions! The wages of success are the divisions about the spoils and possible compromises on principles.

What do the Greens stand for? What unites the Greens of whatever persuasion are the four fundamental principles enunciated in their federal program: ecology, nonviolence, social responsibility, and participatory democracy. Decentralization has also been mentioned in some

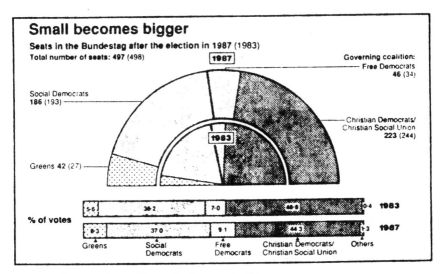

Figure 9.1.   The Green Factor in German Politics
Source: The Economist, January 31, 1987, p. 42.

Green documents as a possible fifth principle. But all of these slogans are subject to a variety of different interpretations, and that is where the division of opinion and factionalism begin. To understand these divisions and their ramifications, we must look at each principle in greater detail.

First, ecology stands as the central, unifying principle in the Green political philosophy. That is also where the Greens have made their profoundest impact on German public opinion and politics. An EMNID Institute poll of August 1984 gave the Greens 40 percent of popular approval on this issue as opposed to 15 percent for the Christian Democratic Union/Christian Social Union (CDU/CSU) and only 11 percent for the Social Democratic Party (SPD) (Langguth, 1986, 62). What had started initially as a series of citizen initiatives on ecological problems in the early 1970s turned into a full-fledged ecology party by the early 1980s. In the meantime, German consciousness of the ecological questions had grown from a fear of radioactivity from nuclear power plants to an increasing concern with ecological catastrophes, including transformation of landscapes into cement highways, toxification of the soil, chemical pollution of the environment, problems of waste disposal, endangering of plants and animals, presence of dangerous pollutants in factories and offices, and acid rains destroying entire forests.

In view of some Green leaders, however, the issues of ecology cut deeper than simple environmental protection policies; they demand a fundamental change of perspective from the limitless growth ideologies of industrialism to a perspective that considers the Planet Earth as sacred and inviolable. In the words of Petra Kelly, as quoted by Capra (1984, 55):

> The spiritual content of Green politics—which unfortunately is not expressed, and is almost opposed, in the party structure—means understanding how everything is connected and understanding your relationship with planet Earth in daily life. We've become so divorced from our ties with the Earth that most people don't even understand what the Greens are fighting for. With the holistic sense of spirituality, one's personal life is truly political and one's political life is truly personal. Anyone who does not comprehend within him- or herself this essential unity cannot achieve political change on a deep level and cannot strive for the true ideals of the Greens.

Second, peace as a principle has also produced a variety of interpretations. The federal program defines peace and nonviolence as follows (Langguth, 1986, p. 78):

We seek a nonviolent society in which the suppression of humans by humans and the use of force by humans against humans has ended. Our highest principle states that humane goals cannot be achieved by inhumane methods . . . the principle of nonviolence does not exclude the fundamental right of self-defense nor social resistance, nor imply passive behavior by its victims. The principle of nonviolence, on the contrary, holds that human beings may defend their vital interests against an authoritarian power structure. Under certain circumstances this might not only legitimate resistance to the demands of the state but make such resistance—e.g., sit-down strikes, road blocks, blocks of vehicular traffic—a necessity.

This clearly places the Greens in the same league as Thoreau on civil disobedience and Gandhi on nonviolent resistance. However, when applied to such a practical policy as the NATO, two distinctly different positions seem to have evolved. These may be called the "unilateralist" and "bilateralist" approaches. In their program, the Greens favor the dissolution of both NATO and the Warsaw Pact. While some Greens are willing to go ahead unilaterally and pull West Germany out of NATO immediately, others prefer a negotiated settlement that gradually achieves the aim of dissolution of military blocs in Europe.

Third, social responsibility covers an even wider gamut of issues and positions. These issues begin with the problems of restructuring the capitalist economy to social, cultural, and communication problems in modern, industrial societies. Decentralization looms large in most of the Green perspectives on these issues. In the words of Joachim Muller, a Green economist and a Bundestag member:

> Expropriation, as Marx demanded it, necessarily implies centralization. But the Green principle is decentrality. For me this is a decisive point, because it is well known that smaller entities are more easily subject to democratic control. This thesis is simply true. This is why we say: no expropriation and central planning, for heaven's sake! Rather, wherever possible, create something like community property. . . .
> The decisive entity in our society has to be, from the perspective of our politics, not the federal government but the traditional notion of community. This could be the traditional Christian community or in a different manifestation, the commune. For us it is interesting that where the connection between life and work is concrete—which is in the community— there and only there do processes of change occur on a long-term basis. This is where consciousness is formed, where learning takes place, where people live together, where people live together, where conflicts arise; and it is here that human beings are really affected.
> (As quoted by Capra & Spretnack, 1984, pp. 100–101)

Social responsibility also means a reorienting of the present capitalist economies from their growth mania towards ecologically and socially responsible strategies of development. As the Economic Program of the Greens argues:

> In 1950, 1 percent growth meant increased goods with a value of 1.9 billion DM. Today 1 percent growth brings with it additional products with a value of 9 billion DM. To cure unemployment by means of growth—a method rejected by the Greens—would require a growth rate of 6 percent per year. This would mean that in ten years we would have to produce and consume twice as much per year as we do now: Twice as many cars, refrigerators, televisions, machines, concrete, nuclear power plants, tanks, cheeseburgers, psychiatric megaclinics, artificial fertilizers, etc. It requires only common sense to see that it is neither possible nor admissible to take this course.
>
> The restructuring of economic conditions includes a change in the totally unequal and unjust conditions of income and wealth in our society. A social redistribution of generated values and income, however, must also be applied on a global basis and must become one of the standards of conduct in our relationship with the Third World.
> (As quoted by Capra & Spretnack, 1984, pp. 89–90, 101)

Green perspectives on social issues encompass some important cultural and communication issues as well. Rudolf Bahro, another Green leader, calls for a cultural revolution not unlike the one Petra Kelly has argued for:

> I am interested in the forces for cultural revolution that lie, in no small way, in Christ, Buddha, and Lao Tzu. Forces that have made history. We need the gnostic tradition—as one aspect, not to fill the whole of life. I have long been drawn to such thinkers as Joachim di Fiore, Meister Eckhart, Spinoza and Pascal on account of the affinity of their mysticism to real freedom of the spirit. I recently read that someone discovered a mystical experience of the young Marx, which would then be analogous to Luther's experience in the tower. I can well see this as possible. Taken realistically, mysticism, at least clear-headed mysticism, means a profound mobilization of emancipatory forces in the human psyche, a phenomenon that has nothing otherworldly about it, and should be made accessible to everyone, for example by the practice of meditation.
> (as quoted by Capra & Spretnack, 1984, p. 56)

The communication concerns of the Greens are focused primarily on the invasions of privacy and freedom that the new information technologies may bring forth. As Capra and Spretnack report (1984, pp. 114–115):

In the spring of 1983 a citizens' movement arose to stop the proposed national census on the ground that the information would be centralized in a "Big Brother" computer file—either within the national police data bank in Karlsruhe, which was supposed to be only for criminals, or in a similar system. The Greens brought the citizens' protest into the Bundestag by introducing a bill to halt the census, and they worked with attorneys who were bringing a suit with the same aim in federal court. As a result, the census was suspended by a court decision in late 1983. The Greens also joined the fight against proposed government-issued, computerized identification cards.

Like some lawmakers in the United States, the Greens are extremely wary of the computer files about one's personal life that will accumulate when—it hardly seems a matter of "if" any more—two-way interactive cable television comes into the home bringing not only selected programs and movies but also certain newspapers—via teletext—and the means for shopping and business transactions—*and* keeps a record of everyone's selections for billing. In 1982, the American Civil Liberties Union, working with the League of California Cities, several city governments, and the cable industry's own organization, the California Cable Television Association, supported a landmark piece of legislation designed to outlaw all invasions of privacy via two-way cable. The bill was introduced in the state assembly by Gwen Moore [D—Los Angeles] and passed in September. It states that a customer's order file may not be released to private or government agencies except under court order, subpoena, or other "legal compulsion," in which case the cable company must notify the subscriber. The Greens, like many Americans, view such safeguards as frail protection once the personal files are established. Their main focus at this time is to require the new cable industry in West Germany to offer one-way cable service in addition to the two-way interactive service the industry is pushing, which would even incorporate one's telephone.

This report suggests a defensive attitude on the part of the Greens towards the new information technologies without considering their democratizing potentials. But the Greens' greatest and perhaps most controversial ideas focus on grass-roots politics and participatory democracy that imply a new public communication system.

Fourth, participatory democracy presents perhaps the Green's most controversial principle. The Green's advocacy of participatory, grassroots, and direct democracy begins with a critique of representative democratic institutions. Despite its apparent efficiency, the Greens suggest, representative democracy has been corrupted into its opposite— unrepresentative bureaucracy. In the passionate words of Petra Kelly (1984, pp. 21–22):

Parliaments have proved themselves incapable of responding to the demands of local action groups. . . All three parties currently represented in the West German parliament—*Bundestag*—have allowed their social democratic, Christian and liberal intentions to disappear into thin air. What they have in common is a hierarchical structure making spontaneous, committed action impossible, so that politically meaningful decisions are only taken at the top and party democracy exists in name only. . .

After years of arduous, detailed work in the committees and working groups of these parties, many of us were driven to despair because, when it finally came to a decision, the party bureaucrats had it all their own way every time. Many established politicians claim that the Greens are drop-outs. Quite the reverse—we have stepped into the system in order to change it. The real drop-outs are the career politicians who have deserted their original professions to work their way up the party career ladder. With their secure incomes behind them, they can deliver themselves of sound advice to working on how savings can be made to pay for yesterday's latest American missile horror.

Thus it can be seen that whole sectors of the population are not represented in parliament, nor elected to it. Representing their interests will only be the first step. Direct democracy means that we will fight for real influence for the people ignored by government.

Under the rubrics of participatory democracy, the Greens are thus calling for deprofessionalization of politics, direct democracy, and dialogic communication. The Greens do not reject parliamentary democracy; they propose to correct it. The political and communication methods by which the Greens have achieved some of their ideals in this respect are rather ingenious but somewhat controversial. Three methods are of particular importance: decentralized party structure, office rotation, and open communication. The structure of the Green Party is designed to prevent, or at least to discourage, professionalization and concentration of power.[3] The Green Federal Program is quite explicit about this: "The new party organization [aims at] permanent control of all office holders, representatives and institutions by the membership-at-large and its policies transparent to all and to counter the ability of individuals to act on their own volition" (as quoted by Langguth, 1986, p. 71). To achieve this objective, the Greens have devised a complex party structure in which the base of the pyramid directs the upper levels while there is no apex embodied in one leader. The Party is administered by two committees—the national executive committee and the national steering committee. The national assembly, at which key issues are voted on, elects the three party speakers as well as the national executive committee. This party structure has worked rather smoothly

---

[3] For a detailed description of that structure, see Appendix A of Capra and Spretnak (1984).

except in one respect. Relations between the 11-person national steering committee and the 27 parliamentarians have gradually become rather strained.

This strain is deeply rooted in the Greens' distrust of all forms of representation that takes authority away from the grass roots. The method of rotation of office is the mechanism by which the Greens have tried to deal with this problem. Wary of "the iron law of oligarchy," as expounded by Robert Michels as early as 1911, the Greens are hoping that a mandatory rotation of officers would prevent the kind of bureaucratic concentrations of power which characterize all modern bureaucracies— including the supposedly revolutionary and democratic political parties. In practice, however, rotation has proved to be a difficult and controversial policy. The midterm rotation of the first Green Bundestag members was an important turning point for the party. Nearly all Green representatives left the Bundestag in March 1985, and gave way to their successors. There were important exceptions, however. Several members, including Petra Kelly, refused to step down on the grounds that "the departure of only two additional members from the parliamentary caucus would endanger the group's recognition as an independent faction and jeopardize numerous financial and parliamentary perquisites. Kelly declared that she would not leave the caucus but would not again be available as a candidate for office (Langguth, 1986, p. 18). Others, such as Wolf-Dieter Hasenclever, have raised some more fundamental issues: "As far as I am concerned," he stated, "the lack of trust disguised by arguments about participatory democracy is nothing more than a dog-in-the-manger attitude" (Langguth, 1986, p. 73).

This "distrust" of power spills over into a distrust of charismatic leaders. Those representatives who are able to obtain favorable or effective media coverage are often accused of being status-hungry. Petra Kelly was, for a while, the target of much of this criticism. Bottom-up and horizontal communication rather than top-down and vertical communication thus presents the Green ideals for an open and dialogic public communication system. Like most enthusiastic movements, the Greens have shown considerable ingenuity and success in this respect. The German electoral system has also helped them to cover the costs of media campaigns much more effectively than their rival parties. West German law provides that a political party shall be paid 3.5 DM (about $1.40) for every vote received in a state or federal election. The major parties conduct expensive campaigns with large paid staffs and so usually incur debts in elections. The Greens, on the other hand, use volunteer workers and typically earn four times more than they spend in elections. The major parties report to the public only infrequently, often just before an election. The Greens are committed to relaying privileged information that usually does not get outside the corridors of power. The Greens have thus become skilled communicators. All levels of the party produce a flood of printed material—on recycled paper, they hasten to add. Their communication strategy seems to consist of three parts: distributing printed materials, working with citizens's movements, and producing a few brief ads for electronic media (Capra & Spretnak, 1984, pp. 127–131).

What are the Greens' prospects? Trend-Radar, a West German research group, has concluded that "there is a greater than 50 percent probability that the Greens will become a well-established party in the Bundestag, a less than 50 percent probability that they will remain largely extra-parliamentary, and less than 30 percent probability that they will soon dissolve" (Capra & Spretnak, 1984, p. 160). Considering their expanding electoral victory in 1987, which gained them 8.3 percent of the votes and 42 representatives in the Bundestag, the Greens seem to have achieved a well-established position in West German politics. In the light of current controversies within the party, however, four scenarios present themselves: cooptation, ineffectiveness, radicalization, and government responsibility.

The co-optation scenario is the one more or less advocated by those Green ecoliberals who argue for a coalition with the Social Democrats. Both major political parties, the Social Democrats and the Christian Democrats, have lost their absolute majorities in the Bundestag. They are consequently in need of coalition partners to form the government. Collaboration between the Greens and the Social Democrats has already been achieved at the state level in Hamburg and Hesse. But it has proved difficult and divisive. The Realist Greens would like eventually to enter into partnership with the social Democrats in the formation of the government, but the Fundamentalist Greens point to the necessary compromises of coalition politics to argue against it.

The ineffectiveness scenario could occur if the Greens continue to split among themselves and achieve nothing more than a negative voice in German politics. But four years of parliamentary experience has shown the Greens to be anything but ineffective so far. Despite their small size, the Greens have often proposed half of the bills and "applications," that is, oral declarations, of a legislative session. They have also posed the greatest number of questions to the government—a third form of parliamentary intervention in the Bundestag. One of the favorite Green tactics is to draw public attention to particular issues by holding public hearings on the budget to which numerous citizens' groups and the media are invited. Through their parliamentary interventions and public communication activities, the Greens have thus left an indelible mark on the German public opinion and beyond.

The radicalization scenario has been inherent in the Green movement ever since its inception, but it can take either of two forms. The Marxist Greens, known as Group Z, tend to focus primarily on class struggle. They see parliament primarily as an instrument, a platform for new social, extraparliamentary movements. However, such views of parliamentary democracy as expressed by Gertrud Schilling ("It is the goal of the Greens to do away with parliament and to practice direct democracy") stand in sharp contrast to the more orthodox view express by Petra Kelly ("We do not exist to do away with parliament. We do want to make parliamentary democracy more trustworthy and more transparent. The Greens want to alter the existing parliaments") (Langguth, 1986, p. 70). On the other hand, radicalization could go the way of the Fundamentalist Greens whose primary focus is on an uncompromising ecology and peace platform rather than class struggle. The two radical groups sometimes merge but they also have distinct identities. Despite the difficulties of making sharp distinctions, Langguth (1986, pp. 58–61) has identified four ideological tendencies and groups within the Green movement that he calls "the red-Greens," the "Green-red realists," the reform ecologists and the fundamentalist oppositionists.

The final scenario, that of a Green government, has not been seriously contemplated by most of the Greens or the literature on the subject. But what if. . . ? What if the Greens grow beyond their wildest imagination into the position of a major party? Their platform can no longer assume the utopian features of an oppositionist group; it would have to take up the realistic tasks of a party that is actually or potentially in charge of the government of a major, industrial power in the world. Can the complex apparatus of an industrial system be dismantled or fundamentally restructured without shock waves in Germany and elsewhere? What would a communitarian government in power look like as opposed to a communitarian movement in opposition? These are intriguing questions to which there are no ready replies.

In the meantime, the profile of the Green voters suggests mostly the politics of reform and not of revolution. Langguth has shown that most Green voters are men rather than women, single rather than married, Protestant rather than Catholic, urban rather than rural, students rather than gainfully employed, white collar rather than blue collar workers, highly educated and of middle- and upper-middle-class origins. "In 1980, 51 per cent of the Greens held at least a secondary school diploma; in 1984, 43 percent. This compares with 13 percent for the CDU, 11 percent for the SPD, and 36 percent for the FDP. Seventy-one percent of the Green voters are members of the middle or upper middle class as compared with 64 percent of the total population" (Langguth, 1986, p. 31).

THE SARVODAYA MOVEMENT IN SRI LANKA

In the communitarian movements of the West, religion and spiritual concerns often play a muted and apologetic role. By contrast, communitarian movements in the Third World place religion and the spiritual life at the very center of their philosophy and program. One of the most fascinating movements of this kind can be found in Sri Lanka. Whereas the Green movement in West Germany primarily focuses on grass-root politics and participatory democracy, the Sarvodaya Shramadana movement in Sri Lanka is primarily concerned with a revival of Buddhism and its teachings for fostering social and economic development. Despite these differences of focus, stemming from differences in stages of material development of the two countries, at a more profound level the two movements share common perspectives on ecology, nonviolence, social responsibility, participatory democracy, and dialogical communication. Both movements owe their success largely to their genius in adapting some of the same communitarian principles and precepts to their own unique cultural and political environments.

In the words of the movement's founder, A. T. Ariyaratne, "Sarvodaya signifies the awakening or liberation of *one and all,* without exception, *Save sata sukhi hontu,* 'May all beings be well and happy,' is the Buddhist wish, in contrast to the Hegelian concept of the welfare of the majority" (Macy, 1983, p. 13). This is also sharply in contrast to the liberal, utilitarian principle of "the greatest happiness of the greatest number," as expounded by Jeremy Bentham and his followers. In this fashion, the Sarvodaya movement sets itself sharply apart from Marxism and Liberalism—the two contemporary, dominant and secular ideologies of development. The second appellation of the movement, *Shramadana,* means "sharing labor" and refers to the village work camps that sponsor the movement's community development projects. The movement has thus a twofold purpose, to awaken community consciousness and to share labor in community projects.

Although the movement's philosophy is steeped in Buddhism, its more recent origins can be traced back to both East and West—to Gandhi as well as to the Quaker work camps of the postwar era in Europe. Inspired by the church-sponsored, youth work camps in the reconstruction of Europe, the first Shramadanas were organized in 1958 and 1959. D. A. Abeysekere and A. T. Ariyaratne collaborated in modeling their first "holiday work camps" in Sri Lanka after them. But Gandhi's philosophy of Satyagraha (truth seeking) and nonviolence was another equally important source of inspiration. Through his firsthand experiences with Vinoba Bhave, Gandhi's spiritual successor in India,

Ariyaratne had come to recognize that the noblest of ideas cannot serve the people unless they are reincarnated in the indigenous cultural tradition.

That is how Sinhalese Buddhism informs the Sarvodaya movement. Sarvodaya's philosophy begins with Buddha's Four Noble Truths: (a) that there is human suffering (dukkha) in the world; (b) that this suffering is caused by human craving (tanha) and greed (lobbha); (c) that this craving and suffering can indeed cease; and (d) that there is a Middle Path to follow for human enlightenment and happiness. This Middle Path or the Noble Eightfold Path consists of Right Understanding, Right Intention, Right Speech, Right Action, Right Livelihood, Right Effort, Right Mindfulness, and Right Concentration. This philosophy has been transformed by the Sarvodaya movement into a theory of development born out of its own practices. Figure 9.2 presents the essentials of this theory in terms of the Four Noble Truths as (a) a pathology of the sufferings of underdevelopment; (b) a diagnosis of the appetites and cravings as its root causes; (c) the promises of healthy development; and (d) a strategy for achieving it.

Since its inception in 1958, the growth of the Sarvodaya movement has been quite remarkable. A movement that had begun in 1958 from a small number of privileged high school students, within a decade had expanded into a national movement. Initially organized as "holiday work camps" to render service to destitute outcast villages, Ariyaratne initiated the Hundred Villages Development Scheme in 1968. Within the next 10 years, the movement had spread to 2,000 villages. In the following three years, it had reached over 4,000. In 1985, the movement was active in more than 7,000 village communities and involved over 2.5 million people. By 1990, the goal of the movement is to reach 12,000 villages and 7 million people. This is about half the population of Sri Lanka (Ariyaratne, 1986, p. 108).

Sri Lanka is one of the smallest and materially poorest countries in the Third World. It has, however, one of the proudest and richest cultural traditions. Before European colonization, this "pearl of the Indian Ocean" was also called the "Isle of Righteousness" and the "Granary of the East." But the country was ravaged by four centuries of colonialism under the Portuguese, the Dutch, and the British before it gained its independence in 1948. Despite its low per capita income ($130 per annum), rural population (80 percent), dependence on commodity cash crops (70 percent of GNP), and vulnerability to the international markets for its exports, the country enjoys relatively high rates of literacy and life expectancy and relatively low-income gaps between the rich and poor. "These factors, rated in the Physical Quality of Life Index as devised by

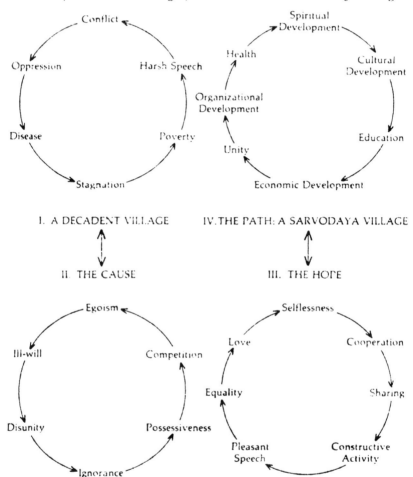

The Dependent Co-Arising of a Decadent and a Sarvodaya Village

I. A DECADENT VILLAGE   IV. THE PATH: A SARVODAYA VILLAGE

II. THE CAUSE   III. THE HOPE

Figure 9.2. The Four Noble Truths of Village Awakening

Source: Macy, 1983, p. 34.
* Adapted from Sarvodaya charts.
Note: Some illustrations in Sarvodaya literature transpose a few of the factors between I and II; they are arranged here to distinguish symptoms I from deeper causes II, in keeping with the gist of Sarvodaya and Buddhist teachings. (Note also how the wheels of coarising change direction when the Movement enters the scene.)

the Overseas Development Council, show Sri Lanka to enjoy a higher quality of life than countries with even ten times the per capita income" (Macy, 1983, p. 22).

There are, however, two polarities that have torn Sri Lankan society apart. One is the polarity between the well-educated, Westernized, English-speaking, urban elite (that often outclasses most elites elsewhere in the Third World) and the Sinhalese-speaking rural masses—the Sinhalese ethnic group constituting more than 70 percent of the population. The second polarity is between the Sinhalese and the Tamil that constitute about 18 percent of the population. Both of these polarities have led to considerable tension and conflict in recent years. The first conflict led to the bloody, Marxist-led uprising of 1971. The second conflict has led to a full-fledged Tamil independence movement and a civil war during the 1980s.

While the Sarvodaya movement is primarily a response to the urban-rural gaps, it has been inevitably caught in the ethnic conflicts between the Sinhalese and the Tamil. Despite its Buddhist origins and philosophy, however, the movement's leaders have attempted to keep it as ecumenical as possible. As Macy (1983, p. 30) has observed:

> That the Movement's religious identification is not exclusively Buddhist is evident in its activities among other religious communities, in its inclusion of Christian, Hindu, and Muslim symbols and rituals [their prayers are usually placed first in the "family gatherings" where religious minorities are present], in its utilization of churches, mosques and kovils [Hindu temples] for its operations (frequently organizing work camps to clean and repair them), in the work of Hindu and Christian priests and Muslim imams in its local programs, and in the ways in which its goals of nonviolence, self-reliance, economic sharing, and social equality are articulated in the thought-forms of these other religions. It is clear that the Movement not only embraces non-Buddhists but also can relate to them in the actual terms of their own religious symbols systems.

To compare Sarvodaya's programs and achievements to those of the Green movement, it might be useful to review them under the same five headings of ecology, nonviolence, social responsibility, participatory democracy, and dialogical communication. On questions of ecology, the Sarvodaya movement is unequivocal. Buddhism refuses to draw a sharp and discontinuous line between human life and life in other forms of nature. This conception is based on *anatta* or the absence of a permanent and immutable self or soul in a human person. Human life does not begin or end with birth or death. Connected with past lives, with possibilities of survival in the future, human life continues to evolve from and into other forms of nature through long periods of time with unpredictable fluctuations. This is called *samsara* or "wandering." In this wandering, each manifest and immediate life (ditta-dhamma, drsta-janman) provides an opportunity for change and improvement, and this opportunity is held sacred in Buddhism (Ariyaratne, 1986, pp. 114–115). All manifestations of life in nature are thus considered sacred. From this perspective, ecological protection is no longer a matter of expedient policy; it is a cosmic duty. The need for this integration of the social and spiritual dimensions of ecologically sensitive strategies of development is something that some Green leaders have also articulated. In the industrial West, where dichotomies between humans and nature have a long history, the ecologists have had to fight an uphill battle. But in Buddhist Sri Lanka, where human domination and exploitation of nature is only a relatively recent idea imported by the colonial powers, Sarvodaya's ecological perspectives have strong, indigenous roots.

Similarly, on nonviolence, Sarvodaya can rely again on the authority of Lord of Buddha (as quoted by Ariyaratne, 1986, pp. 121–122):

> All tremble at punishment; all fear death. Taking oneself as an example for comparison, one should neither strike nor kill. All tremble at punishment; all fear death. Taking oneself as an example for comparison, one should neither strike nor kill. He who, seeking his own happiness, inflicts pain through punishment on beings who are yearning for happiness, does not obtain happiness after death.

The Sarvodaya movement has made its greatest and most significant contributions perhaps in matters of social responsibility by instituting the Shramadana self-help work camps throughout Sri Lanka. According to Ariyaratne (1986, pp. 108–109), the movement has gone through three phases. In the first phase, 1958–68, the movement was basically a study-service program. In this phase, urban students and teachers resided in some of the most depressed villages in order to share their physical labor with the rural people, helping them to satisfy some of their most basic needs such as water for irrigation and drinking. In the second phase, 1968–78, the movement expanded its horizons towards integrated rural development—at first into 100 villages and then into several thousand. In the third phase, from 1978 to present, the movement has directed itself toward a strategy of national development in which growth in output can take place without losing traditional cultural roots. The chief objective of this phase is to reach a "no-poverty, no affluence" society.

The principles of participatory democracy are most cogently expressed in the Sarvodaya's efforts to decentralize all decision making to the smallest units of its organization (Macy, 1983, pp. 26–27). The process of organizing a work camp begins when a village invites a Sarvodaya worker to initiate a program of activity. This worker, in turn, contacts the village monk and key figures to call for a *paule hamua* or "family gathering" of local inhabitants, sometimes in a school, but usually in the temple. As a result of the discussions, in which care is taken by the Sarvodaya worker to assume only the role of a facilitator, village needs and projects are identified. A second phase begins when the local group is formed and assumes its own initiative in identifying their own priorities and programs. The regional and national Sarvodaya organizations assist the local groups in supplying ideas, contacts, skills, and even credit and materials. A third phase is entered when a local leadership has emerged sufficiently strong to provide an alternative to the power of village landlords. The culmination of this phase is reached when the village has its own children's, youth, mothers', farmers', and elders' groups, ready to incorporate its own Village Awakening Council, which then serves as an autonomous legal entity designing its own developmental program. The regional and national Sarvodaya organizations assist the Village Council in legal aid services, library services, the development of community shops, immunization and nutritional programs, and Shanti Sena ("peace keeping army") leagues where volunteers are trained in crowd control, emergency first aid, and conflict resolution.

Finally, dialogical communication forms the basis of all of Sarvodaya's programs and activities. *Priyavachana,* or pleasant and kindly speech, is one of the eight Buddhist noble paths. It calls for listening to people respectfully in order to promote the sense of unity, dignity, and equality that the movement aims to generate. The use of kinship terms is typical among the Sarvodayans (Macy, 1983, p. 60). In "family gatherings," the participants address each other as "older brother," "younger brother," "older sister," "mother," and so on. Along with this goes a conscious effort to avoid pejorative pronouns and verb forms that in the local language reflect class or caste.

In the following schematic model, Wimal Dissanayake (1984, p. 49) has provided an insightful contrast between this Buddhist model of communication to the Aristotelian models of communication prevalent among Western communication theorists and practitioners. As the added brackets attempt to show, these contrasting models could also represent the monologic and dialogic forms of communication:

ARISTOTELIAN [MONOLOGIC] MODEL	BUDDHIST [DIALOGIC] MODEL
1. Emphasis on communicator [sender]	1. Emphasis on receiver [audience]
2. Influence a key notion	2. Understanding a key notion

(continued)

ARISTOTELIAN [MONOLOGIC] MODEL	BUDDHIST [DIALOGIC] MODEL
3. Focus on control	3. Focus on choice
4. Emphasis on outward process	4. Emphasis on both outward and inward process
5. Relationship between communicator [sender] and receiver [of message] asymmetrical	5. Relationship between communicator [sender] and receiver [audience] symmetrical
6. Stress on intellect	6. Stress on empathy

Like the Greens, the Sarvodaya movement is swimming against the dominant currents of national and international politics. Its achievements, problems, and prospects should therefore be measured against this reality. Aside from the natural shortcomings of a nascent, grassroots movement operating in an uncongenial political environment, the Sarvodaya movement has fared rather well. The movement has been notably tolerated by a government that since 1977 has pursued a centralized, capital-intensive, export-oriented, foreign-financed, private enterprise and consumerist strategy of development. The price of this tolerance is that the movement has had to walk on a tightrope between the government's imperatives for economic growth and the people's often-neglected basic needs.

Three major criticisms have been leveled against the movement. First, the movement has consciously pursued a nonpolitical "politics." Formal membership in the movement is contingent upon refusal to join any political parties. While this has been necessary for the unity and survival of the movement, refusal to challenge the national policies and positions of the governing parties may have reduced the movement to a marginal political status in which the government tolerates its local successes while insuring its national ineffectiveness. As a voluntary organization with an emphasis on local self-help, the movement seems to have abdicated its role in regional and national politics that, in fact, set the parameters for the local conditions.

Second, despite its talk of centralization, the movement's major "policies and programs are still made at the central headquarters near Colombo, and regional centers are usually guided by the central program coordinators. This has the adverse effect of discouraging grassroots initiative" (Dissanayake, 1984, p. 50).

Third, despite its talk of self-reliance, Sarvodaya's finances have been heavily dependent (about 80 percent) on foreign assistance from the

Dutch, German, and American agencies. In reply to this criticism, Ariyaratne offers a twofold reply, including (a) the moral obligation of the former colonists to repatriate the colonized, and (b) the enormous generation of resources from the village people that far outweighs the financial aid they receive. "A current Dutch-sponsored study reveals that shramadana camps, for example, create capital many times in excess of the financial input. Thus in one year, Sarvodayans built three times as much roadway as the government did, and at one-eighteenth of the cost." (Macy, 1983, p. 43).

TOWARDS COMMUNITARIAN MEDIA SYSTEMS

In the last two decades, despite its seemingly "utopian" ideals, communitarian democracy has shown some important signs of vitality and practical possibility. As demonstrated by the Green and Sarvodaya movements, these signs have taken on different political configurations and pursued different strategies in different sociopolitical circumstances. But the objectives of the communitarian democratic movements have remained fundamentally similar: (a) revival of community and indigenous cultures in the face of the disintegrating and depersonalizing effects of the modern world; (b) preservation of ecology in the face of the onslaught of unbridled industrialization and developmentalism; (c) peace and nonviolence in the face of a spiraling nuclear arms race and balance of terror; (d) social justice and responsibility in the face of growing gaps within and among nations; (e) direct and participatory democracy in the face of impenetrable technocracies and bureaucratized institutions of representative and corporate democracies; (f) dialogical communication in the face of monologic, mass-media institutions of vertical and one-way message flows from centers of power to the peripheries; and (g) spiritual awareness and growth for the individual in the face of a callous and anomic world.

Information technologies have played a paradoxical role in this incipient process of democratization. The big media (mass circulation press, radio and television, telecommunication, satellites, and mainframe computers) have largely served as instruments of centralization of power, control, and communication. They have provided the modern state and corporation with those indispensable tools of surveillance, control, and communication without which the penetration and administration of their political and market territories would have proved impossible.

On the other hand, the small media (posters, small press, transistor radio, mimeograph machines, copying facilities, public phones, portaback video, the audio and video cassette recorders, and personal computers) have provided the channels to talk back to the dominant structures of power and sometimes to organize resistance and revolutionary movements. The alternative or underground media have served the latter functions. The more recent small media, such as the personal computer and modem, have not yet had sufficient time to reduce prices and penetrate markets to produce mass effects. But there is sufficient evidence in the advanced industrial countries to show that as costs decline and accessibility increases, the new interactive communication technologies (audio, video, and computer teleconferencing) can generate communities of affinity well beyond the communities of vicinity that have so far been the backbone of communitarian democratic movements. The thousands of electronic bulletin boards that have spontaneously emerged throughout the United States during the 1980s are a compelling testimony to the networking and democratic potentialities of such new channels of public communication.

But information technologies, no matter how interactive, cheap, or accessible, do not by themselves lead to democratic formations. The latest U. S. census data demonstrates the point well. (See the figures cited on p.156.)

Technologies have to be accessible and linked to democratic movements and media institutions to augment public discourse and democratic will formation. In other words, the media are not the message! The structure *is* the message. Commercial, government, and "public" media structures have served the commercial, government, and "public" interests. For community media to serve community interests, we need to invent new media structures that put the ownership, management, and operation of the media in the hands of the people themselves. The failure of community cable programming in most parts of the United States demonstrates how a communitarian idea can be undermined when the commercial media continue to set the rules and limits of the game.

Communication and power are inextricably tied together in all societies. The hierarchies of power in society are based on a range of instruments—from brute force to voluntary compliance. In nondemocratic communication systems, they take on the forms of coercion (based on force), terror (based on fear) and manipulation (based on deceit and illusions). In democratic communication systems, power is expressed in the forms of energy (based on love), cognition (based on learning), and cohesion (based on community) (see Table 9.1).

A communitarian media system begins with the energy and power that flows from love—love of the people and their natural and cultural environments. It would organize itself around the great educational principles of learning by doing rather than learning by authority, rote, and persuasion. Once so organized, a communitarian media system would generate a sense of cohesion, community, and power that no degree of exogenous persuasion can produce. In contrast to commercial, government, or public networks, a communitarian media system may be characterized by the following features:

Community ownership and management. The electromagnetic spectrum and the geostationary orbit are natural commons; they belong to all of the people. The publicly constructed channels of communication such as cable and fiber optics also belong to all of the people. A local community is the smallest natural unit of human organization to which we can entrust the ownership and management of these facilities.

Deprofessionalization of programming and production. In a true democracy, public communication is a right—not a privilege. In the face of the scarcity of channels, imposed by the scarcity of electromagnetic spectrum and geostationary orbit, this right has been mostly appropriated by governments and commercial entities. With the introduction of the mass media, media institutions and professionals have intervened between the senders and receivers of messages in order to sell their audiences to the highest bidder. Mediated communication is manufactured communication; mediated realities are reconstructed realities. The myth of professional neutrality in the mass media has served as an ideology of self-justification for media institutions, professionals, and their sponsors. It has mystified the fact that media institutions are no exception to any other institution in society; they serve the interests of those who control them. As A. J. Liebling aptly put it, "The freedom of the press belongs to those who have one!" (Isaacs, 1986). Democratic

Table 9.1. Authoritarian vs. Democratic Modes of Communication

Authoritarian Power & Communication (Bottom-Up Vertical)	Democratic Power & Communication (Top-Down Horizontal)
Coercion (based on force)	Energy (based on love)
Terror (based on fear)	Cognition (based on learning)
Manipulation (based on deceit/illusion)	Cohesion (based on community)

communication therefore demands some measure of deprofessionaliza-tion. It requires of every citizen to develop her/his communication com-petencies, including skills in production and programming in the mod-ern media. Visual and computer literacies are as vital today to survival in an information society as print literacy has been in industrial societies. The emerging abundance of public communication channels and media promises the practical possibility of widespread citizen literacy, but left to its own devices it can degenerate into further political manipulation and commercial exploitation.

Empowerment of audiences. But certain oppressed sectors of the au-dience have been historically conditioned to silence. To develop their communication competencies, they need to empower themselves. As Freire had discovered among the poor peasants of Northern Brazil, the pedagogy of the oppressed consists of a process of awakening, of cons-cientization, to their true conditions and interests through literacy. As the Greens in West Germany and the Sarvodayans in Sri Lanka have also discovered, this process primarily takes place through discussion groups and "family gatherings," that is, through interpersonal commu-nication and networking based on community organization and devel-opment. The very concept of "audience" also needs to be challenged in this context. "Audience" is an Aristotlian, rhetorical concept in which the sender of a message attempts to influence, persuade, or manipulate a passive receiver. Mass audiences of the mass media are presumed to be the inert consumers to be delivered to advertisers—at a price some-times exceeding half a million dollars for three seconds. Empowerment means the creation of communicators rather than audiences *cum* consumers or subjects; it demands full, active, communicative citizen-ship.

Interactive technologies and networks. Empowerment means, there-fore, interactive communication. Communitarian media are interactive media. Communitarian media may use the one-way channels, such as print or broadcasting, but they will use them always in the context of interactive communication networks and feedback—letters to the edi-tors, phone-ins, radio and television discussion groups, and so on. Communitarian media would also take full advantage of the new tech-nological breakthroughs in interactive, mediated communication in order to foster direct and participatory democracy. But communitarian media are not based on a blind faith in technologies. Communitarians know how interactive technologies can be placed at the service of com-mercial interests as they have been in the Qube System of Ohio. They also know that the new interactive media can be used to create an Orwellian world of mind and behavior control. Communitarians, how-ever, do not subscribe to a Luddite position. They are not afraid of new information technologies; they see in them contradictory potentialities and attempt to tame them for democratic purposes.

Decentralization. To achieve this objective, communitarian media would promote the Schumacherian motto of "Small is Beautiful!" Although there are exceptions, big media generally tend to concentrate power; small media generally tend to disperse it. Local community media would, therefore, be the nerve centers of communitarian media systems. National and indeed global radio and television networks are possible, but they would emanate from local community media organizations. Just as the Greens seem to have achieved in their party organization, communitarian media organizations would subordinate the centers to the peripheries rather than the other way around.

Cultural and structural pluralism. Despite the predominance of community media structures, a communitarian media system would not preclude commercial, government, or public media and networks. Since, however, public communication channels are considered a common property, access to these channels by private interests would have to be conditioned upon payment of rent. Income from rent would thus be channeled to support the work of the media. This principle has already been accepted by many municipal governments in the United States in their regulation of cable television. A portion of the commercial cable fees, usually no more than 5 percent, is reserved to support community cable programming. The extension of this principle to all of the electronic media would make it possible for community media to thrive instead of just survive.[4] The right of commercial, government, and public networks to establish themselves would insure structural and cultural pluralism without endangering the fundamental rights of the public to the ownership and management of public communication channels. As the example of countries with multiple media structures demonstrates, programming would also be of higher quality and diversity. To encourage pluralism and creativity, the concept of copyright would also have to be radically revised. In recognition of community support, artists, writers, and scientists would submit their creations and inventions to community chest funds that would pay them royalties based on the market returns on uses and applications.

Think globally, act locally. Communitarian media systems would be grass-roots media, but not parochial and localist media. The new interactive communication technologies have already created a global network that transcends national and cultural boundaries. Community media would be local in structure but global in scope and networks.

---

[4] However, with the Cable Deregulation Act of 1987, this principle is facing extinction.

240 TECHNOLOGIES OF POWER

CONCLUSION

In recent decades, the search for democracy and development has taken on a new turn. Wherever we look, whether in the capitalist democracies or in the socialist democracies or in the postcolonial Third World, there is a sense of dissatisfaction with the old regimes and remedies. The old regimes and remedies have not worked—sometimes not well enough, sometimes not at all. Capitalist democracies have led everywhere to systems of well-entrenched privilege, well-protected by the institutions of representative democracy that have led, on the one hand, to cynical manipulations of the electoral process and, on the other, to political apathy on the part of a vast majority of the marginalized groups. Socialist democracies have fared no better. Following the leveling effects of the revolutionary experience, socialist democracies have also been corrupted into bureaucratic politics of the single-party system in which the absence of competition has led to both economic stagnation and political apathy. In the Third World, where mixes of capitalism and socialism have produced a variety of etatist formations, the exploitative character of private enterprise has often combined with the inertia and inefficiency of the state bureaucracies to produce parasitic ruling cadres that profit on dualistic economies and societies. These systems have come together in the formation of a world economy in which the centers of power in the industrial, industrializing, and preindustrial world have developed a common interest in keeping the rural and semiurban peripheries at bay.

Out of this abysmal situation, a variety of different democratic social movements have emerged that call themselves by different names but exude a common purpose. The counterculture movement in the United States, the Green movement in Germany, the Ecology Party in England, the Solidarity movement in Poland, the Sarvodaya Movement in Sri Lanka, the Theology of Liberation in Latin America, the Nuclear Freeze Movement in the Pacific, and hundreds of other smaller and less well-known groups, parties, and movements—all promise a new politics. As analyzed in this chapter through a closer examination of the Green and Sarvodaya movements, the new politics has a threefold purpose: (a) to discover the roots of the current democratic malaise in a serious analysis of the social, economic, and cultural causes of technocratic domination, (b) to infuse into politics a new sense of purpose from the deepest sources of traditions of civility unique to each country (Transcendentalism in the United States, Buddhism in Sri Lanka, Catholicism in Poland and Latin America, Islam in the Muslim world), and (c) to construct the new democratic purposes and projects on grass-roots, direct, community-based participation and dialogue. I have taken this last feature of the new politics as its most fundamental feature and called this entire phenomenon "communitarian democracy."

It has taken a few centuries for the other two democratic formations, liberal and socialist democracies, to unfold. It will take at least a few decades for the new communitarian democratic formations to work themselves out in different sociohistorical circumstances. But it is already clear that the new democratic impulse is in response to counter-democratic forces that have manifested themselves in a variety of guises and disguises, including some of the models of democracy outlined by David Held (1987) and others (Bowles & Gintis, 1986). The new democratic and totalitarian formations would not necessarily follow the patterns of the past. The democratic movements of the last few decades have demonstrated some of their unique features in their concerns with community, ecology, peace, and dialogical communication. The new totalitarian formations, by contrast, rely heavily on further atomization of society through a further closing of the public sphere while extending the consumer society and its boundless channels of self-gratification (Ewen & Ewen, 1982).

The role of information technologies in these contradictory formations is just an aspect of a larger social struggle. The new information technologies have opened up an unprecedented historical opportunity for the revitalization of all forms of democracy, but particularly those forms we have here called communitarian—grass-roots, direct, and participatory. But the new information technologies also have created historically unprecedented opportunities for totalitarian surveillance and domination. The new electronic democracy can link up horizontal and interactive communication among citizens at the local, national, and global levels. For that potential to be realized, however, we need open and equal access for all. By contrast, the new electronic tyranny allows the citizen to receive instant gratification from "pushbutton fantasies" (Mosco, 1982) while denying access to the public sphere. A breakdown of political community would be the eventual outcome of such a system of domination. In such a scenario, totalitarian domination would arrive, as T. S. Eliot prophesied in "The Hollow Men," "not with a bang but a whimper."

Totalitarianism is, however, the worse-case scenario. The new communitarian democracy also faces two other possible scenarios: a scenario of limited success and a scenario of cooptation. The Green Party in Germany and the Sarvodaya Movement in Sri Lanka demonstrate the examples of limited success. However, neither movement has managed to translate its ideals into national policy. There are serious impediments on the way to that project. West Germany presents a major Western industrial country committed to the postwar policies of nuclear armament and acquisitive capitalism. To change its course takes more than a small party which is already divided in its own ranks. The government in Sri Lanka has followed an acquisitive, development policy that runs counter to the Sarvodaya ideals (Goulet, 1981). The civil war between the Sihalese and the Tamils has also gone against the Sarvodaya ideals of nonviolence and peaceful cooperation among peoples of all religions and ethnicity.

A third scenario facing communitarian democracy lies in cooptation. Many of the ideals of the Green movement in ecology have already been coopted in Western industrial democracies by environmentalist legislation. But as Porrit (1985) points out, there is a big difference between environmentalist (how to preserve nature in order to exploit it better) and ecological politics rooted in a deep reverence for all living creatures. Many of the Buddhist rhetorics of the Sarvodaya movement have also been coopted by the secular, Sri Lankan government. But as Goulet (1981) has pointed out, there is also a big difference between limiting the arena of Sarvodaya action to small villages and trying to translate its values into practice at the larger, regional, and national terms. The battle can be won while the war is lost!

To avoid these pitfalls, the new communitarian democracy needs to begin with an awakening—a sarvodaya of its own—to the new sociotechnological environment and the new historical possibilities. Information technologies need to turn into communication technologies in all three senses of the word—as interactive hardware, software, and cognitive modes. We need to learn a great deal more about how technologies can lock into institutions of participatory democracy to yield both a sense of community and a participatory democratic outcome. Technologies can be excellent masters but also capricious masters. What determines their outcome is not some inherent purpose, a *telos*, in their design or function but, rather, it is the social purposes that command their use and abuse. In that fashion, the origin, development, and uses of technologies must be problematized. Technologies lock into institutional arrangements and social forces; they link up with those perennial structures of power and hierarchies of class, ethnicity, race, and gender that have dominated much of the substance of politics in history. Information technologies play an auxiliary role in the maintenance of these structures and hierarchies and challenges to them. By themselves they can neither explain nor rectify the malaise of democracy.

References

Abramson, N. (1979). *PALAPA for data communications.* Unpublished manuscript, University of Hawaii, Honolulu, HI.

Alfian, & Chu, G. C. (1981). *Satellite television in Indonesia.* Honolulu: East West Communication Institute.

American Library Association. (1988). *Less Access to Less Information By and About US Government.* Washington, DC: American Library Association.

Amin, S. (1974). *Accumulation on a world scale: A critique of the theory of under-development.* New York: Monthly Review Press.

Arendt, H. (1966). *The origins of totalitarianism* (new ed.). New York: Harcourt & Brace & World.

Ariyaratne, A. T. (1986). Learning in Sarvodaya. In Thomas & Ploman (Eds.), *Learning and development: A global perspective.* Toronto: Ontario Institute Studies in Edun.

Armstrong, B. (1979). *The electronic church.* Nashville: Thomas Nelson.

Arterton, F. C. (1987). *Teledemocracy: Can technology protect democracy?* Newbury Park, CA: Sage.

Bagdikian, B. H. (1983). *The media monopoly.* Boston: Beacon Press.

Bagehot, W. (1900). *The English Constitution.* London: Thomas Nelson & Sons.

Baran, P. M. (1958). *The political economy of growth.* New York: Monthly Review Press.

Barnet, R. J., & Muller, R. E. (1974). *Global reach: The power of the multi-national corporations.* New York: Simon & Schuster.

Batra, R. (1987). *The Great Depression of 1990.* New York: Dell.

Bateson, G. (1975). *Steps to an ecology of mind.* New York: Ballantine.

Becker, T. et al. (1981, June). *Report on New Zealand Televote.* Unpublished manuscript, Victoria University, Wellington, New Zealand.

Becker, T. (1981, December). Teledemocracy: Power to the people. *The Futurist,* pp. 6–9.

Becker, T., & Scarce, R. (1987). Teledemocracy emergent: State of the American art and science. In B. Dervin & M. Voigt (Eds.), *Progress in Communication Sciences* (Vol. VIII, pp. 263–287). Norwood, NJ: Ablex.

Becker, T., & Slaton, C. (1981). Hawaii Televote: Measuring Public Opinion on Complex Policy Issues. *Political Science* (New Zealand), *33,* 52–83.

Bell, D. (Ed.). (1964). *The radical right.* New York: Doubleday Anchor Books.

Bell, D. (1973). *The coming of the post-industrial society: A venture in social forecasting.* New York: Basic Books.

Bell, D. (1978). *The cultural contradictions of capitalism.* New York: Basic Books.

Bellah, R. N., Madsen, R., Sullivan, W. M., Swidler, A., & Tipton, S. M. (1986). *Habits of the heart: Individualism and commitment in American life.* Berkeley, CA: University of California Press.

243

Berger, P. L. (1973). *The homeless mind: Modernization and consciousness.* Harmondsworth: Penguin Books.

Berger, P. L. (1967). *The sacred canopy: Elements of a sociological theory of religion.* Garden City, NY: Doubleday & Co.

Bernstein, E. M. (1984, Spring/Summer). Harvard economics at the Bretton Woods conference. Cambridge, MA: *Harvard Graduate Society Newsletter.*

Berrigan, F. J. (Ed.). (1977). *Access: Some Western models of community media.* Paris: UNESCO.

Berrigan, F. J. (1981). *Community communications: The role of community media in development.* Paris: UNESCO.

Binder, L. (1978). *In a moment of enthusiasm: Political power and the second stratum in Egypt.* Chicago: University of Chicago Press.

Blomstrom, M., & Hettne, B. (1984). *Development theory in transition.* London: Zed Books.

Bloom, A. (1987). *The closing of the American mind.* New York: Simon & Schuster.

Bloom, B. (Ed.). (1956). *Taxonomy of educational objectives.* New York: David McKay Co.

Blumler, J. G., & Katz, E. (1974). *The uses of mass communications.* Beverly Hills & London: Sage.

Bok, D. (1986). *Higher learning.* Cambridge, MA: Harvard University Press.

Bookchin, M. (1987). *Modern crisis.* Montreal: Black Rose Books.

Boormand, S. A., & Levitt, P. R. (1983, November 20 & 27). The computer as judge and jury. *The New York Times,* F3.

Bowles, S., & Gintis, H. (1986). *Democracy and capitalism.* New York: Basic Books.

Boyd, D. A. (1982). *Broadcasting in the Arab world: A survey of radio and television in the mid east.* Philadelphia: Temple University Press.

Brand, S. (1987). *The media lab: Inventing the future at MIT.* New York: Viking.

Brandt, W. et al. (1980). *North-south: A program for survival.* London: Pan Books.

Brandt, W. et al. (1985). *Common crisis: North-south co-operation for world recovery.* Cambridge, MA: The MIT Press.

Bretz, R. (1983). *Media for interactive communication.* Beverly Hills: Sage Publications.

Britain has a go at linking telecom and computing. (1983, March 5–11). *The Economist,* p. 91.

Brock, G. W. (1981). *The telecommunications industry: The dynamics of market structure.* Cambridge: Harvard University Press.

Browne, E. G. (1966). *The persian revolution, 1905–09.* Cambridge: Cambridge University Press.

Bunyard, P. et al. (1987). *The Green alternative: A guide to good living.* London: Methuen.

Campbell, V. (1974). *The televote system for civic communication: First demonstration and evaluation.* Palo Alto: American Institutes for Research.

Campbell, V., & Santos, J. (1975). *Televote: A new communication system.* Palo Alto, CA: American Institutes for Research.

Capra, F. (1977). *The tao of physics.* Toronto: Bantum Books.

Capra, F., & Spretnak, C. (1984). *Green politics: The global promise.* New York: E. P. Dutton.

Carey, J. W. (1981). *Culture, technology and communications*. Unpublished manuscript, University of Illinois, Champaign, IL.

Casting light on super fast computing. (1983, February 25–March 24). *The Economist*, pp. 91–92.

Clarke, C. (1940). *The conditions of economic progress*. London: Macmillan.

Cohen, S. S., & Zysman, J. (1987). *Manufacturing matters: The myth of post-industrial economy*. New York: Basic Books.

Compaine, B. M. (1984). *Understanding new media: Trends and issues in electronic distribution of information*. Cambridge, MA: Ballinger.

Comstock, G. et al. (1972). *Television and social behavior: A technical report to the Surgeon General's scientific advisory committee on television and social behavior.* Washington, DC: Government Printing Office.

Dator, J. (1979). The future of culture or culture of the future. In A. J. Marsella et al. (Eds.), *Perspectives on Cross-Cultural Psychology*. New York: Academic Press.

Dator, J. (1983). The 1982 Honolulu electronic town meeting. In G. D. Page (Ed.), *The future of politics*. London: Frances Pinter.

Davidge, C. (1987). America's talk-back television experiment: Qube. In W. H. Duttoon, J. G. Blumler, & K. L. Kraemer (Eds.), *Wired Cities*. Boston: G. K. Hall.

Dissanayake, W. (1984). A Buddhist approach to development: A Sri Lankan endeavor. In G. Wang & W. Dissanayake (Eds.), *Continuity and Change in Communication Systems* (pp. 39–51). Norwood, NJ: Ablex.

Dordick, H. S., Bradley, H. G., & Nanus, B. (1981). *The emerging network marketplace*. Norwood, NJ: Ablex.

Draper, T. (1987, June 29, October 8, December 17). The Iran-Contra affair. *New York Review of Books.*

Dutton, W. H., Blumler, J. G., & Kraemer, K. L. (1987). *Wired cities: Shaping the future of communications*. Boston: G. K. Hall & Co.

The Economist, p. 15. (1985, November 30).

The Economist, p. 89. (1983, December 17).

Eisenstein, E. L. (1979). *The printing press as an agent of change* (Vols. 1–2). Cambridge: Cambridge University Press.

Ellul, J. (1983). *The technological system*. New York: Continuum.

Enzenberger, H. M. (1974). *The consciousness industry: On literature, politics and the media*. New York: Continuum.

Ewen, S., & Ewen, E. (1982). *Channels of desire: Mass images and the shaping of American consciousness*. New York: McGraw-Hill.

Feather, F. (Ed.). (1980). *Through the '80s: Thinking globally, acting locally.* Washington, DC: World Future Society.

Ferguson, M. (1981). *The Aquarian conspiracy: Personal and social transformation in the 1980s*. Los Angeles & New York: J. P. Tarcher.

Filep, R. T., & Haq, M. S. (1977). Communications development in India. In M. Tehranian et al. (Eds.), *Communication policy for national development*. London: Rouledge, Kegan & Paul.

Foucault, M. (1978). *The history of sexuality* (Vols. 1–2). New York: Pantheon.

Foucault, M. (1979). *Discipline and punish: The birth of the prison*. New York: Pantheon.

Frank, A. G. (1969). *The development of underdevelopment.* New York: Monthly Review Press.

Frankfort, H. et al. (1964). *Before philosophy: The intellectual adventures of ancient man.* Hammondsworth: Pelican Books.

Freire, P. (1979, August). Cultural action and conscientisation. *Harvard Education Review* (40)3.

Freire, P. (1972). *Pedagogy of the oppressed* (trans. by Myra Bergman Ramos). New York: Herder & Herder.

Freire, P. (1973). *Education for critical consciousness.* New York: Seabury Press.

Freire, P. (1976). Acevca de la Educacion Popular. In *Tema de Educacion y Politica.* Lima: Centro de Publicacion Educativas, TAREA.

Freire, P. (1978). *Pedagogy in process: The letters to Guinea-Bissau.* New York: Seabury Press.

Freire, P. (1985). *The politics of education: Culture, power and liberation.* Hadley, MA: Bergin & Garvey.

Frey, F. (1973). Communication and development. In I. S. Pool et al. (Eds.), *Handbook of communication.* Chicago: Rand McNally.

Friberg, M., & Hettne, B. (1983). *The greening of the world: Towards a non-deterministic model of global process.*

Friedrich, C. J. et al. (1969). *Totalitarianism in perspective: Three views.* New York: Praeger.

Fromm, E. (1963). *Escape from freedom.* New York: Harper & Row.

Fuller, R. B. (1983). *Grunch of giants.* New York: St. Martin's Press.

Galbraith, J. K. (1956). *American capitalism: The theory of countervailing power.* Boston: Houghton Mifflin.

Galbraith, J. K. (1978). *The new industrial state* (3rd rev. ed.). Boston: Houghton Mifflin.

Galtung, J. (1971). A structural theory of imperialism. *Journal of Peace Research, 8* (2), 81–118.

Galtung, J. (1980, June). Remarks. *Proceedings of the World Forum,* Union of International Associations, Brussels.

Galtung, J. (1979). *Development, environment and technology: Towards a technology of self-reliance.* New York: United Nations.

Galtung, J. (1983). *Keynote Address.* Conference of the World Future Studies Federation, University of Hawaii, Honolulu, HI.

Galtung, J. (1987). *Democracy and development.* Unpublished manuscript.

Ganley, O. H., & Ganley, G. D. (1982). *To inform or to control: The new communications network.* New York: McGraw-Hill.

Garnham, N. (1986, January). The media and the public sphere. *InterMedia* 14(1), 28–33.

Geertz, C. (1973). *Interpretation of cultures: Selected essays.* New York: Basic Books.

Gerbner, G. (Ed.). (1985, Winter). The mediated ministry. *Journal of Communications* 35(1).

Gibbons, A. (1985). *Information, ideology and communication.* Lanham, NY & London: University Press of America.

Giddens, A. (1984). *The constitution of society: Outline of the theory of structuration.* Berkeley & LA: University of California Press.

Gilligan, C. (1984). *In a different voice: Psychological theory and women's development.* Cambridge, MA: Harvard University Press.

Gore, M. S. (1983). *The Site experience.* Paris: UNESCO, Reports and Papers on Mass Communication.

Gouldner, A. W. (1982a). *The dialectic of ideology and technology: The origins, grammar, and future of ideology.* New York: Oxford University Press.

Gouldner, A. W. (1982b). *The future of intellectuals and the rise of the new class.* New York: Oxford University Press.

Gouldner, A. W. (1982c). *The two Marxisms: Contradictions and anomalies in the development of theory.* New York: Oxford University Press.

Goulet, D. (1981). *Survival with integrity: Sarvodaya at the crossroads.* Colombo: Marga Institute.

Gramsci, A. (1971). *Selections from the prison notebooks.* London: Lawrence & Wishart.

Gross, B. (1980). *Friendly fascism: The new face of power in America.* New York: M. Evans.

Gross, L. S. (1983). *Telecommunications: An introduction to radio, TV and the developing media.* Dubuque, IA: W. C. Brown Company Publishers.

Grossberg, L. (1985). *Strategies of Marxist cultural interpretation.* Unpublished manuscript.

Habermas, J. (1972). *Knowledge and human interests.* Boston: Beacon Press.

Habermas, J. (1975). *Legitimation crisis.* Boston: Beacon Press.

Habermas, J. (1979). *Communication and the evolution of society* (trans. by T. McCarthy). Boston: Beacon Press.

Habermas, J. (1983). *A theory of communicative action* (3 vols.). Boston: Beacon Press.

Hall, E. T. (1977). *Beyond culture.* New York: Doubleday.

Hamelink, C. J. (1983). *Cultural autonomy in global communications: Planning national information policy.* New York & London: Longman.

Have West Germany's greens found a future. (1984, August 11). *The Economist,* pp. 37–43.

Head, S. W. (1985). *World broadcasting systems: A comparative analysis.* Belmont, CA: Wadsworth.

Held, D. (1987). *Models of democracy.* Stanford: Stanford University Press.

Hettne, B. (1983, Autumn). Peace and development: What is the relationship? *Development and Peace,* 4(2), 149–163.

Hirsch, E. D. (1987). Cultural literacy: What every American needs to know. Boston: Houghton Mifflin.

Hollander, R. (1985). *Video democracy: The vote-from-home revolution.* Mt. Airy, MD: Lomond Publications.

Hungary: The lessons for Mr. Andropov. (1983, March 19–25). *The Economist,* p. 78.

Huntington, S. (1968). *Political order in changing societies.* New Haven & London: Yale University Press.

Illich, I. (1971a). *Celebration of awareness: A call for institutional revolution.* Harmondsworth: Penguin Books.

Illich, I. (1971b). *Deschooling society.* Harmondsworth: Penguin Books.

Illich, I. (1973). *Tools for conviviality.* London: Calder.

Illich, I. (1974). *Energy and equity: The paradox of speed.* London: Calder.

Illich, I. et al. (1977). *Disabling professions.* New York: M. Boyars.

Illich, I. (1978). *The right to useful unemployment and its professional enemies.* London: Marion Boyars.

Illich, I. (1983, Winter). Silence is a commons. *Co-Evolution Quarterly, 40,* 4–9.

Inkeles, A., & Smith, D. H. (1974). *Becoming modern: Individual change in six developing countries.* Cambridge, MA: Harvard University Press.

Innis, H. (1950). *Empire and communications.* Toronto: University of Toronto Press.

Innis, H. (1951). *The bias of communication.* Toronto: University of Toronto Press.

Isaacs, N. E. (1986). *Untended gates: The mismanaged press.* New York: Columbia University Press.

Ito, Y. (1984). Community media in Japan. In P. Lewis (Eds.), *Media for people in cities.* Paris: UNESCO.

Ito, Y. (1983). The "Johoko Shakai" approach to the study of communication in Japan. In G. C. Wilhoit (Ed.), *Mass Communication Review.* Beverly Hills: Sage.

Ito, Y. (1980). *Community media in Japan.* Unpublished manuscript, Institute of Communication Research, Keio University, Tokyo.

Jacobs, P., & Landau, S. (1966). *The new radicals: A report with documents.* New York: Vintage Books.

Jankowski, N. W. (1982). Community television: A tool for community action? *Communication, 7,* 33–58.

Jonscher, C. (1983). Information resources and economic productivity. *Information Economics and Policy, 1,* 13–35.

Jonscher, C. (1984). Productivity and growth of the information economy. In M. Jussawalla & Ebenfield (Eds.), *Communication and Information Economics.* Amsterdam: North Holland.

Joshi, S. R. (1978, December). Mode of Operation. *Another TV Seminar,* p. 232.

Katz, E. (1981). In defense of media events. In R. W. Haigh, G. Gerbner, & R. B. Byrne (Eds.), *Communication in the 21st Century.* Glencoe, IL: The Free Press.

Katz, E., & Lazarsfeld, P. (1964). *Personal influence: The part played by people in the flow of mass communications.* Glencoe: The Free Press.

Katz, E., & Szecsko, T. (Eds.). (1981). *Mass media and social change.* Beverly Hills: Sage.

Kelly, P. (1984). *Fighting for hope.* Boston: South End Press.

Klapper, J. (1960). *The effects of mass communication.* Glencoe, IL: The Free Press.

Kuhn, T. S. (1962). *The structure of scientific revolutions* (2nd ed.). Chicago: University of Chicago Press.

Kumar, K. (1978). *Prophecy and progress: The sociology of industrial and post-industrial society.* New York: Penguin.

Kuznets, S. (1971). *Economic growth of nations: Total output and productive structure.* Cambridge: Harvard University Press.

Langguth, G. (1986). *The green factor in German politics: From protest movement to political party.* Boulder, CO: Westview Press.

Lasswell, H. D. (1927). *Propaganda techniques in the world war.* New York: Knopf.

Lauden, K. (1977). *Communication technologies and democratic participation.*

Lazarsfeld, P. F., Berelson, B., & Gaudet, H. (1948). *The people's choice: How the voter makes up his mind in a presidential campaign.* New York: Columbia University Press.

Lenin, V. I. (1969). *What is to be done?* New York: International Publishers Company.

Lerner, D., & Pevsner, L. W. (1958). *The passing of traditional society.* Chicago: The Free Press of Glencoe.

Levi-Strauss, C. (1966). *The savage mind.* London: Weidenfeld and Nicholson.

Lewis, P. (Ed.). (1984). *Media for people in cities: A study of community media in the urban context.* Paris: UNESCO.

Lima, V. A. de, & Christians, C. G. (1979). Paulo Freire: The political dimension of dialogic communication. *Communication, 4,* 133–155.

MacBride, S. et al. (1980). *Many voices, one world: Communication and society today and tomorrow.* Paris: UNESCO Press.

Machlup, F. (1962). *The production and distribution of knowledge in the United States.* Princeton, NJ: Princeton University Press.

Machlup, F. (1980–1984). *Knowledge: Its creation, distribution and economic significance* (vols. 1–3). Princeton, NJ: Princeton University Press.

Macpherson, C. B. (1973). *Democratic theory: Essays in retrieval.* Oxford: Clarendon Press.

Macy, J. (1983). *Dharma and development: Religion as resource in the Sarvodaya self-help.* West Hartford: Kumarian Press.

Malinovsky, S. (1927). *Sex and repression in savage societies.* London: Kegan Paul.

Marcuse, H. (1964). *One-dimensional man: Studies in the ideology of advanced industrial society.* Boston: Beacon Press.

Margolis, M. (1979). *Viable democracy.* New York: Penguin Books.

Marx, C., & Engels, F. (1970). In C. J. Arthur (Ed.), *The German ideology.* New York: International Publishers.

Marx, K., & Engels, F. (1959). The Communist Manifesto. In L. S. Feuer (Ed.), *Marx and Engels: Basic Writing on Politics and Philosophy* (pp. 1–41). New York: Anchor Books.

Masuda, Y. (1981). *The information society: As post-industrial society.* Washington, DC: World Future Society.

McGinniss, J. (1969). *The selling of the president, 1968.* New York: Trident.

McLaughline, J. F., & Birtinyi, A. E. (1980). *Mapping the information business.* Cambridge, MA: Center for Information Policy Research, Harvard University.

McLuhan, M. (1964). *Understanding media: The extensions of man.* Boston: McGraw-Hill.

McLuhan, M. (1969). *The Gutenberg galaxy: The making of typographic man.* New York: Signet Books.

McLuhan, M., & Fiore, Q. (1967). *The medium is the massage: An inventory of effects.* New York: Bantum Books.

McQuail, D. (1984). *Mass communication theory: An introduction.* Beverly Hills: Sage.

McRobie, G. (1981). *Small is possible.* New York: Harper & Row.

Melody, W. H. (Ed.). (1981). *Culture, communications and dependency: The tradition of H. A. Innis.* Norwood, NJ: Ablex.

Michels, R. (1966). *Political parties* (trans. by E. Paul & C. Paul). New York: Hearst's International Library.

Mill, J. S. (1956). *On liberty.* New York: Bobbs.

Mills, C. W. (1956). *The power elite.* New York: Oxford University Press.

Mintz, A. (1987). *Online newsletter '87,* pp. 106–112.

Montesquieu, C. de. (1978). *The spirit of the laws: A compendium of the first English edition.* Berkeley: University of California Press.

Moore, Jr., B. (1967). *Social origins of dictatorship and democracy.* Boston: Beacon Press.

Moore, S. (1983, September). *Participatory communication in the development process.* Unpublished manuscript, The Netherlands Ministry of Housing.

Mortimer, E. (1982). *Faith and power: The politics of Islam.* New York: Vintage Books.

Mosco, V. (1982). *Pushbutton fantasies: Critical perspectives on videotex and information technology.* Norwood, NJ: Ablex.

Mowlana, H. (1986). *Global information and world communication. New Frontiers in international relations.* New York: Longman.

Muggeridge, M. (1977). *Christ and the media.* Grand Rapids, MI: William B. Eerdmans.

Mumford, L. (1962). *Technics and civilization.* New York: Harcourt, Brace & World.

Murdock, G. (1982). Large corporation and the control of the communication industries. In M. Gurevitch, T. Bennett, J. Curran, & J. Woolacott (Eds.), *Culture, Society and the Media.* London & New York: Methuen.

Naisbitt, J. (1982). *Megatrends: Ten new directions transforming our lives.* New York: Warner Books.

National Citizens Committee for Broadcasting (NCCB). (1979). *New technologies and their application to individual and community uses.* Washington, DC: National Citizens Committee for Broadcasting.

Nerfin, M. (1977). *Another development: Approaches and strategies.* Uppsala: The Dag Hammerskjold Foundation.

Neuman, W. R. (1986). *The paradox of mass politics: Knowledge and opinion in the American electorate.* Cambridge, MA: Harvard University Press.

Nimmo, D., & Combs, J. E. (1983). *Mediated political realities.* New York & London: Longman.

Nisbet, R. A. (1953). *The quest for community.* London & New York: Oxford University Press.

Nyererre, J. K. (1968). *Ujamaa: Essays on socialism.* London: Oxford University Press.

O'Sullivan-Ryan, J., & Kaplun, J. (n.d.). *Communication methods to promote grassroots participation.* Paris: UNESCO.

Olsen, R. J. (1986). The digital pacific—Evolution or revolution? In D. J. Wedemeyer & A. Pennings (Eds.), *Pacific Telecommunication Conference 86 Proceedings* (pp. 22–24). Honolulu: Pacific Telecommunication Council.

Orwell, G. (1981). *1984.* New York: Signet Classics.

Pal, Y. et al. (1978, December). *Another TV: A report on the experiences of the space application center. Seminar*, 232.

Pelton, J. N. (1981). *Global talk*. Rockville, MD: Sijthoff & Noordhoff.

Perry, R. (1984). *The programming of the president*. London: Aurum Press.

Peterson, R. A. (1976). The production of culture. *American Behavioral Scientist, 19*, 669–684.

Plato. (1936). *Phaedrus* (trans. & commentary by C. J. Rowe). Wiltshire: Aris & Phillips Ltd.

Ploman, E. (1983, January). *National needs in an international setting*. Keynote address at the Pacific Telecommunications Conference.

Pool, I. de Sola. (1973). *Talking back: Citizen feedback and cable technology*. Cambridge, MA: MIT Press.

Pool, I. de Sola. (Ed.). (1983). *Technologies of freedom*. Cambridge, MA: Harvard University Press.

Porat, M. (1977). *The information economy*. Washington, DC: U.S. Office of Telecommunications.

Porat, M. (1978). Communication policy in an information society. In G. O. Robinson (Ed.), *Communications for Tomorrow* (pp. 3–60). New York: Praeger.

Porrit, J. (1985). *Seeing green: The politics of ecology explained*. Oxford: Blackwell.

Poster, M. (1984). *Foucault, Marxism and history: Mode of production vs. mode of information*. Cambridge, UK: Polity Press.

Qvortrup, L. (1984). *The social significance of telematics: An essay on the information society*. Amsterdam/Philadelphia: John Benjamins Publishing Company.

Rogers, E. N. (1987, July). *Communication and development revisited*. Paper presented at the Conference on Communication and Change, East West Center, Institute of Culture and Communication, Honolulu, HI.

Rogers, E. N. (Ed.). (1976). *Communication and development: Critical perspectives*. Beverly Hills: Sage.

Rogers, E. N., & Shoemaker, F. F. (1971). *Communication of innovations*. New York: Free Press.

Rogers, E. (1983). *The Silicon Valley fever*. New York: Basic Books.

Rohatyn, F. (1983, August 18). Time for change. *The New York Review of Books, 30*, p. 13.

Rosengren, K. E. (1981). Mass media and social change: Some current approaches. In E. Katz & T. Szecsko (Eds.), *Mass Media and Social Change*. Beverly Hills: Sage.

Rostow, W. W. (1960). *The stages of economic growth: A non-communist manifesto*. London and New York: Cambridge University Press.

Roszak, T. (1969). *The making of the counter-culture*. New York: Anchor Books.

Roszak, T. (1972). *Where the wasteland ends*. Garden City, NY: Doubleday.

Roszak, T. (1986). *The cult of information*. New York: Pantheon.

Rousseau, J. J. (1968). *Social contract*. New York: Penguin Books.

Sale, K. (1980). *Human scale*. New York: Putnam.

Sartori, G. (1987). *The theory of democracy revisited* (2 vols.). Chatham, NJ: Chatham House Publishers.

Schiller, D. (1982). *Telematics and government*. Norwood, NJ: Ablex.

Schiller, H. I. (1981). *Who knows: Information in the age of Fortune 500.* Norwood, NJ: Ablex.

Schiller, H. (1985). *Information and the crisis economy.* Norwood, NJ: Ablex.

Schlesinger, A. (1984, August 16). The Election and After. *The New York Review of Books, 31,* p. 13.

Schramm, W. (1964). *Mass media and national development.* Stanford: Stanford University Press.

Schumacher, E. F. (1973). *Small is beautiful: Economics as if people mattered.* New York: Harper & Row.

Schumacher, E. F. (1977). *A guide for the perplexed.* New York: Harper & Row.

Servaes, J. (1987). *Habermas and the critique of ideology.* Unpublished manuscript.

Shannon, C. E., & Weaver, W. (1959). *The mathematical theory of communication.* Urbana, IL: University of Illinois Press.

Shattuck, J., & Morisey, M. (1988). *Government information controls: Implications for scholarship, science & technology.* Report for Association of American Universities. Washington, DC.

Siebert, F. S. et al. (1974). *Four theories of the press.* Urbana: University of Illinois Press.

Slack, J. (1984). *Communication technologies and society.* Norwood, NJ: Ablex.

Slack, J. D., & Ferjes, F. (Eds.). (1987). *The ideology of the information age.* Norwood, NJ: Ablex.

Smith, A. (1984, November). The self and post-industrial society. *Intermedia, 12,* p. 6.

Smythe, D. (1977, Fall). Communications: Blindspots of western Marxism. *Canadian Journal of Political and Social Theory,* pp. 1–27.

Smythe, D. (1981). *Dependency road: Communications, capitalism, consciousness and Canada.* Norwood, NJ: Ablex.

Southern California Association of Governments (SCAG). (1983, October 18–November 1). *A Report on the Los Angeles Televote.* Unpublished manuscript.

Sturm, R. W. (1987). *Telecommunication and the emerging global corporation.* Paper presented at the Pacific Telecommunication Conference.

Tehranian, M. et al. (Eds.). (1977). *Communications policy for national development.* London: Routledge, Paul & Kegan.

Tehranian, M. (1979). Development theory and communication policy: The changing paradigms. In M. J. Voigt & G. J. Hanneman (Eds.), *Progress in Communication Sciences* (Vol. I, pp. 119–166). Norwood, NJ: Ablex.

Tehranian, M. (1980a). The curse of modernity: The dialectics of communications and modernization. *International Social Science Journal, 32*(2).

Tehranian, M. (1980b, Spring). Communication and revolution in Iran: The passing of a paradigm. *Iranian Studies, 13,* 1–4.

Tehranian, M. (1981). *Socio-economic and communication indicators in development planning.* Paris: UNESCO.

Tehranian, M. (1984). *Electronic democracy: Promises and perils.* Unpublished manuscript, UNESCO, Paris.

Tehranian, M. (1985). Communication development indicators. In J. Middleton & D. Wedemeyer (Eds.), *Communication planning methods.* Paris: Unesco.

Tehranian, M. (1986, Autumn). Thoughtfully Ambivalent, Review of Video Democracy. *Journal of Communication*, pp. 180–181.

Teicher, J. S. (1984). Urban community media in North America. In P. Lewis (Ed.), *Media for People in Cities*. Paris: UNESCO.

Telecommunications survey. (1987, October 17). *The Economist*, p. 3, 13.

Thompson, J. B. (1984). *Studies in the theory of ideology*. Berkeley, CA: University of California Press.

Thompson, W. I. (1971). *At the edge of history*. New York: Harper Torchbooks.

Thompson, W. I. (1985). *Pacific shift*. San Francisco: Sierra Club Books.

Tocqueville, A. de (1956). *Democracy in America* (Abridged & ed. by R. D. Heffner). New York: Mentor Books.

Toffler, A. (1970). *Future shock*. New York: Bantam Books.

Toffler, A. (1980). *The third wave*. New York: Bantam Books.

Toynbee, A. (1972). *A study of history* (abridged in one vol.). New York: Oxford University Press.

Tunstall, J. (1977). *The media are American*. New York: Columbia University Press.

Tunstall, J. (1986). *Communications deregulation: The unleashing of America's communications industry*. Oxford & New York: B. Blackwell.

UNESCO. (1961). *Mass media in the developing countries: A UNESCO report to the United Nations*. Paris: UNESCO.

Vask, T. (1988). *The long wave debate*. Berlin: Springer-Verlag.

Voge, J. (1983). From information society to communication society. *Pacific Telecommunication Conference 83 Proceedings*. Honolulu: Pacific Telecommunication Conference.

Voge, J. (1985). *Crise, Information et Communictions dan l'economie des Etats-Unis*. Unpublished manuscript.

Wallerstein, I. (1974). *The modern world system*. New York: Academic Press.

Wallerstein, I. (1979). *The capitalist world economy*. Cambridge: Cambridge University Press.

Weizenbaum, J. (1976). *Computer power and human reason: From judgement to calculation*. New York: W. H. Freeman.

Wicklein, J. (1981). *Electronic nightmare: The home communications set and your freedom*. Boston: Beacon Press.

Will optical fibers ever forget? (1987, September 26). *The Economist*, p. 91.

Wills, G. (1988). *Reagan's America*. New York: Penguin.

World Almanac. (1984). *The world almanac and book of facts 1984*. New York: Newspaper Enterprise Association.

World Almanac. (1986). *The world almanac and book of facts 1986*. New York: Newspaper Enterprise Association.

Biographical Note

MAJID TEHRANIAN is formerly Chairman and currently Professor of Communication and Director-Elect of the Institute for Peace at the University of Hawaii. A political economist by education, he received his PhD and master's degree from Harvard University and his bachelor's degree from Dartmouth College. He has served at both national and international organizations, as Director of Iran Communications and Development Institute (Tehran), Program Specialist at UNESCO (Paris), and trustee of the International Institute of Communications (London). He has also served as faculty or visiting scholar at Harvard, MIT, Stanford, Oxford, and Tehran Universities. His publications include *The Middle East: Its Governments and Politics,* with A. Al-Marayati et al. (Belmont: Duxbury Press, 1972); *Towards a Systemic Theory of National Development* (Tehran: Industrial Management Institute, 1974); *Communications Policy for National Development: A Comparative Perspective,* edited with F. Hakimzadeh and M. L. Vidale (London: Routledge, Kegan & Paul, 1977); and *Socio-Economic and Communication Indicators in Development Planning: A Case Study of Iran* (Paris: UNESCO, 1981). His numerous articles have appeared in a variety of scholarly journals; they have been also translated into French, Spanish, German, Norwegian, Polish, Korean, Japanese, Indonesian, Arabic, and Persian.

Author Index

Subject Index

Cuba, 187
Cultural
  industries, 29
  homogenization, 30
  lag, 43–44
  revolution, 87
Cybernetic, 6, 52, 77
  control of production, 10
Cycles,
  of American history, 83–84
  historical cycles, 185, 186, 193, 196
Czechoslovakia, 188

D
Das Kapital, 3
Databases, 102, 169, 223
Democracy,
  capitalist, 79–84
  communist, 84–87
  communitarian, 87–92, 208–242
  conditions of, 52
  corporate, 113, 115, 119
  cultural, 13, 86, 149
  direct, 70, 87–93, 208–242
  electronic, 50
  liberal, 79–84
  political, 13, 86, 148
  potentials of, 46
  representative, 25, 30, 70, 113, 115, 119,
    192, 240
  social, 13, 86, 148
  tele-, see Teledemocracy
  will formation, 52
Democratization, 9, 12, 17, 45, 165
Democrats,
  Keynesian, 26
Dependency, 32, 60
Depoliticization,
  of economy, 24–25
  of state, 24, 26, 28
  of culture, 24
Design
  computer-assisted, see Computer
Desktop Publishing, 29
Development, 13, 44, 75, 174–185, 197,
  203
  another, 32, 100
  developmentalism, 174–184, 201
  economic, 181 ff
  indicators, 176–180

participatory, 76, 87–92
political, 181 ff
repressive, 76, 92–93
self-reliant, 198
sociocultural, 181 ff
Dialogical, 32, 234
Diffusion, 32
Discourse, 19, 21, 28, 40–44, 52, 68, 153,
  170
  critical public, 28, 45
  private vs. public, 21, 119, 173
  power-free, 38 ff
  theory, 52
Dissociation, 185–186
Distantiation, 28–29
Doordarshan (Indian TV), 199

E
Ego, 76, 78
  Alter-, 76
  Super-, 76, 78
Electronic publishing, 48, 101
Elite, 18, 51, 64, 66, 68–69, 80, 84–85, 183
  secular, 24
  technocratic, 10, 88, 179, 236
Enclosure Movement, 49, 169
Enlightenment, 21
Empirical, 32, 35
Empiricist, 32, 95
Epistemological lag, 43–44
Empowerment,
  of audiences, 238
Expropriation, 221

F
Facsimile, 46–47, 102
Falklands War/Crisis, 83, 171
Fascism, 75–78, 86, 93, 114, 147
Federal Bureau of Investigation (FBI), 150
Federal Communications Commission
  (FCC), 129–130, 152
Financing,
  of media, 105–109
Film, 46–47, 67
First Amendment, 49, 87
Federalist Papers, 80
Food and Agricultural Organization
  (FAO), 204
Fourth Estate, 79, 80, 81, 88
France, 163–164
Frankfurt School, 32–35

DATE DUE

L.-Brault